TBS
THE**BLACK**SCHOLAR®

Volume 43 • Number 4   W I N T E R   2 0 1 3

THE **BLACK** SCHOLAR (ISSN 0006-4246) is a peer-reviewed journal, published four times a year by the Black World Foundation, a non-profit educational organization, in association with Paradigm Publishers in Boulder, Colorado. Postal address: The Black Scholar, Box 1001, 4739 University Way, N.E., Seattle, WA 98105-4412. Website: www.the blackscholar.org. Books for review should be sent to this address. Correspondence can be sent to this address or by email to chrisman@theblackscholar.org.

The Black Scholar encourages unsolicited submissions of articles and proposals for special issues. Contributors are encouraged to contact the editors (chrisman@theblackscholar.org, chajua@theblack scholar.org, chukwu@theblackscholar.org) to discuss their ideas and to look at the submissions guidelines on the website www.theblackscholar.org.

Subscription Rates

Print Subscriptions for Libraries/Institutions
  Domestic: $148.00 (U.S. and Canada)
  International: $163.00

Print and Online Subscriptions for Libraries/ Institutions
  Domestic: $226.00 (U.S. and Canada)
  International: $250.00

Online Only Subscriptions for Libraries/Institutions
  Domestic: $216.00

Print Subscriptions for Individuals
  Domestic: $35.00
  International: $48.00

Single Copy Pricing
  Individual: $12.00 (plus $3.00 S&H)
  Institutional: $40.00 (plus $3.00 S&H)

For subscriptions, address changes, and advertising rates and schedules, contact Paradigm Publishers at meganm@paradigmpublishers.com or Paradigm Publishers, 5589 Arapahoe Ave., Suite 206A, Boulder, CO 80303.

Contents

Introduction

Black Philosophy and the Crucible of *Lived* History

GEORGE YANCY

The black experience, history, and culture are the controlling categories for a black philosophy—not chromosomes.

—William R. Jones

It is with honor and humility both to be the guest editor[1] of this special issue of *The Black Scholar* and to have had the freedom to frame the philosophical motif to be critically discussed within its pages. "The Role of Black Philosophy" constitutes the organizing theme of this special issue of *TBS*. While the systematic exploration of the role of black philosophy and the broad array of majority "professional" black philosophers gathered here to theorize such a role might be unique to the pages of *TBS,* the *spirit* of this issue as one that critically addresses the importance of the magnitude and complexity of black thought and existence, and the importance of conceptually grappling with these, is not. Concerned with self-determination, liberation, sociopolitical critique, and broad grassroots political praxis—all of which implicates the power and ethical fortitude of sociopolitical agitation against various national and international instantiations of injustice—*TBS* has a rich historical legacy in terms of its focus and concern with issues such as black power, racist oppression and hegemony, movements instigated by black students, the vitality and importance of black studies, issues involving black politics, black educational progress and inclusion, and black diasporic literature. Because of this rich diachronic and synchronic concern with black cultural material history and thought, this special issue of *TBS* is *not* inaugural. Not only does this special issue comprise diverse/heterogeneous philosophical voices on the theme of the role of black philosophy, but the contributions are consistent with the *pluralist* and *activist* thrust of *TBS*.

Consistent with the idea of an open-ended perspective and a diversity of voices, I conceptualize black philosophy within the crucible of *lived* history. This raises the interrelated themes of context, situation, and philosophical thought. Indeed, this dynamic interrelation points to the dialectical relationship between philosophical thought and socio-existential setting. On this score, and as philosopher William R. Jones's epigraph implies, black philosophy is protean and historically contextual. To refer to "black" philosophy is not to imply a chromosomal matrix out of which philosophical thought *causally* proceeds. There is no genetic substratum (or biological *telos*) that inexorably dictates the existence of black philosophy

George Yancy is professor of philosophy at Duquesne University. He has authored, edited, and coedited seventeen books, including *Black Bodies, White Gazes: The Continuing Significance of Race* (2008), *Look, a White! Philosophical Essays on Whiteness* (2012), and (coedited with Janine Jones) *Pursuing Trayvon Martin: Historical Contexts and Contemporary Manifestations of Racial Dynamics* (2013).

r the diverse philosophical content and trajectories of black philosophy, though the process of racialization is central to thinking about the meaning of black philosophy and its role. And since "blackness" is itself an identity category that has its origins within history, the idea of a black philosophy and its role must be couched within a hermeneutic lens that takes seriously the dimension of black *Erlebnis,* through a form of *lived* experience that is not homogenous for all of those who identify as black people even as there are shared dimensions of historical and contemporary forms of black oppression, marginalization, and dehumanization.

In my book *Black Bodies, White Gazes,*[2] I point to the middle passage as the crucible in terms of which black identity is marked and the black body is ontologically truncated and returned to itself as distorted and monstrous, thus locating the black body within a context of anti-black racism. Theorizing the black body from this location critiques an ontogenic perspective and raises the issue of the sociogenic. The middle passage, I argue, functions as that space of death, docility, amalgamation, and resistance that is important for comprehending black people in North America. So, it becomes a central existential and social ontological motif through which I theorize what it means to be black and how I understand black philosophy and its role. Yet, it is important to note that those black bodies were scattered and not confined to North America. So, I think that it is important to theorize the ways in which that oceanic experience shaped other black bodies that were dispersed throughout the world. As such, then, one must be attentive to and examine the different genealogies

and phenomenological configurations that speak not only to those bodies that were not enslaved in North America, but also speak to those black bodies that did not arrive at their "destinies" through the transatlantic slave trade at all. This raises important questions regarding the *lived* meaning of "blackness" and how blackness is differentially defined diachronically and in terms of points of geographical origin, suggesting that blackness is dynamically protean.

Although above I point to the middle passage as the matrix in terms of which black identity is shaped, we must be cognizant of how black identity and black subjectivity can be erroneously tethered to *that* moment in time and physical space,[3] which then raises the issue of how a specific black historical narrative can function monolithically and thus exclude those black bodies that don't narrativize the middle passage in the same way or even at all. While I will not pursue this issue here, I want to be clear that there is a diverse "terrain of blackness" in terms of the changing landscape and meaning of blackness and that this change impacts differential experiences for those who consider themselves black people. Indeed, such differential experiences have an impact on how we think about the dynamics of black identity and black philosophizing, and the latter's key normative assumptions, modalities, and different morphologies of questions and responses that emerge. My point is to remain critically cognizant of the ways in which I privilege the middle passage and how that privileging might function as a historical gap for black people who nevertheless see themselves as black and yet whose experiences are shaped differently, though not incommensurably vis-à-vis other black people who contend with anti-black racism.

Black philosophy and its role are fundamentally linked with existential struggle. The lived experiences of struggle and resistance (etymologically, "to take a stand") speak to the fact that the social ontological structure of the world is not a metaphysical *fait accompli*. Black philosophy acknowledges its historical conditionality and emergence against the backdrop of white racism, violence, colonialism, dehumanization, enslavement, oppression, and objectification. It recognizes this backdrop as constituted through lived embodiment and configurations of thought and action that were not *necessary,* but that are predicated upon contingent sites of power and hegemony that are linked to oppressive ideologies and the possession of material power to superimpose such oppressive ideologies. Hence, relevant to black philosophy is its clarion call: *"The world is not as it ought to be!"*

It is the power of "ought" that points to the openness of human history, agency, and counter-hegemonic praxis. The "ought" implies slippage, excess, lacunae, and the capacity to create. The subtext here is that one *can* reconfigure the world, reshape its direction, undo its normative repetitions, and create new and ever freeing forms of political formation, relationality, and performance. The role of black philosophy, then, having its point of origin within a matrix of oppression, even as this oppression was/is diasporic, is antagonistic and iconoclastic; indeed, resistant to claims of philosophical universality that are actually forms of discourse that are predicated upon a philosophical anthropology that is, in this case, underwritten by whiteness as the transcendental norm and that valorizes its vision of the world and the meaning of humanity at the exclusion of others. Hence, to engage in black philosophy on conceptual terms set forth here is to affirm one's humanity in the face of those who deem you a sub-person, ersatz, ontologically nugatory.

Black Arts Movement (BAM) theorist Larry Neal says, "The light is black (now, get that!) as are most of the meaningful tendencies in the world."[4] In short, blackness functions as a corrective to those procrustean philosophical assumptions-in-white. It is this corrective dimension that was achieved in my book *Reframing the Practice of Philosophy,*[5] where both black and Latino philosophers, those marked as "different" and "ersatz" bodies, engage significant meta-philosophical concerns of identity, political philosophy, language, canon formation, and so on. The themes explored within that text are primarily obscured (indeed, placed under erasure) by traditional Anglo-American and European philosophical perspectives. Not to deploy the history of black people as the lens that shapes their philosophical concerns and through which they pose their philosophical intuitions is an issue of self-denial. As Jones contends, "It is unobscure that blacks dehumanize themselves if they do not insist upon the right to make their history the point of departure for their philosophizing."[6]

In my book *African-American Philosophers, 17 Conversations,* Leonard Harris shared with me when he taught his first course in black philosophy in 1970 at Miami University. In teaching that course, he relates, "What I did was that I would show slides of Black people being hanged. That's how I started off the course. Then I would play blues music. And I'd say, 'We're studying Black philosophy here.'"[7] Though we did not pursue this point any further, his point is profoundly instructive and raises important meta-philosophical concerns. As with Jones, Harris insisted upon the right to make his history in North America (and the history of millions of other black people) the point of departure for his philosophizing. As such, this act was a site of counter-dehumanization. Within this context, Harris frames black philosophy through the agony of the spectacle of lynching black bodies—both male and female. The point here is that to teach black philosophy requires the contextualization of its emergence within white terror and resistance to that terror. This raises the issue of freedom and justice fought for in the face of "strange fruit"—black bodies mutilated and burned to death. Think here of Mary Turner, a pregnant black woman who in 1918 had her ankles tied together and then was hung upside down. The white mob then used gasoline to burn her alive. She was then disemboweled. Her baby fell to the ground crying as one white man crushed the black baby with his heel. Or think of Claude Neal, who in 1934 was castrated and had his penis and testicles stuffed in his mouth, and was then made to say that he liked them before he was eventually killed. How does one philosophize in the abstract given the existential gravity and horror of thousands of black bodies lynched? Indeed, how did European and Anglo-American philosophers continue to theorize during this period without their philosophies becoming moribund under the weight of their collective failure (perhaps indifference) to address white ter-ror? The reality of such white racist spectacles, white racist technology, constitutes an indispensable site of the crucible of *lived* history where the role of black philosophy is to contest such forms of barbarity and moral ineptitude, to deconstruct the assumptions that support such forms of white terror, to rethink manifestations of "reason" vis-à-vis modernity's support of the dehumanization of nonwhite people, to affirm one's humanity and dignity (and those of others), and to rethink, to reimagine, and to work to actualize a world in which the oppressive racist trauma experienced by black people no longer exists. The role of black philosophy, then, is committed to dwelling near the existential stench of human existence. This closeness is exemplified in the case of Harris, who taught black philosophy through the display of lynched bodies. To turn one's back on the stench of human existence, and in this case, the reek of white supremacy in the historical and contemporary lives of black people—assuming, of course, that one thinks that he/she is doing black philosophy—is to delude oneself.

One will also note that Harris mentions the blues. He telescopes the existential sorrow of these lynched bodies through the musical venue of the blues, a form of musical praxis that not only *dwells near* the stench of human existence, but exemplifies ways of rethinking that reality, responding differently to that reality, touching the pain of that reality and yet transcending it. Hence, black philosophy has a transcendent modality, one that pushes forward toward liberationist ends even as black life might present itself as a structural impossibility within the context of white racism. In the face of this absurdity, black philosophy can become protean, perhaps recognizing, as Joy James argues, that "the black matrix *maroon* is terrifyingly beautiful because it is violently transcendent. It ruptures conventional political protest."[8]

The role of black philosophy must also keep track of ways in which black women specifically undergo multiple forms of oppression, objectification, social castigation, humiliation, and marginalization. In *African-American Philosophers, 17 Conversations,* Anita Allen says, "With all due respect, what does philosophy have to offer to Black women? It's not obvious to me that philosophy has *anything* special to offer Black women today."[9] I think that this is where the role of black philosophy must be broadened to self-reflect, especially given its commitment to liberation, on its own blinkers to the ways in which black male hegemony (inside and outside of the professional space of philosophy) functions vis-à-vis black women and women of color. This is a case where black male philosophers are "signatories" of a contract borne out of a male supremacist "inverted epistemology."[10]

After all, how can we valorize the philosophical fruits of black philosophy without valorizing the philosophical fruits of black women—those who are deemed embodiments of "maternal pathology," "hyper-reproductivity," and "irresponsibility"? Indeed, they are also deemed "inferior" in their attempts to do philosophy in the abstract because they are seen as reduced and reducible to mere experience and the body, and who lack any reality independently of the racist and sexist images that have been superimposed upon them, and whose primary

function it is to *work under* (an intentional double entendre) black and white male philosophers and *work for* white women philosophers as a source of raw material that they, white women, are only "good" at theorizing. Black women must also fight for *philosophical, physical, and psychological space within the academy*. They also fight for respect—personal and epistemological.

As black male philosophers, we must not inhibit *when and where they enter*. As Desirée H. Melton writes, "Non-white men are not privileged by race but they are privileged by gender. Invested in preserving gender domination, they will be blind to the patriarchy that positions them above non-white women. Non-white women will look to their brothers for community and find that the sights of those men are not on their sisters but instead on getting to the top of the hierarchy alongside their brothers in gender domination, white men."[11] Allen's question shifts the burden to philosophy "to explain why it is good enough for [black women]."[12] Melton's critique shifts the burden—or certainly the share of responsibility—onto *black men*.

The articles within this issue address the theme of the role of black philosophy from multiple viewpoints. In some of the articles, the theme is implicit. However, this does not detract from the implications that those pieces convey regarding the role of black philosophy. While there is a consistent theme throughout all of the articles—that black philosophy engages ontology, political philosophy, ethics, aesthetics, axiology, and so on as a critical framework for rethinking epistemic blinkers vis-à-vis traditional Western philosophy, and struggles to create spaces for greater freedom and liberation through critical reflection and praxis—the collection here does not constitute a homogeneous and non-dynamic discursive space, but makes it clear that black philosophy is rich in diversity and universal in scope precisely because of its angular perspective, its capacity to speak courageously to what has been neglected, ignored, and many times rejected, in traditional philosophy.

The articles within this special issue, written by black men and black women philosophers/scholars, demonstrate the importance of black philosophy as a site of *parrhesia* that has universal implications for both philosophy and extra-philosophical concerns, concerns that burn at the level of the quotidian, the everyday existential complexities of life. Each article consists of deep and broad philosophical, critical, and theoretical analyses that are sharp and unapologetic. Indeed, they carry on the critical tradition of *The Black Scholar*. It is with profound delight and a sense of mission that I introduce these critical voices to you here.

Notes

1. I am indebted to literary figure and philosopher Charles Johnson for making it possible for my path to cross with that of Louis Chude-Sokei, senior editor of *The Black Scholar*.

2. George Yancy, *Black Bodies, White Gazes: The Continuing Significance of Race* (Lanham, MD: Rowman & Littlefield, 2008).

3. I thank Michelle M. Wright for theorizing black identity through the deployment of space and time in ways that critically open new questions and concerns.

4. L. Jones and L. Neal, *Black Fire: An Anthology of Afro-American Writing* (New York: William Morrow & Company, 1968), p. 652.

5. George Yancy, ed., *Reframing the Practice of Philosophy: Bodies of Color, Bodies of Knowledge* (Albany: SUNY Press, 2012.

6. William R. Jones, "The Legitimacy and Necessity of Black Philosophy: Some Preliminary Considerations," *Philosophical Forum* 9 (Winter–Spring 1977–1978): 157.

7. "Interview with Leonard Harris," in *African American Philosophers, 17 Conversations,* ed. George Yancy (New York: Routledge, 1998), p. 212.

8. See Joy James's "Afrarealism and the Black Matrix: Maroon Philosophy at Democracy's Border" in this issue.

9. "Interview with Anita Allen," *African American Philosophers,* ed. George Yancy, p. 172.

10. Charles Mills, *The Racial Contract* (Ithaca, NY, and London: Cornell University Press, 1997).

11. Desirée H. Melton's "Are You My People? The Surprising Places This Black Woman Philosopher Did Not Find Community," in this issue.

12. "Interview with Anita Allen," *African American Philosophers,* ed. George Yancy, p. 172.

The Role of Black Philosophy

A Personal Retrospective

LUCIUS T. OUTLAW (JR.)

I.

Taking up the task set by George Yancy and as delineated in the title for contributions to this special issue of *The Black Scholar* necessitates, for me, first setting out important aspects of the historical context of the emergence of the call for, and agendas regarding, the very notion of black philosophy. For at the basis of the call, what had to be foundational to taking up the call, was the resolution of a profound *existential* challenge, namely, the reworking of the terms, meanings, and significances of one's racialized personal and social *identities:* What is it to become and be *black?* This was the self-understanding called for as the basis for praxis in academic philosophy if one were self-consciously *black,* necessarily so for the work of articulating *black* philosophy. There is the additional need, then, to sketch out some of the ways in which the very idea of, and efforts to conceptualize, black philosophy brought to the fore a number of very serious epistemological and political challenges. These challenges had to be resolved to bring into clearer conception, and bring into *being,* within and beyond institutions of higher education, a field of discourse of and for knowledge-production and articulation by black persons that would be of primary service to black peoples while meeting the credible challenges within such institutions (and for various publishers) of satisfying criteria that would certify the instances as "philosophy" in successful defiance of those who would invalidate the efforts to construct black philosophy as a fallacious *ad hominem* project. Thus, in profoundly significant ways matters personal and social (racial identity and associated responsibilities), epistemological (racially conditioned validation of philosophical productions and articulations), and political (recognition, legitimation, and institutionalization of the productions and articulations of philosophical efforts and understandings by black folks) were conjoined in struggle.

In what follows I offer a sketch of the history of my own development in taking up the call for black philosophy and, in doing so, help to work out the role(s) of the enterprise and the standards of fulfillment. However, given the limitations set for this writing, I will not be able to rehearse my efforts over

Lucius Turner Outlaw (Jr.) is professor of philosophy and of African American and diaspora studies at Vanderbilt University, having joined the faculty in July 2000. (Outlaw was formerly the T. Wistar Brown Professor of Philosophy at Haverford College in Pennsylvania.) Outlaw teaches, researches, and writes about race and ethnicity, American philosophy, African American philosophy, critical social theory, social and political philosophy, and the history of philosophy in the West. Born in Starkville, Mississippi, he is a graduate of Fisk University (BA, 1967) and of the Graduate School of Arts and Sciences of Boston College (PhD, philosophy, 1972).

several decades, with others, to wrestle with the complex epistemological and political challenges, or to rehearse our accomplishments, in the decades-long development from the initial call and quests for black philosophy to the establishment of "Africana philosophy" as a vibrant and still developing field of discourse now recognized by professional organizations of academic philosophy, including the American Philosophical Association and such international organizations as UNESCO, the World Congress of Philosophy, and others. (Readers who wish to know more should consult my essay on "Africana Philosophy.")[1]

II.

The historical context in which the call and quest for black philosophy emerged was constituted by transformative historic eruptions of intricately related organized political, social, and cultural movements for *freedom* and *justice* by and for "colored" peoples who were influencing and being influenced by equally historically transformative intellectual and ideological developments, by movements and developments conditioning and being conditioned by the emergence and coalescence of new modes of consciousness, and, thus, by transformed and revalorized personal and social identities ("colored" and "Negro," for example, being rejected by more than a few persons for "black" and "African/Afro-American" as notions of identification): the twentieth-century instances of the Freedom/Civil Rights Movement; the Black Power/Black Consciousness Movement; decolonizing

National Liberation Movements throughout the African continent and the African diaspora; and in the Middle East, Southeast Asia, elsewhere. . . . It was out of the confluences of these cauldrons of transformative historic forces that the call for black philosophy emerged and the forces mined for heuristic guidance by those inspired to take up and fulfill the demands and aspirations of the call.

So it was, and has been, for me. From 1963 to 1967, I was a student majoring in philosophy at Fisk University in Nashville, Tennessee. During these years the city, Fisk, and other institutions of higher education—American Baptist College, Meharry Medical College, Tennessee Agricultural and Industrial University (designated Tennessee State University in 1968), Scarritt College, and Vanderbilt University—were important sites, along with local black churches and other organizations, within and from which conceptions of and commitments to the historic transformations were nurtured and taken up by students, faculty, staff people, administrators, and other citizens. The conceptions and commitments were guides for the extraordinarily well-organized, ethically principled, and trained-for-discipline successful Nashville instantiation of the national nonviolent movement for much fuller *Freedom!* through full recognition of the just and full dignity and integrity of the personhood of Negro people in civic and political life. As well, during all four years of my residency in transformative education at Fisk, there were the accumulative influences of the Annual Spring Arts Festival that showcased extraordinary achievements of Negro/black people in the fine arts of music, plastic arts, dance, and creative literature. There were, too, the subtle and explicit influences of the embodiments of principled and disciplined accomplishment, white racial supremacy notwithstanding, in the embodied persons and teaching of the Negro/black, brown, and white teacher-scholar-artists on the faculties, a number of whom also were pivotal in the movements. And my last year—from the summer of 1966 through the spring of 1967—was the opening period of the explosive ruptures of the call for, and the development of, responsive efforts by various individuals and organizations, locally and nationally, to conceive, forge, and sustain the movement to acquire and employ Black Power as the means by which to achieve and sustain full freedom and justice in struggles against white racial supremacy. This call required a new mode of self-consciousness, thus necessitating the recalibration and revalorization of the terms of recognition and respect, of identity, for black peoples. Consequently, before the end of my senior year, I, along with a significant number of my classmates and other Fisk students, and a significant number of persons in my generational cohort from other colleges and universities in Nashville and other cities across the country influenced by the historic transformations under way—including what would very soon become a powerfully influential movement opposing a war in Vietnam being waged by US military forces, and a second-wave women's movement—had to struggle through profound existential challenges to our personal and social racialized identities prompted by the movements and, *especially,* by the call for *Black Power!*

In my own case, neither the literature of the discipline of philosophy nor the formal classes and seminars were of immediate help even when I continued my studies at the graduate level (1967–1970 at Boston College) on the way to a PhD as certification of the learnedness acquired that qualified me to pursue a career as a college or university teacher. Moreover, while I had significantly influential teacher-scholar-artist role models at Fisk, none of my undergraduate and graduate philosophy professors were of African descent, and none of the texts assigned for study in all of the classes and seminars I endured during my undergraduate and graduate years were authored by a Negro/black person. As I worked my way through the existential challenges toward a new self-consciousness and identity as a black person, any readings that were resourceful for the strenuous effort had to be procured beyond the disciplinary context of academic philosophy; so, too, for my accessing black thinkers who in their persons and through their articulations might serve me as role models and examples. Graduate study was, then, weighted with "double duty": that is, mastering the assigned texts *and* searching out for, acquiring, reading critically, and digesting masterfully the articulations of critically minded black thinkers who would aid me in coming to clarity, of purpose and effort, of what was to be done in my being able to think *blackly* with integrity and rigorous competence.

While on this quest for self-definition and articulation, several crucial encounters in close succession (1969) would prove decisive. The first was attending a lecture at Boston College given by Harold Cruse, who spoke with incisive insightfulness and pointedness out of his reflected-on extensive experiences and weighty considerations that he had set forth in *The Crisis of the Negro Intellectual* [2] and in reviews and essays collected and republished under the title *Rebellion or Revolution*.[3] Inspired and challenged by Cruse's lecture, I was *compelled* to take on *The Crisis,* a text in whose very title a mode of being was given prominent naming—*Negro+Intellectual*—while being subjected to strenuous critical analysis for such persons having failed at leadership. Indeed, I *had* to learn what constituted the failure and why, what made for the situation of crisis, in the hope that I might become a black intellectual not crippled by either failure or crisis. I delved deeply into *The Crisis,* and while doing so experienced another encounter that was to be of equal significance. While perusing a bookstore in Harvard Square near the end of the year I came upon a boldly graphic rendering of a journal's title that I experienced as though it had leapt off the rack and landed in the unsettled core of an intellect I was working with strenuous effort to forge in keeping with my evolving consciousness-of-being-black: the very first issue of *The Black Scholar.* I quickly purchased the issue and rushed back to the environs of my apartment (where I shared life with a confident young woman working out her own notion of being black, had purchased a copy of Cruse's *The Crisis* before I did, and who, but a week or two earlier, had become my wife and first-friend and continues to provide my life with a much-desired form of completeness). I devoured the inaugural issue of *The Black Scholar,* immediately became a subscriber, and for years thereafter looked forward with great anticipation to the delivery of each subsequent issue.

A third encounter: reading in an issue of *Ebony* magazine an article about the coming together in Atlanta, Georgia, of a decidedly select, international group of principled activist teacher-scholar intellectuals and activists in the formation and conferencing of an especially intriguing think tank: the Institute of the Black World (IBW). The principals of the IBW and the participants in its first conference were participants and contributors to movements bringing about historic transformations of societies that had been distorted for centuries by white racial supremacy through regimes of racial apartheid and Jim Crow, European colonialism and Eurocentrism, and capitalist exploitation of lands and peoples throughout Africa and the African diaspora, and elsewhere. (Several years later, 1974, in one of the signal publications by the IBW, founding director historian Vincent Harding would set out the *calling* of the black scholar: "To speak truth to our people, to speak truth about our people, to speak truth about our enemy—all in order to free the mind, so that black men, women, and children may build beyond the banal, the dangerous chaos of the American spirit, towards a new time.")[4]

A fourth encounter of lasting significance: attending a lecture by Herbert Marcuse at Boston University that would inspire me to immediately find, purchase, and begin the work of understanding and digesting the significance for my own aspirations for enhanced critical thinking of his *One Dimensional Man,* then other writings by him. And as I learned more about a particular posse of intellectuals with whom he had been associated in pre-Holocaust Frankfurt, Germany—the Institute for Social Research—I began a program that, across most of a decade, would have me delving into writings by several members of the posse: Max Horkheimer, Theodore Adorno, Eric From, and Jürgen Habermas. Finally, a fifth encounter of profound significance: becoming aware of struggles being waged by black students, faculty, and administrators at predominantly white institutions of higher education—often with the support of other students, faculty, and administrators of color, and even with the support of some white students, faculty, and administrators—to revise and correct missions, curricula, and pedagogies through the development of programs of black studies. Older and younger generations of black teacher-scholars, artists, and activist administrators and community activists made transformative demands on the production, validation, legitimation, and mediation of the disciplinary knowledge-enterprises of history, psychology, sociology, political science, English, religion, music, art, the study of languages. . . . The movements of previous years that had drawn human and other resources from institutions of higher education were now resources for radical critiques and transformative renovations of many of those same institutions, and of others that previously had not been implicated directly or involved. So it was at Boston College: while still a graduate student I was hired as the university's first director of black studies and tasked with developing a program of studies, including mission, objectives, and courses. Consequently, only by strenuous

denial or disregard of the momentous challenges and transformations in flux would I have been unaffected. I *was* affected.

Taking up the existential challenges of the calls for Black Power, black consciousness, and black studies while endeavoring to keep faith with those who led and waged the struggles for freedom and justice in civic and political life in the United States, in colonial Africa, and throughout the African diaspora had profound consequences for my setting a mission and agenda for myself in academic philosophy. I set off on the mission with my dissertation, *Language and the Transformation of Consciousness: Foundations for a Hermeneutic of Black Culture,* an exploration, drawing on W. E. B. Du Bois's notion of "double consciousness" and Franz Fanon's exploration of "Language and the Negro" in *Black Skin, White Masks,* of the significances of the willful displacement of "Negro" by "black" as the term and concept for historically and politically compelled redefinition and revalorization of self- and social-group identities and life-agendas for black people.

III.

I began my career as a professional in academic philosophy in 1970, called back to Fisk University to teach and quite excited to be off on an adventure, convinced by the encounters described as well as in combination with others not referenced but of great significance, that I *must* contribute to forging a way in and through which philosophical explorations of the lives, histories, contributions, and future possibilities of black people, with honesty and integrity, would gain respect and legitimacy within the discipline. As well, I was convinced that in my teaching an essential core of the curriculum through which young black folks gained both radically critical historical knowledge and enhanced skillful competences in critical analysis, creative thoughtfulness, and insight-bearing oral and written communications while studying and practicing academic philosophy must include representative works by black thinkers. More than four decades later, having long ago resolved my existential challenges and taken on those epistemological and political while serving on the faculties of several institutions, with periods of visitation at several others, I am even more convinced of the pertinence the *callings* have been, and remain, for my own career and life as a teacher and scholar in academic philosophy with much of my work having been devoted to challenges of Africana philosophy. And so shall it be until I am done working. . . .

Notes

1. Lucius Outlaw, "Africana Philosophy," *Stanford Encyclopedia of Philosophy* (http://plato.stanford.edu/entries/africana/), Stanford University, 2010.

2. Harold Cruse, *The Crisis of the Negro Intellectual: A Historical Analysis of the Failure of Black Leadership* (New York: William Morrow, 1967).

3. Harold Cruse, *Rebellion or Revolution* (New York: William Morrow, 1968).

4. Vincent Harding, "The Vocation of the Black Scholar," *Education and Black Struggle: Notes from the Colonized World,* edited by the Institute of the Black World, *Harvard Educational Review,* Monograph No. 2, 1974, p. 6.

African-American Philosophers and the Critique of Law

ANITA L. ALLEN

I am sure that none of you would want to rest content with the superficial kind of social analysis that deals merely with effects and does not grapple with underlying causes. . . . Negroes have experienced grossly unjust treatment in the courts. There have been more unsolved bombings of Negro homes and churches in Birmingham than in any other city in the nation. These are the hard, brutal facts of the case.[1]

—Martin Luther King,
African-American theologian, from a
jail in Birmingham, Alabama, 1963

When someone asks me about violence, I just, I just find it incredible. Because what it means is that the person who's asking that question has absolutely no idea what black people have gone through, what black people have experienced in this country since the time the first black person was kidnapped from the shores of Africa.[2]

—Angela Davis, African-American philosopher,
from a jail in Marin County, California, 1972

During the past half century a new field of specialization has emerged within the academic discipline of philosophy: African-American (or, more broadly, "Africana")[3] philosophy.[4] The field has appeared in tandem with an increase in the number of professionally trained philosophers of African and African-American ("black") descent holding PhDs in philosophy.[5] While there were barely a handful of black academic philosophers teaching and writing in 1960,[6] among the American Philosophical Association's estimated ten thousand PhD-trained philosophers in the United States today, at least one hundred are thought to be of African descent or African American, and about twenty of those individuals are black women.[7]

Some contemporary African-American philosophers teach and write about topics that do not explicitly or directly relate to African or African-American history and culture, in the traditional fields of philosophy. These fields include metaphysics and epistemology, ethics, history of philosophy, logic, aesthetics, philosophy of language, philosophy of mind, philosophy of science, ancient philosophy, and so on. A greater number of African-American academically employed philosophers publish scholarly articles and books on topics directly related to race or other aspects of the African-American experience. Indeed, at some point in their careers, most African-American philosophers have found themselves deeply engaged in "social analysis" that deals with what M. L. King referred to in my opening quotation as "the hard, brutal facts of the case." Work by black philosophers has addressed the ignorance Angela Davis identified in the

Anita L. Allen is vice provost for faculty and Henry R. Silverman Professor of Law and professor of philosophy at the University of Pennsylvania. Her books include *Unpopular Privacy: What Must We Hide?* (Oxford University Press, 2011).

second of my opening quotations, of those who purport fairly and objectively to judge and legislate concerning blacks while having "absolutely no idea" about the depth of African-American deprivation and vulnerability. A body of rigorous, often publicly engaged scholarship now describes, explains, critiques, and evaluates African-American culture, slavery, oppression, and discrimination, and the significance of race discourse to identity, morality, ethics, politics, culture, public policy, law, science, medicine, and the arts.[8] In this vein, a journal of "critical race philosophy" published its first issue in 2012, to provide a regular forum for scholarship by and about people of color.[9]

The University of Pennsylvania, a large Ivy League private university located in central Philadelphia, has a unique relationship to African-American philosophy. To start, it is worth noting that the university's current president, political philosopher Amy Gutmann, has meaningfully contributed to the national conversation about the significance of race and color consciousness in the United States in a book written with a prominent co-author of African ancestry.[10] In 2012 Penn posthumously awarded Harvard's first black PhD, W. E. B. Du Bois (1868–1963), an honorary professorship in sociology.[11] Neither sociologist Du Bois nor philosopher Alain LeRoy Locke (1885–1954) was awarded Penn professorships in their lifetimes. One of the nation's most accomplished twentieth-century intellectuals, Locke received his PhD in philosophy from Harvard in 1918 and for many years chaired the philosophy department at Howard University. The nation's first black Rhodes Scholar, Locke grew up in Penn's shadow, but with no op-

portunity to make a career there. Yet Penn was among the first institutions of higher learning outside of the historically black colleges and universities to hire an African-American philosopher onto its tenure-track faculty: William T. Fontaine. Interest in Fontaine's complex relationship with Penn was revived a few years ago by the publication of a biography, *Black Philosopher, White Academy: The Career of William Fontaine*. Penn historian emeritus Bruce Kuklick depicted Fontaine with nuance as a man whose life at Penn was burdened by intractable racism and chronic tuberculosis.[12]

William Fontaine passed away in 1968. I joined Penn's tenured faculty as a professor of law and philosophy exactly thirty years later, in 1998. Honored to have been among the first African-American women to receive a PhD in philosophy after Angela Davis, Joyce Mitchell Cook, and Lavern Shelton,[13] I am only the second African-American PhD philosopher, after William Fontaine, to serve on Penn's standing faculty. After earning a PhD in philosophy from the University of Michigan and a Juris Doctor from Harvard, and teaching at two other law schools, I was hired by Penn with a primary appointment in law, and a secondary appointment in philosophy. I regularly teach philosophy courses at Penn.[14]

I am an example of an African American trained in philosophy who has not made issues of race and the African-American experience the centerpiece of her work. I am best known as a scholar of the law and ethics of privacy and data protection.[15] My contributions to African-American philosophy have been modest,[16] but I have written a few dozen articles and book chapters about issues of racial identity, interracial intimacy, multiculturalism, affirmative action and diversity, equal and fair access to sexual and reproductive services, and the legal protection of minorities through constitutional and common law. I have given lectures, talks, and panel presentations on normative philosophical dimensions of race. I have served as a mentor to several black philosophers, reading dissertations, book manuscripts, and writing tenure letters. I have very occasionally been part of Philosophy Born of Struggle and Alain Locke Society events. I have frequently been invited to speak at American Philosophical Association meetings on topics related to affirmative action and the profession. In 2011 I was asked to serve on a keynote plenary panel at Purdue University, funded by the United Nations Educational, Scientific and Cultural Organization, at a conference titled "Philosophical Dialogue Between Africa and the Americas." I have been recognized with an Alain Locke award from Howard University for work in legal philosophy, and by the Collegium of Black Women Philosophers for being the first African-American woman to hold both a JD and a PhD in philosophy.

Against this background, last year I decided to bring African-American philosophy to Penn after an overly long dormancy.[17] In the fall of 2012, I offered a new course that was cross-listed by the Department of Philosophy and the Department of Africana Studies in the School of Arts and Sciences. The course was a thematic introduction to African-American philosophy since 1960. Its main goal was to structure a knowledge-based critical appreciation of the diverse contributions of recent and contemporary

PhD-trained African-American philosophers. By the end of the semester, I hoped participants would have, first, substantive knowledge of previously unfamiliar American philosophy and of the challenges to entering, remaining in, and flourishing in the profession of academic philosophy; and, second, a foundation for future work in philosophy and African-American philosophy. The course focused on the work primarily of recent and living philosophers of African descent working in the United States, quite deliberately not limited to work about race and African diaspora experience.

Until I assembled my course, I did not have a clear perspective on the role of African-American philosophy. But I am coming to have such a perspective. Construed to mean the scholarly work of African-American academic philosophers, African-American philosophy has played at least six broad roles: (1) to critique law and government authority; (2) to critically analyze power, and institutions and practices of oppression, subordination, slavery, class, caste, colonialism, racism, sexism, and homophobia; (3) to articulate the bases of African-American identities and the grounds of responsibility, community, solidarity, and collective action; (4) to express African-American existential, spiritual, psychological, and moral joys and discontents; (5) to celebrate and interpret African-American art and culture; (6) to assess the discipline, canon, and history of Western philosophies, by reference to gaps, logical and moral inconsistencies, methodological limitations, epistemologies, and exclusions.

The first of the six roles I have identified is of particular interest to me as a lawyer. African-American philosophers have often proffered urgent critiques of the law and the exercise of government authority. African-American philosophers have taken the lead in pointing to the injustice of substantive and procedural rules of law (such as the laws that maintained slavery and segregation). African-American philosophers have called out injustice in the application of legal power (profiling, over-incarceration of blacks, overlooked violence, poverty, and health disparities). While philosophers of any color could engage these concerns, white male philosophers who dominate the field have seldom made it their mission to articulate flaws in the legal system and advocate constructive changes; a number have taken up the topics of affirmative action and capital punishment.

Angela Davis and Martin Luther King Jr. both went to jail. I paired jailhouse quotations from Dr. Davis and Dr. King at the beginning of this article to stress that the critique of law and coercive government authority is an important role for Africana philosophy—descriptively and prescriptively. American philosophers have often found themselves on the wrong side of the positive law, literally and figuratively. We are on the wrong side of the law figuratively any time we write and speak out against positive laws and its official acts and omissions. American law has been deeply prejudicial to African Americans. Through its original eighteenth-century Constitution, the country condoned and facilitated slavery. Through laws enacted before and after the Civil War, it created rigid systems of race-based segregation in housing, schools, employment, and places of public accommodation. Those charged to make, enforce, and interpret the

law have often failed blacks. They have construed rights narrowly and as negative liberties. They have overlooked violence against blacks, and they have perpetrated acts of violence against blacks. They have manipulated facially neutral laws to disparately punish, control, and marginalize blacks and to undercut our political participation.

The "mother" of black philosophy was at one time on the wrong side of the positive law, and this is meant literally. She was placed on the FBI's most wanted list, captured, and thrown into prison. A student of Herbert Marcuse, Professor Angela Davis (born 1944) received her doctorate in philosophy from Humboldt University in East Berlin and made her career as a professor in the Department of the History of Consciousness and the feminist studies program she created at the University of California, Santa Cruz. Like Martin Luther King, Angela Davis was jailed by legal authorities fearful of black radicalism. Davis was tried for kidnapping and murder carried out with guns she had purchased. She was acquitted. "Free Angela Davis" was a slogan on a political button before I had ever read a word of philosophy written by a black man or woman. (I recall thinking, as a college student, that my chances of getting into graduate school to study philosophy were somehow greater because of the notoriety of Angela Davis. She may have been a communist, a Black Panther sympathizer, an accused murderer, and advocate of defensive violence, but because of her fame, white university philosophers on admissions committees could finally *imagine* such a thing as a black woman philosopher.)

Angela Davis was a politically radical critic of liberal law, with its dependence on capitalist markets, traditions of patriarchy, and thin conceptions of rights and freedoms. Like Davis, Penn's Dr. William T. Fontaine was a remarkable critic of the law. But Fontaine stayed carefully and cautiously on the "right" side of the law by advocating logic, philanthropy, and the market to address black inequality. Fontaine's solutions were radical, but at a distance from the ideals of Black Power, Marxism, or separatism. Fontaine offered stunning solutions to housing segregation that invoked liberal market ideals of social order bluntly rejected by his contemporary Angela Davis.

Fontaine stressed that moral and intellectual truth demand an end to segregation advocated by segregationist whites and black radicals alike, since "segregation as a way of life commits its followers to misology, the hatred of reason, and to misanthropy, the hatred of man." He was persuaded that the material betterment of urban African Americans required the use of moral suasion and market incentives to prompt people of different races to choose voluntarily to live among one another.[18] In the only book he published, *Reflections on Segregation, Desegregation, Power and Morals,* Fontaine rejected additional civil rights statutes as the key to speeding progress for "ghettoized" blacks. Instead he proposed public and private partnerships under the umbrella of "a body to be known as the Organization for an Open Progressive Society."[19] These partnerships would raise money for local funds to literally pay white people to live in majority black communities and blacks to live in majority white communities. Fontaine maintained, as would my friend the great legal scholar Derrick Bell a number of years later,

that only a convergence of interest between blacks and whites would prompt whites to participate in measures to uplift African Americans: "When the moral and economic power of philanthropy are employed in such a way as to render desegregation attractive to both white persons as well as to Negroes, we shall begin to make progress."[20]

Fontaine did not believe moral idealism or a sense of justice would be adequate to prompt swift and fundamental change. And like so many African Americans of his generation, he was skeptical of the ability of law to do all the work that needed to be done:

> The letter and penalties of law are not enough; they are necessary conditions but not sufficient conditions. Laws are frequently compromises, for legislators invariably subject their consciences to the practical test and end up sparing the life of a social evil. Administration of the law is subject to the delays inherent in litigation, and to distortion by officers influenced by their own interests. Finally, by the same genius with which some men fashion the law, others can devise ways of evading it. And to tighten the loopholes so as to prevent evasion frequently runs the risk of destroying personal liberty.[21]

This compact half paragraph contains a deeply insightful critique of the law. Fontaine's critique is striking and all the more striking in light of its emergence from the pen of a man who rejected black separatism and violent radicalism, and wrote in the wake of the War on Poverty and the Civil Rights Act of 1964. Fontaine masterfully executed the critique of law and legal authority, a vital role for African-American philosophy. The rule of law ideal is a persistent feature of political, social, economic, and moral reality. Nearly fifty years after Fontaine's death, philosophers of diverse ideological stripes must continue to assess legal solutions to intractable problems of inequality and injustice in and beyond the United States.

Notes

1. www.africa.upenn.edu/Articles_Gen/Letter_Birmingham.html, last visited March 21, 2013.

2. newwavefeminism.tumblr.com/post/18499 037796/angela-davis-on-violence, last visited March 21, 2013.

3. See generally, Lewis R Gordon, *An Introduction to Africana Philosophy* (Cambridge: Cambridge University Press, 2008). Compare "Africana Philosophy," en.wikipedia.org/wiki/List _of_African_American_philosophers#List_of_ Africana_philosophers, last visited March 27, 2013.

4. Tommy Lott and John Pittman, eds., *Blackwell Companion to African American Philosophy* (Oxford: Blackwell, 2003); Tommy Lott, *African-American Philosophy* (Upper Saddle River, NJ: Prentice Hall, 2002); Leonard Harris, ed., *Philosophy Born of Struggle: Anthology of Afro American Philosophy from 1917* (Dubuque, IA: Kendall-Hunt, 2000); John P. Pittman, ed., *African American Perspectives and Philosophical Traditions* (New York: Routledge, 1997). Organizations of African-American philosophers include the Alain Locke Society, alainlocke.com; Philosophy Born of Struggle, pbos.com; Society for the Study of Africana Philosophy, www.africanaphilosophy. net; the Caribbean Philosophical Society, www. caribbeanphilosophicalassociation.org/index. html; the Institute for the Study of Race and Social Thought, www.temple.edu/isrst/events/CPA.

asp; and the Collegium of Black Women Philosophers, web.me.com/ktgphd/CBWP/Welcome. html. Indicative of an emergent field is a publication series, African American Philosophy (AFAM), edited by J. Everet Green: "African American Philosophy (AFAM) solicits manuscripts in all areas of philosophy within the African-American Experience and on emerging paradigms within the broader tradition of Africana Philosophy."

5. See generally, Carlin Romano, *America the Philosophical* (New York: Alfred Knopf, 2012). Romano devotes chapters to African-American (male) philosophers and includes a section on black women philosophers in a larger chapter on women in philosophy.

6. See generally, Bruce Kuklick, *Black Philosopher, White Academy: The Career of William Fontaine* (Philadelphia: University of Pennsylvania Press, 2008).

7. See "Situated Black Women's Voices in/on the Profession of Philosophy," ed. George Yancy, *Hypatia* 23, no. 2 (Spring 2008): 155–159.

8. See, e.g., Derrick Darby, *Rights, Race, and Recognition* (Cambridge: Cambridge University Press, 2009); Tommie Shelby, *We Who Are Dark: The Philosophical Foundations of Black Solidarity* (Cambridge, MA: Belknap Press of Harvard University Press, 2007); Tommie Shelby and Derrick Darby, eds., *Hip Hop and Philosophy: Rhyme 2 Reason* (Chicago: Open Court, 2005); Jorge Garcia, *Race or Ethnicity? On Black and Latino* (Ithaca, NY: Cornell University Press, 2007); George Yancy, *Black Bodies, White Gazes: The Continuing Significance of Race* (Lanham, MD: Rowman & Littlefield, 2008); George Yancy, *Look, a White! Philosophical Essays on Whiteness* (Philadelphia: Temple University Press, 2012); George Yancy, ed., *What White Looks Like: African-American Philosophers on the Whiteness Question* (New York: Routledge, 2004); Naomi Zack, *Thinking About Race* (Wadsworth, 2005); Naomi Zack, *Philosophy of Science and Race* (New York: Routledge, 2002); Naomi Zack, *Race*

and Mixed Race (Philadelphia: Temple University Press, 1994); Charles W. Mills, *The Racial Contract* (Ithaca, NY: Cornell University Press, 1997); Lucius Outlaw, *On Race and Philosophy* (New York: Routledge, 1996); Charles Mills, *Blackness Visible: Essays on Philosophy and Race* (Ithaca, NY: Cornell University Press, 1998).

9. *Critical Philosophy of Race,* see www.psupress.org/Journals/jnls_CPR.html, last visited March 22, 2013.

10. Kwame Anthony Appiah, Amy Gutmann, et al., *Color Conscious: The Political Morality of Race* (Princeton, NJ: Princeton University Press, 1998).

11. W. E. B. Du Bois, *The Souls of Black Folk* (New York: New American Library, 1969). Other works by Du Bois include *The Philadelphia Negro: A Social Study* (New York: Schocken Books, 1967).

12. See also Anita L. Allen, "Bruce Kuklick's Black Philosopher, White Academy: The Career of William Fontaine," *Pennsylvania Magazine of History and Biography* 133, no. 2 (April 2009): 213.

13. I was a graduate student in residence in philosophy at the University of Michigan from 1974 to 1978. My PhD in philosophy from the University of Michigan was officially conferred in 1980, about the same time as another black woman, Adrian Piper, received hers from Harvard. Piper, who lives in Germany, taught in the philosophy departments of the University of Michigan, Georgetown University, the University of San Diego, and Wellesley College. Joyce Mitchell Cook (Yale), the first black woman to earn a PhD in philosophy, and Laverne Shelton (Wisconsin), the second, did not receive tenure when they entered teaching at Howard and Rutgers, respectively. Piper appears to have been the first black woman to be tenured by a philosophy department. She was tenured in philosophy at Georgetown about the time I was tenured in law by Georgetown—around 1989. Cf. Robin Wilson, *Chronicle of Higher Education,* "Black Women Seek a Role in Philosophy" (2007), chronicle.com/article/Black-Women-Seek-a-Role-in/24971.

14. Cf. George Yancy, ed., *African-American Philosophers: 17 Conversations* (New York: Routledge, 1998).

15. Chapters of my books about privacy delve into issues of race; see *Unpopular Privacy: What Must We Hide* (New York: Oxford University Press, 2011), which includes a chapter on the concept of racial privacy; and *Why Privacy Isn't Everything: Feminist Reflections on Personal Accountability* (Lanham, MD: Rowman & Littlefield, 2004), which includes long discussions of interracial marriage and the impact of drug use on black families.

16. See https://www.law.upenn.edu/cf/faculty/aallen.

17. Michael Eric Dyson, who has a PhD in religion, was appointed to Penn's faculty to teach religion and Africana studies in 2002, but moved his base of operations to Georgetown University a few years later.

18. William T. Fontaine, *Reflections on Segregation, Desegregation, Power and Morals* (Springfield, IL: Charles C. Thomas, 1968), p. 41.

19. Ibid., pp. 117ff.

20. Ibid.. p. 117.

21. Ibid., p. 117.

A Westian Vision of the Role of Black Philosophy

CHIKE JEFFERS

The role of black philosophy? I believe Bro. Cornel West pointed us down the right path. In 1977 he wrote: *"Afro-American philosophy is the interpretation of Afro-American history, highlighting the cultural heritage and political struggles, which provides desirable norms that should regulate responses to particular challenges presently confronting Afro-Americans."*[1] Where he spoke of "Afro-American philosophy," I would speak of *Africana philosophy,* a term I will treat as interchangeable with "black philosophy."[2] In what follows, I will use West's definition to build a vision of the role of Africana philosophy in the intellectual life of the black world. I will also provide an example of what I would see as the fruitful development of the field by briefly exploring the prospects for increased work on the topic of Pan-Africanism.

I would define philosophy in a general sense as the activity of raising and trying to answer, in a reflective and critical fashion, fundamental questions about the nature and value of things, about how we gain knowledge, and about how we ought to live our lives. Africana philosophy in the broadest possible sense is, on this definition, immeasurably old, as I see no reason to doubt that this activity has been carried out by people on the African continent for as long as our species has possessed the linguistic and cognitive capacities we associate with being human. Ancient Egyptian thought serves, I believe, as the initiating source of Africana philosophy as a historically ascertainable tradition, given the difficulty of measuring the age of sources in the oral tradition.[3] In the modern era, as Africans and African descendants confronted the slave trade, slavery, segregation, and colonization, Africana philosophizing developed a strong sociopolitical focus. The modern period also brings us the first black professional philosophers, people like Anton Wilhelm Amo, from what is now Ghana, who received the equivalent of a doctorate in philosophy in Germany in 1730, and Thomas Nelson Baker, who became the first African American in the United States to receive a PhD in philosophy in 1903.[4]

I shall concentrate here on Africana philosophy as a professional enterprise, that is, on the work of trained philosophers. I should explain right away, though, that I do not take all work in philosophy by black professional philosophers to count as *black philosophy*. I count only work that is distinctively Africana, in the sense that it is concerned with issues arising out of the black experience and/or it participates in a philosophical tradition associated primarily with black people.[5] Works by black philosophers

Chike Jeffers is an assistant professor of philosophy at Dalhousie University (Halifax, Nova Scotia). He specializes in Africana philosophy and philosophy of race, with broad interests in social and political philosophy and ethics. He is the editor of *Listening to Ourselves: A Multilingual Anthology of African Philosophy* (Albany: SUNY Press, 2013).

that fit into the standard categories of Western philosophy and are not plausibly related to the racial/ethnic identity of their authors in any interesting way are best classified, in my view, as simply contributions to Western philosophy.[6]

With this brief historical overview and classificatory clarification in place, I can turn to explaining why I think Cornel West's conception of Afro-American philosophy is so helpful for figuring out the proper function of Africana or black philosophy. West's vision has three vital components I wish to highlight. Two of these components concern the temporal direction of our attention when doing Africana philosophy: West evokes, on the one hand, a backward-looking orientation ("the interpretation of Afro-American *history*") and, on the other hand, a sense of engagement with the present ("responses to particular challenges *presently* confronting Afro-Americans"). These different directions are not held in tension but rather smoothly reconciled: we are asked to look into the past to determine how best to deal with the present. The other component that I wish to highlight is not temporal but a matter of content, that is, a point about the subject matter of Africana philosophical inquiry: West calls for a focus on the "*cultural heritage*" and "*political struggles*" of black people.

I endorse this vision of black philosophy. I believe Africana philosophy maximizes its relevance and usefulness to black people's individual lives and the collective life of black people as a whole when it serves as a kind of powerful mirror we can use to *critically reflect upon who we are and where we stand*. The Westian vision of black philosophy helps us achieve this by encouraging the cultivation of the historical consciousness we need to understand how we became who we are, the awareness of present-day challenges needed to ensure that we are contributing to the ongoing struggles of our people, and the sensitivity to varying cultural and political dimensions of black life necessary to paint appropriately complex images of a healthy black future.

Let us consider, first, the importance of turning to the past. Part of the point here is that Africana philosophy must of necessity have concern for the past because it is only by grappling with our unique historical experience with slavery and colonialism that we can begin to address the issues black people face today. Another primary concern, though, is the need to retroactively *build a canon*.[7] It is a hugely important task for Africana philosophers to explore the black intellectual tradition and uphold within it those works they find valuable from a philosophical point of view. In his 1977 essay, for example, West critically engages with, among others, W. E. B. Du Bois, James Weldon Johnson, R. R. Wright Jr., Marcus Garvey, Martin Luther King Jr., E. Franklin Frazier, Sutton Griggs, Charles Chesnutt, Nella Larsen, Rudolph Fisher, Wallace Thurman, Richard Wright, James Baldwin, Gayl Jones, Toni Morrison, Jean Toomer, Langston Hughes, Sterling Brown, Zora Neale Hurston, and Ralph Ellison.[8] A number of these figures are, of course, already canonical in the study of African-American literature. In a manner that is not opposed to but rather complementary to the literary critic's examination of the ability of such figures to creatively render and reinterpret African-American experiences through the art of language, philosophers have the task of drawing analytical and critical attention to their ability to insightfully conceptualize various phenomena and make persuasive arguments, whether implicit or explicit in their writing.[9] Novels, poetry, plays, and other forms of creative writing may be usefully subjected to this kind of reading, but it is, of course, the nonfiction prose stream of black intellectual thought that is most readily amenable to this treatment.

Why is it so important that we turn to this historical chain of ideas, embedded most often in texts not generally recognized as philosophy? We turn back in this way because we as professional philosophers, self-consciously dedicated to the task of clarifying and addressing tough questions, have an extremely rich legacy of philosophical thinking behind us that must be reckoned with if we do not wish our contributions to be impoverished reinvents of the wheel. We do ourselves a number of disservices when we fail to examine the riches of the black intellectual tradition. First of all, despite my comment above about the most amenable sources, I mean to refer here not only to black writing, but also to oral traditions. Engaging with traditional African thought as best we can through its modern reconstruction is vital to avoiding a Eurocentric conception of Africana philosophy's roots.[10] Among the oral traditions of the diaspora, we might single out musical works as especially significant repositories of reflective thought that philosophers would do well to take more seriously.[11] Finally, a central reason for building up a canon through exploring the black intellectual tradition is the fact that, as previously noted, our problems

today are connected to past injustices. For this reason, when we engage with modern black thought and its past attempts to comprehend and do battle with our systematic oppression, we encounter ways of thinking that remain strikingly relevant.

Take Robert Gooding-Williams's recent book, *In the Shadow of Du Bois: Afro-Modern Political Thought in America* (2009). Gooding-Williams contributes to the canon-building project I have described by treating Du Bois's *The Souls of Black Folk* (1903) as an "outstanding contribution to modern political philosophy" that must furthermore be recognized as belonging particularly to the "*Afro-modern* tradition of political thought, an impressively rich body of argument and insight that began to emerge late in the eighteenth century" with the work of Afro-British figures like Quobna Ottobah Cugoano and Olaudah Equiano.[12] Gooding-Williams offers us a careful and well-argued reconstruction of the theory of politics in *Souls* (what he calls Du Bois's "politics of expressive self-realization").[13] He then reaches past Du Bois back to Frederick Douglass, specifically the Douglass of *My Bondage and My Freedom* (1855), in order to claim that Douglass has a theory of politics (a "politics of radical reconstruction") that can be used to challenge Du Bois and reveal the latter's "limitations and blind spots."[14] Having thus engaged, in great depth, with two canonical thinkers and having thereby cast new light on their texts by juxtaposing them as he does, Gooding-Williams then explores what he sees as the problematic shadow of Du Bois over black thought today and the need for his Douglass-derived alternative view through a critical discussion of "ongoing debates about the nature of African American politics, the relevance of black identity to black politics, and the plight of the black underclass."[15]

Through efforts like these, Africana philosophers bring the past to bear on the present. They do this not in a manner that chains us to the past or blinds us to the present but in a way that carefully sifts the past for what is most informative and illuminating in understanding our current predicament and discerning possible paths forward. I should note that I, unlike Gooding-Williams, believe the influence of Du Bois on contemporary black political thought ought to be extended rather than lessened. I believe that we can and should draw on Du Bois in learning how to maintain a careful balance when confronting white supremacy between, on the one hand, constantly *demanding an end to racial difference* in access to power and resources and, on the other hand, constantly *defending the value of racial difference* in rejection of Eurocentrism.[16] One way to think of this is as a balance between seeking *political sameness* and affirming *cultural difference*. My belief that these two concerns, which pull in different directions, must be carefully balanced contrasts with Tommie Shelby's prominent position, according to which the cultural nationalist investment in affirming black cultural difference is an unproductive distraction.[17] These disagreements with Gooding-Williams and Shelby are symbolic, I believe, of the ultimate centrality in modern Africana philosophy of the question of *the relationship between culture and politics*.[18] Africana philosophy has, by necessity, a certain broadness of vision, a concern for the nature of what it is to be black that makes every aspect of black life of

potential importance and also raises tough questions about how it all fits together. This broadness of vision helps make Africana philosophy relevant to thinking through an amazing variety of questions: from large questions of political economy to small, personal questions of daily habits, with not only everything in between but the infinitely intricate question of the whole also at stake.[19]

I would like to use the remainder of this comment to discuss an example of the kind of political and cultural issue that I believe Africana philosophy is well placed to address through clarifying, criticizing, and defending positions on what is at stake and what ought to be done. What is the contemporary relevance of the notion of Pan-Africanism? Is it a living political movement? Can it be used to describe our current cultural reality or a reality that we ought to be striving to attain? From a political perspective, some might see Pan-Africanism as a historical movement whose call for black unity was most pressing when we were faced with the task of overcoming racist political structures that formally subjected black people to white domination. Following the defeat of apartheid in South Africa, in a world with many countries run by black people (not to mention a black US president), black unity on a global scale may seem less important. From a cultural perspective, the idea that all black people are and ought to feel culturally connected may seem rooted in completely outdated notions of racial essentialism. Pan-Africanism might therefore seem, overall, simply a thing of the past.

In response to this, I would first like to point out why conditions in the black world today make the question of unifying black people across ethnic and national boundaries increasingly rather than decreasingly significant. In the majority-white countries of North America and Europe, immigration trends over the past half-century have consistently increased the diversity of black populations. Whether the majority of black people in the country are of recent immigrant background, as in European countries, or not, as in the United States, there is no escaping anywhere the reality that "the black community" in Western countries is drawn from various parts of the black world, making relations between black people of various backgrounds an important issue.[20] While immigration thus makes the local more global, the global has famously become more local through economic and technological transformations that reduce the significance of national borders. The future development of majority-black countries in Africa and the Americas will not be toward greater and greater independence, even if we defeat pernicious forms of neocolonialism, but greater interdependence. This raises the question of what role unity on the basis of African heritage might play in forming global linkages.

I believe Africana philosophy can and should help to organize and develop the conversation about Pan-Africanism that needs to happen in light of these political and cultural realities. Some may bring philosophical perspectives to this issue that lead to conclusions unfavorable to the Pan-Africanist stance, but I support Pan-Africanism and believe its philosophical foundations can be clarified and strengthened. Despite my space limitations, I wish to sketch two arguments showing this.

First, in relation to worries about essentialism, I would argue that embracing Pan-Africanism need not be about ignoring differences between black people and can, in fact, be valued precisely for the way it makes plain the diversity of blackness. What unifies black identity is a particular history, one that involves global dispersion and a series of recombinations under conditions of slavery and/or colonial rule. The amount of variation in the cultures brought together under this umbrella or newly created by this historical experience need not embarrass the Pan-Africanist. Indeed, in light of the reshaping and revaluing of what it means to be black through the agency of those so categorized, this diversity can and should be a source of pride.

Second, we should be wary of how resisting Pan-Africanism may mean perpetuating divisions that are not natural but rather, to a significant extent, products of anti-black racism. Misunderstandings and antagonisms between black people of different backgrounds do not arise simply because of the bare fact of being different. Especially when they have been brought together in societies full of anti-black stereotyping, much of the discord between black groups can plausibly be related to acceptance of or at least the failure to challenge the distorting images of racist ideology. Pan-Africanism's call for unity is partly a call to transcend rather than naturalize and resign ourselves to the existence of this type of invidious division.[21]

In closing, let me note that the African Union has declared itself open to the increasing participation in African affairs of the African diaspora, affirming even the possible future recognition of the diaspora as an official "sixth region."[22] I call upon Africana philosophy to aid in thinking through the aims and implications of this possible participation, drawing upon and critically engaging with the rich history of Pan-Africanist thought represented by figures like Du Bois and Garvey and relating the political issues here to cultural questions like those raised by the immense popularity of hip-hop in Africa. There is much to consider and discuss.

Notes

1. Cornel West, "Philosophy and the Afro-American Experience," *Philosophical Forum* 9 (Winter–Spring 1977–1978): 122–123.

2. For the pioneering usage and theorization of the term "Africana philosophy," see Lucius Outlaw, "African, African American, Africana Philosophy," *Philosophical Forum* 24 (Fall–Spring 1992–1993): 63–93. For a book-length study of the field, see Lewis R. Gordon, *An Introduction to Africana Philosophy* (Cambridge: Cambridge University Press, 2008).

3. On philosophy in ancient Egyptian thought, see Théophile Obenga, "Egypt: Ancient History of African Philosophy," in *A Companion to African Philosophy,* ed. Kwasi Wiredu (Malden, MA: Blackwell, 2004), pp. 31–49. Obenga makes a strong case for seeing a passage in a text from the Twelfth Dynasty (1991–1782 BC) known as the *Inscription of Antef* as offering us the "first definition of a 'philosopher' in world history" (ibid., p. 35).

4. See William E. Abraham, "Anton Wilhelm Amo," in *A Companion to African Philosophy,* pp. 191–199, and George Yancy, "Thomas Nelson Baker: Toward an Understanding of a Pioneer Black Philosopher," *American Philosophical Association Newsletter on Philosophy and the Black Experience* 95 (Spring 1996): 5–9.

5. Stephen C. Ferguson II has similarly drawn a distinction between "*Africana philosophers* and the *philosophy of the Black experience.*" I think we disagree, however, with regard to whether all work by Africana philosophers counts as Africana philosophy, given what Ferguson goes on to say while arguing that "the philosophy of the Black experience" is one part of the larger project of "Africana philosophy." Note, though, that my narrower definition, according to which not all work by black philosophers counts as Africana philosophy, nevertheless refrains from limiting Africana philosophy to work focused on the experiences of African and African-descended peoples, as I count any tradition of thought as Africana philosophy—whatsoever its themes—as long as it can be seen as distinctively tied to the work of black thinkers. See Stephen C. Ferguson II, "Philosophy in Africa and the African Diaspora," in *The Oxford Handbook of World Philosophy* (New York: Oxford University Press, 2011), p. 463. My view on what ought to be counted as Africana philosophy is partly influenced by Kwasi Wiredu's thoughts on how work that does not concern traditional African culture might come to be rightly called African philosophy. See Kwasi Wiredu, "On Defining African Philosophy," in Tsenay Serequeberhan, *African Philosophy: The Essential Readings* (New York: Paragon House, 1991), pp. 92–93.

6. So, for example, Ghanaian philosopher Kwame Anthony Appiah has greatly contributed to Africana philosophy through efforts like *In My Father's House: Africa in the Philosophy of Culture* (New York: Oxford University Press, 1992). His first two books, however, I would not consider contributions to Africana philosophy but rather simply examples of philosophy of language in the Western tradition. See Anthony Appiah, *Assertion and Conditionals* (Cambridge: Cambridge University Press, 1985) and *For Truth*

in *Semantics* (Oxford: Basil Blackwell, 1986). It is perhaps harder to decide how to classify some of his more recent work on matters like cosmopolitanism, empirical evidence in ethics, and the moral significance of honor. I would at least count his work on cosmopolitanism as forming part of Africana philosophy, given the ways in which he draws on aspects of his cultural background in making his arguments. For more on that topic, see my "Appiah's Cosmopolitanism," *Southern Journal of Philosophy* 51 (December 2013): 488–510.

7. I echo Howard McGary: "I can't emphasize enough that what I think is crucial now is that African-American philosophers spend the time creating the canon." Note, however, that McGary is perhaps not speaking solely about historically oriented work here, so I may, to some extent, be appropriating his words for my own purposes. See "Howard McGary," in *African-American Philosophers: 17 Conversations,* ed. George Yancy (New York: Routledge, 1998), p. 91.

8. The presence of Larsen, Jones, Morrison, and Hurston on this list is important, as it is imperative that in constructing the canon of African American philosophical thought, we ensure that women thinkers are amply represented. We are aided in doing so by collections of writing like Beverly Guy-Sheftall's landmark volume, *Words of Fire: An Anthology of African-American Feminist Thought* (New York: New Press, 1995).

9. For an example of an attempt to make this sort of complementary philosophical move in relation to a significant text in ancient Egyptian literature, see my "Embodying Justice in Ancient Egypt: *The Tale of the Eloquent Peasant* as a Classic of Political Philosophy," *British Journal for the History of Philosophy* 21 (May 2013): 421–442.

10. The need for diasporic traditions in Africana philosophy to engage with traditional African thought is nicely defended and demonstrated in Paget Henry's *Caliban's Reason: Introducing Afro-Caribbean Philosophy* (New York: Rout-

ledge, 2000). For an alternative view, see Cornel West, *Prophesy Deliverance! An Afro-American Revolutionary Christianity,* anniversary ed. (Louisville, KY: Westminster John Knox Press, 2002 [1982]), p. 24. The significance of traditional African thought for contemporary African philosophy has, of course, long been a central topic and source of controversy in the field. One way the issue has come up is the question of what difference it would make for African philosophy to be carried on in indigenous African languages rather than European ones. I have tried to contribute to moving the field from discussion to action on this issue by editing *Listening to Ourselves: A Multilingual Anthology of African Philosophy* (Albany: State University of New York Press, 2013).

11. For an example of taking this type of source seriously, see Angela Y. Davis, *Blues Legacies and Black Feminism: Gertrude "Ma" Rainey, Bessie Smith and Billie Holiday* (New York: Random House, 1998).

12. Robert Gooding-Williams, *In the Shadow of Du Bois: Afro-Modern Political Thought in America* (Cambridge, MA: Harvard University Press, 2009), pp. 1, 2. Emphasis mine.

13. Ibid., p. 4.

14. Ibid., pp. 18, 5.

15. Ibid., p. 8. Gooding-Williams intervenes in these contemporary debates by engaging with a number of important black thinkers of today, including John Brown Childs, Joy James, Adolph Reed, Paul Gilroy, Tommie Shelby, Eddie Glaude, William Julius Wilson, Cathy Cohen, and Henry Louis Gates Jr.

16. For more on this, see my "The Cultural Theory of Race: Yet Another Look at Du Bois's 'The Conservation of Races,'" *Ethics* 123 (April 2013): 403–426.

17. See Tommie Shelby, *We Who Are Dark: The Philosophical Foundations of Black Solidarity* (Cambridge, MA: Belknap Press of Harvard University Press, 2005). Note that while Shelby rejects the cultural nationalist element of Du Bois's

work, he simultaneously draws on other aspects of his work in support of the view that there can be stable black solidarity across class lines (see chapter 2).

18. West, for his part, speaks of culture as a matter of "self-image" or "the perennial human attempt to define who and what one is" and politics as a matter of "self-determination" or the "struggle to gain significant control over the major institutions that regulate people's lives." He argues further that "culture is more fundamental than politics" in the sense that "Afro-American cultural perceptions provide a broader and richer framework for understanding the Afro-American experience than political perceptions," which helps to explain the large number of literary figures and other artistic types in his essay. See West, "Philosophy and the Afro-American Experience," pp. 123, 125.

19. For an example of tackling a question concerning daily habits in the light of the broad question of the relationship between race, culture, and politics, see my "Should Black Kids Avoid Wearing Hoodies?" in *Pursuing Trayvon Martin: Historical Contexts and Contemporary Manifestations of Racial Dynamics*, eds. George Yancy and Janine Jones (Lanham, MD: Lexington Books, 2012).

20. Canada, the country I call home, is an interesting case, as the majority of the black population is of recent immigrant background (as in Europe) but there are also long-standing black populations and, in the province of Nova Scotia, where I live, the situation is somewhat similar to that of the United States: the majority of the black population is not of recent immigrant background but rather descended from people who arrived in this province centuries ago, and yet recent immigration has made the black population increasingly diverse. For more on the significance of the diversity of black Canada, see the final section of my "Do We Need African Canadian Philosophy?", *Dialogue: Canadian Philosophical Review/Revue canadienne de philosophie* 51 (December 2012): 643–666.

21. As Du Bois put it in 1933, "American Negroes, West Indians, West Africans and South Africans must proceed immediately to wipe from their minds the preconcepts of each other which they have gained through white newspapers." W. E. B. Du Bois, "Pan-Africa and New Racial Philosophy," *Crisis* 40 (November 1933): 247.

22. See section I.A.(k) of the Declaration of the Global African Diaspora Summit, held in Johannesburg, South Africa, May 25, 2012: www.au.int/en/content/declaration-global-african-diaspora-summit-sandton-johannesburg-south-africa-25-may-2012.

An Illuminating Blackness

CHARLES W. MILLS

If philosophy is definitionally an exercise in enlightenment, the illumination of oneself and the world, then how could philosophy ever be *black?* Surely this is the very color of the darkness that we want illuminated and eliminated, both internally and externally. It is whiteness that is classically the color of enlightenment, not to mention Enlightenment. Moreover—in terms of actual electromagnetic radiation—any physicist will be happy to inform us that white light already includes all the colors of the visible spectrum, while blackness turns out to be not really a color at all, but the *absence* of all light and color. So it would seem that any metaphors drawn from this realm already conceptually foredoom the enterprise. Whiteness is light; whiteness is all-encompassing; whiteness is the universal. How could genuine philosophy be anything *but* white?

And the obvious answer is . . . it all depends on how you choose your metaphors.[1]

Consider another way of looking at things, another set of linked metaphors, though still within the realm of the optical: whiteness as glare, whiteness as dazzle, whiteness as blinding, whiteness as the "Monopolated Light & Power" of Ralph Ellison's *Invisible Man.*[2] In the prologue to Ellison's novel, his nameless black narrator—surrounded in his secret basement by 1,369 lightbulbs—tells us: "I've illuminated the blackness of my invisibility—and vice versa."[3] But the illumination he has attained over the novel's quest (as he looks back in a prologue that is really a postscript) has been achieved despite, not with the help of, the Jim Crowed white power source represented by Monopolated, and its attempted totalitarian control of his vision. Whiteness here is constructed not by inclusion of the other colors but by their official exclusion, an "Optic White" for "Keeping America Pure," even if an unacknowledged black base lies at the heart of its "purity."[4] Figuring whiteness in this way demystifies its chromatic pretensions and the related illusions of the Eurocentric worldview that has biased objective inquiry into the workings of the world. Seen through this alternative prism, whiteness is a willed darkness; whiteness is segregated investigation; whiteness is the particular masquerading as the universal.

From this revisionist perspective, then, we can appreciate how a philosophy coming out of blackness could actually be better situated to carry out the Enlightenment project than its designated "legitimate"

Charles W. Mills is John Evans Professor of Moral and Intellectual Philosophy at Northwestern University. He works in the general area of oppositional political theory, with a particular focus on race. He is the author of numerous journal articles and book chapters, and five books: *The Racial Contract* (1997); *Blackness Visible: Essays on Philosophy and Race* (1998); *From Class to Race: Essays in White Marxism and Black Radicalism* (2003); *Contract and Domination* (with Carole Pateman) (2007); and *Radical Theory, Caribbean Reality: Race, Class and Social Domination* (2010).

representatives. But first we need to clarify: What is black philosophy? To begin with, it is not simply the philosophy produced by people of (recent) African origins, whether in Africa or the diaspora. If race is a product of the modern period, as many postwar commentators have argued,[5] black philosophy cannot exist before blackness exists. Thinkers in the Africa of, say, 1000 CE would not have been black, and so would not have been doing black philosophy when they philosophized.

But the second and more important point is that even after the emergence of blackness as a social category and social reality, it seems dubious to categorize all the philosophizing of blacks as black philosophy. If the mere identity of the practitioners constituted a sufficient condition, then work by blacks in mainstream metaphysics, epistemology, logic, philosophy of language, value theory, history of philosophy, and so on, that is in no way informed by blackness or race or the African-American experience would count as "black" philosophy even if it were indistinguishable from work produced by European and Euro-American philosophers. Clearly such a conclusion is quite counterintuitive. So we need to differentiate the identity of the philosophers from the identity of the philosophy, and separate the question of *who they are* from the question of *what it is*. Black philosophy will, of course, predominantly be done by black philosophers—this is not a contingent correlation. But it cannot be turned into a definitional truth.

In my opinion, the best way to conceptualize the defining features of black philosophy is as the philosophy that develops out of the distinctive experience of racial subordi-nation in modernity—a philosophy that in its effort to understand and end that subordination, illuminates modernity more thoroughly and relentlessly, more free from illusions, than its white antagonist. Blackness really indicates not a particular band of wavelengths but a particular social position, and not just any subordinated nonwhite position but a peculiar location within the nexus of multiple oppressions created by white supremacy. And if, as "standpoint theorists" in epistemology have been arguing for several decades now (though largely white feminists with respect to gender), social subordination affords one distinctive insight, this means that blacks have been peculiarly well placed to theorize, from the underside (think of Ellison's narrator in his basement), the actual material and normative topography of this racialized world.

Consider the "big three" of structural social oppression: gender, class, and race. Of these, both gender and class clearly predate the modern period, in patriarchal systems of various kinds stretching back to the early formation of the species, and in class societies evolving in separate continents out of hunter-gatherer communities. But race is different. Controversy exists as to whether race as a concept and shaper of thought is distinctively modern or goes back to antiquity.[6] But even if race as an idea is older than the conventional postwar narrative would claim, race as a planetary system is unambiguously modern. It is European expansionism in the modern period that internationalizes race, creating a white supremacy that becomes global by the early twentieth century.[7] So although gender and class are, of course, also part of this matrix of interlocking oppressions generated by empire, race is the element that is new and whose synthesizing effect shapes the transmutation of these premodern categories into their distinctively modern forms. To the extent that white supremacy gradually spreads, in material structures and overarching norms, across the planet, it henceforth ceases to be possible to speak simply of "gender" and "class," for these identities will now be racialized.

And this means, as the disproportionately black and female pioneering theorists of "intersectionality" have taught us,[8] that insofar as white racial identity tends to trump gender and class—with the white woman and the white worker generally making common cause with the white male bourgeois directors of the colonial project rather than with their sisters and brothers of color in resistance to it—both white feminism and white class theory will be cognitively handicapped. White women and the white working class will generally find it harder to recognize and theorize racial oppression, from which they benefit, whether through the land and resources from indigenous expropriation, the racial exploitation of African slavery and the subsequent social denial to blacks of equal opportunities, or their privileged European citizenship of the imperial powers. This is not to deny the existence of that historic handful of white progressives, male and female, who have overcome their socialization to demand an end to *all* forms of subordination. But the reality is that white racial privilege has generally distorted the clarity of vision one would have hoped for from those experiencing intra-white gender and class oppression. While white feminism and white Marxism have produced distinc-

tive and invaluable insights as oppositional bodies of thought within the Western tradition, they have usually failed to see white supremacy as a system in itself.

Black philosophy, then, particularly in its intersectionalist rather than its dominant black male form, emerges as the philosophy of those at the bottom of this interlocking set of oppressions. And I would suggest that the distinctive racialization of blacks offers insights into the workings of white supremacy not always as readily available from other nonwhite cognitive locations in this system.

Consider the major varieties of white Western racism of the modern period: anti-Semitism in its racial form; anti-black racism; anti–Native American racism; anti-Arab racism; anti-Asian racism; anti-Latino racism; anti–Australian Aborigine racism. Anti-Semitism is generally judged to have been discredited in the West, except for racist fringe groups, by the Holocaust, and Jews are today accepted as "white" in Western nations, certainly in the United States. Moreover, anti-Semitism was never integral to the colonial project. Anti–Native American racism was, obviously, central to the creation of the United States, but the genocide of Native Americans and the creation of the reservation system means that today they are a marginal presence in the daily life of the white polity. In addition, though their racial categorization—"Indians"—was crucial to white settler ideology, it is not generally one that they have embraced themselves, except for contingent reasons of political solidarity against the white man, since they retain their preconquest civilizational identities. The same could be said about Australian Aborigines, who have sometimes self-identified as "blacks"—both as a reclamation and positive inversion of the derogatory white settler term used for them and in partial emulation of the black American struggle—but have their diverse ethnic belongings to fall back on. Islamophobia has been judged by some theorists to be a form of medieval cultural anti-Arab racism, and thus long embedded in the Western tradition, even before its renascence in recent decades as a result of Middle East politics and the growth of anti-Western terrorist movements. But in part because of the legacy of the Arab slave trade, blacks have themselves often been seen in racist terms by Arabs, and religion rather than race was the banner under which the Arab anticolonial struggle was fought. "Asians" as a racial, as against continental, category attempts to subsume into one group people from very different nations with different languages, cultural histories, and in some cases traditions of extensive conflict with one another. And again, their national identities, even in immigrant communities in the United States, often trump their imputed/constructed "racial" identity, since unlike (some) Native Americans and Native Australians, they suffered less damage from Western colonialism's attempted eradication of their national cultures through violence and the lure of assimilation. Finally, Latinos are not only, like Asians, citizens of many different nations, but do not even have the "racial" commonalities that would justify a clear-cut racial category. Hence the ongoing debate as to whether they should really be seen as a race in the first place or as an ethnic group composed of many races, with "whiteness" a preferred choice for many of them, and a tradition of derogation of Afro-Latinos.[9] *The position of blacks is unique among all the groups racialized as nonwhite by the modern West; for no other nonwhite group has race been so enduringly constitutive of their identity and so enduringly central to white racial consciousness and global racial consciousness in general.*[10]

My claim is, then, that black philosophy is more likely to be systematically devoted to the project of developing a consistently antiracist understanding of race than the "racial" philosophies (to the extent that they exist) of other nonwhite racialized groups. The peculiar experience of Africans under Western modernity, which originally turned them into "negroes" (lowercase), creating a race where previously none had existed, impressed a forced diaspora on them that took them to Europe and the Americas (unlike Amerindians and Native Australians, who generally remained at home), made the extraction of their labor central to the making of the modern world,[11] thus requiring them to be part of the Western polity while simultaneously excluding them from equal membership in that polity (aboriginal land is also central to this making, but the presence of its inhabitants is not necessary), attempted to deprive them of their original civilizational and national identities, so that race in the diaspora became the central "practical" identity[12] for them, oppositionally resignified from stigma to badge of pride, while still leaving them globally identifiable as the people who were appropriately designated a "slave race" in modernity, the very period when slavery was dead or dying in the West, their physical features instantly recognizable across the planet both because of a higher degree of phenotypical distinctiveness (whites/blacks as a polar contrast) and because of this slave legacy and its associations, reinforced moreover by the seeming fact that even today no other continent of origin continues to have the problems of the African one, which remains "Dark," while China and India are global success stories. In sum, no other group has had the distinctive combination of experience, motivation, lack of alternative identitarian resources, and intimate and quotidian familiarity with the ideologies and practices of the West to be better positioned to understand race from the inside. It is no accident, then, that what has recently been christened "critical philosophy of race"[13] has been pioneered by blacks, for no other "race" has felt so imperatively the need to make sense of a world that has been more thoroughly and unforgivingly structured by race for them than for any other group, with no way out except to turn race to emancipatory purposes. Black philosophy is primarily critical philosophy of race drawing on the experience of black racial subordination.

And that brings us back to the promise of the universal. As the phrase implies, "standpoint theory" is a theory about epistemic locations, not individuals. The claim is not that "blackness" confers any kind of automatic veridical insight upon you: blacks are as capable of being racist and sexist as everybody else. After all, black womanism arose in large measure precisely because of the need to combat black male sexism. What standpoint theory presumes is that taking up a perspective shaped by social subordination, especially when it is open to multiple varieties of subordination, orients one epistemically in a way *more likely to be* illuminating of the true nature of the social system than

viewpoints taking for granted class, race, and gender privileges and their accompanying phenomenology. Onora O'Neill has famously argued that the problem with mainstream ethics and political philosophy is that it typically employs *idealizing* abstractions, not in the innocuous sense of selecting certain features of reality to take to the higher level of the model (since any theoretical abstraction necessarily does this), but in the problematic sense of abstracting away from social oppression and its fundamental shaping effect on people and society in carrying out such modeling.[14] The flawed abstractions typical of white social and political philosophy are of this form; they whitewash, they white-out, crucial aspects of social reality, above all the fact of white racial domination and its holistic impact over the past few hundred years. In the useful phrase of Joe Feagin's recent book, they give us a "white racial frame" through which to (mis) apprehend the world.[15] So what are being represented as abstract universals are really whitewashed particulars that have been polished up and Platonized. In theorizing the intersection of gender, class, and race, black philosophy thus holds the potential for a correction of the deficiencies that white racial privilege introduces into other bodies of oppositional theory, such as white feminism and white class theory. It is in this respect that black philosophy is potentially better positioned to realize the genuine (as against bogus) universal.

Finally, as a closing example (to allay fears of a black chauvinism), let me cite Nick Nesbitt's recent account of the Haitian Revolution.[16] Nesbitt demonstrates both how the Haitian Revolution was the most universal of its time, eclipsing the American and French Revolutions, and why it was necessary for a coordinated North Atlantic "Monopolated" white power to darken its universalist emancipatory beacon. And in the process he also shows how he, a white scholar, can adopt the illuminating vision, the radical enlightenment viewpoint, of a transformative black philosophy—a rainbowed vision, potentially containing all colors, for all of us.

Notes

1. See George Lakoff and Mark Johnson, *Metaphors We Live By,* 2nd ed. (1980; Chicago: University of Chicago Press, 2003).

2. Ralph Ellison, *Invisible Man* (1952; New York: Vintage, 1995), p. 5.

3. Ibid., p. 13.

4. Ibid., pp. 196, 212–218.

5. George M. Fredrickson, *Racism: A Short History* (Princeton, NJ: Princeton University Press, 2002).

6. Ibid.; Benjamin Isaac, *The Invention of Racism in Classical Antiquity* (Princeton, NJ: Princeton University Press, 2004).

7. W. E. B. Du Bois, *The Souls of Black Folk,* eds. David W. Blight and Robert Gooding-Williams (1903; Boston: Bedford Books, 1997); Victor Kiernan, *The Lords of Human Kind: European Attitudes to Other Cultures in the Imperial Age,* 4th ed. (1969; London: Serif, 1996); Howard Winant, *The World Is a Ghetto* (New York: Basic Books, 2001); Marilyn Lake and Henry Reynolds, *Drawing the Global Colour Line: White Men's Countries and the International Challenge of Racial Equality* (New York: Cambridge University Press, 2008).

8. Beverly Guy-Sheftall, ed., *Words of Fire: An Anthology of African-American Feminist Thought* (New York: New Press, 1995).

9. See, for example, Jorge J. E. Gracia, ed., *Race or Ethnicity: On Black and Latino Identity* (Ithaca, NY: Cornell University Press, 2007).

10. It is generally recognized that of all the many problematic claims in Jean-Paul Sartre's *Anti-Semite and Jew,* trans. George J. Becker (New York: Schocken Books, 1976), the most egregious is that the anti-Semite creates the Jew. (See, for example, Richard H. King, *Race, Culture, and the Intellectuals, 1940–1970* [Baltimore: Johns Hopkins University Press, 2004], chapter 2.) But the Negrophobe does create the negro.

11. David Brion Davis, *Inhuman Bondage: The Rise and Fall of Slavery in the New World* (New York: Oxford University Press, 2006).

12. Christine M. Korsgaard, *The Sources of Normativity* (New York: Cambridge University Press, 1996).

13. See the editors' letter introducing the new journal *Critical Philosophy of Race* 1, no. 1 (2013).

14. Onora O'Neill, "Justice, Gender, and International Boundaries," in *The Quality of Life,* eds. Martha Nussbaum and Amartya Sen (New York: Clarendon Press, 1993).

15. Joe R. Feagin, *The White Racial Frame: Centuries of Racial Framing and Counter-Framing* (New York: Routledge, 2010).

16. Nick Nesbitt, *Universal Emancipation: The Haitian Revolution and the Radical Enlightenment* (Charlottesville: University of Virginia Press, 2008).

Radical Love

Black Philosophy as Deliberate Acts of Inheritance

KRISTIE DOTSON

We can say with conviction that anything . . . [our children] love can be sheltered by their love. . . . They have to make their love inseparable from their belief. And both inseparable from hard work.[1]

—Alice Walker,
Anything We Love Can Be Saved

Introduction

Black philosophy requires radical love for black people. It is radical love not because it is rabid or obsessive. Rather, it is radical love because it results in a steadfast commitment, unwavering trust, and, in some contexts, a daring that defies current dominant reason. As I understand it, *one* of the roles of black philosophy is to dare to demonstrate radical love for black people.[2]

Though I do not mind speaking in generalities, the voice you hear is located somewhere, belongs to someone, and is influenced by some such embodiment. To that end, let me provide a more particular narrative. I am a black woman professional philosopher in the United States.[3] More specifically, my relationship to black philosophy is through the study and creation of black feminist philosophy, in which I center the lives and work of black women. So although I speak here of black philosophy, in general, I speak as a black feminist professional phi-

losopher, in particular. As such, I find that radical love for the lives and cultural artifacts of black women takes a steadfast commitment to centering black women, an unwavering trust that such centering will reap theoretical fruit, and a willingness to stake these claims in the face of many who would find my orientation, quite frankly, ludicrous. It is radical love and, at times, only radical love that brings me to black philosophy and it is from radical love that I produce it. *In this vein, I claim that one of the roles of black philosophy is to demonstrate radical love for black people by performing acts of inheritance of theoretical production created and maintained by black peoples.*[4]

In what follows, I will articulate three aspects of how demonstrating radical love can

Kristie Dotson is an assistant professor of philosophy at Michigan State University. Her research interests are primarily in feminist philosophy, African-American philosophy (especially black feminism), and epistemology. She edited with Robert Bernasconi a series of books titled *Race, Hybridity, and Miscegenation*. Some of her recent essays include "Tracking Epistemic Violence, Tracking Practices of Silencing" (*Hypatia*), "How Is this Paper Philosophy?" (*Comparative Philosophy*), "A Cautionary Tale: On Limiting Epistemic Oppression" (*Frontiers*), "Knowing in Space: Three Lessons from Black Women's Social Theory" (*Labrys*), "Querying Leonard Harris' Insurrectionist Standards" (*Transactions of the Charles S. Peirce Society*), and "Considering Epistemic Oppression" (forthcoming, *Social Epistemology*).

be perceived as one of the roles of black philosophy. First, I will articulate a commitment to centering black people and, in particular, black women's theoretical production. Second, I will locate the necessity of a kind of trust without which black feminist philosophy becomes difficult to identify. It is here I will develop the notion of acts of inheritance. Third, I will gesture to the daring such a centering and trust demands within professional philosophy in anti-black contexts. I conclude with a fleshed-out restatement of my claim that one of the roles of black philosophy is to demonstrate radical love for black people by performing acts of inheritance of black people's theoretical production with an attitude of, at times, brazen disregard for the status quo.

I. A Commitment to Black Peoples

To do black philosophy that centers the lives and work of black women requires that one is committed to valuing the theoretical production of black people, in general, and black women, in particular. Theoretical production, here, is a kind of cultural product that hearkens to organizing principles, discursive strategies, and/or broad observations for explaining or orienting phenomena. In a US context, which is an anti-black context, tracking and attending to the theoretical production of black women is not as easy as it sounds. As Audre Lorde explains:

It is not that we [black women] haven't always been here, since there was a here. It is that the letters of our names have been scrambled when they were not totally

erased, and our fingertips upon the handles of history have been called the random brushings of birds.[5]

Lorde highlights here that black women's work and contributions are often subject to a number of practices of unknowing that serve to render such contributions invisible. These ignorance-producing practices include misreading, erasure, and obfuscation. She is neither the first nor the last black woman to comment on process-based invisibility.[6] Process-based invisibility, on my account, refers to manufactured forms of invisibility that can be traced by the very processes that affect the disappearances in question. Often, engaging in black philosophy requires identifying and unpacking the many process-based invisibilities shrouding black theoretical production.

When centering the theoretical production of black women, which is often taken to be nonexistent, tackling and dismantling process-based invisibility is absolutely necessary. This includes, but is not limited to, archival investigations uncovering black women's theoretical production and, often, creating systems of interpretation that highlight rather than render abstruse that production. The amount of creative philosophical work that goes into creating systems of interpretation that feature rather than obscure black people's theoretical production should not be underestimated. It includes a set of tasks and abilities that are infrequently taught in graduate programs in philosophy, where there is often a presumption that "standard" interpretive strategies are sufficient for every kind of theoretical production.[7] The philosophical labor involved in creating or identifying interpretive strategies that do justice to black theoretical production is rarely fully appreciated. Yet, to even begin to engage in this kind of labor one needs to possess the second aspect of radical love to be discussed here, that is, trusting black people.

II. Trusting Black People: Making Love Inseparable from Belief

It may seem strange that I posit trusting black people as a named aspect of the radical love demonstrated by black philosophy. However, I take this to be the most important part of black philosophy, in general, and black feminist philosophy, in particular. Too often, in anti-black contexts, there is a denial of the existence of black theoretical production. Although with respect to black women persisting in climates with multifarious devaluations of black womanhood, there are relatively few specific denials. It is often assumed that black women in a US context have no significant body of philosophical literature. In both of these estimations, process-based invisibilities are ignored, and the resulting disappearing of black theoretical production is taken as evidence that no such production exists. Certainly, many who are philosophy-trained in a US context are encouraged to believe that there is no, "properly speaking," black philosophy at all. As a result, engaging in black philosophy in US professional philosophy, specifically, and in anti-black contexts, more generally, takes immense acts of inheriting.

Acts of inheriting, here, refers to the activity of stripping, shifting, and re-creating black cultural production to identify theo-

retical positions and/or orientations. In her article "Coalition Politics: Turning the Century," Bernice Johnson Reagon provides a general outline for acts of inheriting when she writes:

> The thing that must survive you is not just the record of your practice, but the principles that are the basis of your practice. If in the future, somebody is gonna use that song I sang, they're gonna have to strip it or at least shift it. I'm glad the principle is there for others to build upon.[8]

Here Johnson Reagon identifies not only what one should expect to leave of themselves and their work, but also what one should expect to receive. She calls this "throwing ourselves into the future."[9] Doing black philosophy, in general, and black feminist philosophy, in particular, requires one to trust that our ancestors have indeed thrown their theoretical production (i.e., their practice and their principles) into this century, as we, by engaging in black theoretical production and beyond, throw ourselves into future centuries.[10]

Johnson Reagon, a civil rights singer and renowned folk artist, highlights that her songs carry her practice and her principles, thereby indicating that the cultural production of black people relevant for black philosophy is exceedingly diverse. From songs to visual art, from poems to prose, and from comedy sketches to philosophical tracts, the range of cultural production carrying theoretical contributions is exceedingly vast.[11] There is one caveat, of course. One must trust black people to have lived deliberately in such a way that one understands that black cultural production, in all its many forms, *does* hold the potential to carry theoretical production; that black people's practice ought to be read to hold principles. And though this seems like a given, many conceptions of what counts as philosophy or "properly" philosophical implicitly or explicitly disallow this kind of trust due to either pernicious conceptions of philosophical engagement or unabashed anti-black sentiment.[12] As such, to do black philosophy one must make their "love inseparable from belief," which I understand here as "belief in."[13] When love is inseparable from belief in black people, the kind of trust in black people required to do black philosophy emerges. Black philosophy, in my estimation, requires a trust of black people, which, in a US context (anti-black with a persisting devaluation of black womanhood), is constantly in peril. This is why doing black philosophy, in general, and black feminist philosophy, in particular, requires a kind of daring that should not go unnoticed.

III. Because We Dare: Making Love and Belief Inseparable from Hard Work

In professional philosophy contexts, like the US, where appeals to false objectivity carry more authority than positions that acknowledge the situatedness of perspectives, making a commitment to and belief in black people, in general, and black women, in particular, runs the risk of turning one into the laughingstock of the profession. The pressure this reality can exert has been acknowledged.[14] The daring it takes to pursue black philosophy in some professional philosophy contexts, however, has received relatively less attention.[15] This daring can often manifest as either engaging or eschewing politics of respectability that prevail in a given professional philosophy context.

A *politics of respectability* is a discourse, usually within a black community, that demands one's overall behavior not feed into prevailing negative stereotypes of black peoples. For example, E. Frances White explains that a politics of respectability can manifest as a "discourse within the black community demanding the end of open expressions of sexuality . . . [and] shows of laziness," for example.[16] By no means is such a politics universally shared across all black communities or among all black professional philosophers. In fact, some would identify politics of respectability as issuing from middle-class conceptions of proper conduct—a position I am decidedly sympathetic to, actually. However, the concept of a politics of respectability is useful for understanding some of the pressure placed on those engaged in black philosophy within professional philosophy contexts embedded in anti-black intellectual marketplaces.

When professional philosophical cultures assume that black philosophy, in general, and black feminist philosophy, in particular, does not exist, one is placed in the position of having to, at the very least, (1) counter these assumptions in some way and/or (2) operate as if they do not exist. To think that these choices run no significant risks amounts to a radical underestimation of how one's engagement in acts of inheriting can be compromised or fostered by prevailing professional landscapes. That is to say, addressing the misconception that black philosophy does not exist, which was necessary to create a specialization in black or Africana philosophy in US professional philosophy, can suppress one's own creative engagement with black philosophy. It can induce, and continues to induce, academic passing.[17] In short, it can compromise the fullness of one's engagement in acts of inheriting. A far more sinister problematic, however, follows from the possibility that one's message can become lost to those who inherit that work. Daring to specifically counter prevailing trends of thought existing today, easily become the "apologies" castigated tomorrow—castigated because the climate that required specific defenses of black philosophy, for example, has been changed by those very defenses. This leaves the defenses or, as some would say, "apologies" without significant context for interpretation making them vulnerable to easy, destructive critique, thereby compromising one's very acts of inheriting.[18]

One is not "out of the woods" if one chooses to ignore current challenges to the existence of black philosophy. Ignoring such rejections is, of course, warranted. Such challenges are ridiculous, after all. Philosophical engagement is a basic human activity and we, none of us, are humanistically neutral. To claim that there is no distinctive black philosophy is but one other manifestation of an anti-black intellectual marketplace. However, ignoring such charges may serve to compromise one's acts of inheriting as well, albeit differently. I think here of Bill Lawson's print work. In his articles, he writes what he is interested in. His body of work looks at topics from US slavery to jazz. And his recent work on the profession of philoso-phy does not take the structure of a philosophical apology, but is rather an accusation of "playa hatin'" among white professional philosophers. His work, however, is already being subject to process-based invisibilities by virtue of not being considered philosophy "proper." Not abstract enough, not "deep" enough, not playing the game of the politics of respectability enough. Those who chose this path can have fruitful careers, but are often ostracized in their own eras and their work obscured by its refusal to engage anti-black aspects of our intellectual marketplaces. It remains to be seen if this relative obscurity will compromise the appreciation of Lawson's work over time. However, one would be remiss to not take note that such a risk exists.

To be clear, I do not take the appreciation of acts of inheritance to be something as simple as "one's work being read after one's death" or "one's work being taken seriously while one is alive." Rather, I understand acts of inheritance to concern serving our people by *actively* existing in a cultural and social life larger than ourselves, where our labor continues projects started before us and, hopefully, ending when such labor is no longer needed. It is likely that the labor of "apologies" for black philosophy is no longer needed and it is likely that writing on one's understanding of black experiences cannot be passed down, but neither of these possibilities removes the daring it takes to forward acts of inheritances along these lines in an anti-black intellectual marketplace. That is to say, where one's efforts may be doomed to the kind of process-based invisibilities that make a deliberate commitment to and infallible trust in black people necessary requirements for black philosophy one also exists in a circumstance where engaging in black philosophy takes a brazen will to do so. And this will, for me at least, follows from the radical love of black people that is required to engage in black philosophy at all. To produce black philosophy, then, is hard work. In anti-black contexts, it is daring work. It is work that requires a commitment to and trust in black people, in general, and black women, in particular, along with the daring to produce in accordance with this commitment and trust.

A commitment to black people, an unassailable trust in black people, and the daring it takes to produce black philosophy in anti-black intellectual contexts is a manifestation of radical love. It is an act of inheriting that attempts to respect our inheritances while throwing ourselves into the next century for future acts of inheritance. As a result, I believe *one of the roles* of black philosophy is to demonstrate radical love.

Notes

1. Alice Walker, *Anything We Love Can Be Saved: A Writer's Activism* (New York: Random House, 1997), p. 49.

2. I am deliberate in my use of "one of the roles" because, as this special issue will no doubt suggest, there are many roles of black philosophy. Here I aim to outline but one such role.

3. I use the term "professional philosopher" to designate the fact that I derive my wages from academic philosophy credentials and expertise. I take the time to make this distinction because not every black philosopher is, nor need be, a black professional philosopher. Black professional philosophers are but one population among many

that engage in black philosophy. Here, I speak as a black woman professional philosopher.

4. To say that one of the roles of black philosophy is to demonstrate radical love for black people is not to say that only black philosophy serves this role. The same, in many ways, can be said for any endeavor that takes its departure from blackness in places where anti-blackness is pervasive. However, black philosophy takes on the specific role of performing acts of inheritance of decidedly *theoretical* production created and maintained by black peoples.

5. Audre Lorde, "Foreword," in *Wild Women in the Whirlwind: Afra-American Culture and the Contemporary Literary Renaissance,* eds. Joanne Braxton and Andree McLaughlin (New Brunswick, NJ: Rutgers University Press, 1990), p. xi.

6. See also Patricia Hill Collins, "The Social Construction of Black Feminist Thought," *Signs* 14, no. 4 (1989); Valerie Smith, "Black Feminist Theory and the Representation of the 'Other,'" in *Changing Our Own Words: Essays on Criticism, Theory and Writing by Black Women,* ed. Cheryl Wall (New Brunswick, NJ: Rutgers University Press, 1989); Michele Wallace, *Invisibility Blues: From Pop to Theory* (New York: Verso, 1990); Gloria T. Hull and Patricia Bell Scott, eds., *All the Women Are White, All the Blacks Are Men, but Some of Us Are Brave: Black Women's Studies* (Old Westbury, NY: Feminist Press, 1982); Rebecca Wanzo, *The Suffering Will Not Be Televised: African American Women and Sentimental Political Storytelling* (Albany: SUNY Press, 2009); Melissa Harris-Perry, *Sister Citizen: Shame, Stereotypes, and Black Women in America* (New Haven, CT: Yale University Press, 2011); Anna Julia Cooper, "Our Raison D'etre," in *The Voice of Anna Julia Cooper: Including a Voice from the South and Other Important Essays, Papers, and Letters,* eds. Charles Lemert and Esme Bhan (New York: Rowman & Littlefield, 1992).

7. I leave open what "standard" interpretative strategies include. Different approaches to philo-

sophical engagement give rise to different conceptions of "standard" interpretative strategies. For example, Continental approaches to philosophical engagement have very different interpretative strategies than Analytical approaches. It is hard to say that those who engage in black philosophy are, in principle, committed to interpretative strategies that are either Continental or Analytic, even if the influences of these kinds of approaches can be seen in the work of professional black philosophers. See Tommy L. Lott, "Comparative Aspects of Africana Philosophy and the Continental-Analytic Divide," *Comparative Philosophy* 2, no. 1 (2011).

8. Reagon, "Coalition Politics: Turning the Century," *Home Girls: A Black Feminist Anthology,* ed. Barbara Smith (New York: Kitchen Table Press, 1983), p. 366.

9. Ibid., p. 365.

10. This formulation, some may think, presupposes that anyone producing black philosophy must be a historian of black philosophy as well. I admit to a bias here. Because black philosophy in anti-black contexts is so heavily suppressed, doing work in black philosophy requires some inclination toward seeking and engaging historical black theoretical production. That is to say, simply being black and doing philosophy, on my account, does not qualify one as doing black philosophy. One has to be in a tradition of such thought, whether one's tradition is reconstructed and reimagined or fairly standardly represented.

11. A very good example of this is Angela Davis, *Blues Legacies and Black Feminism: Gertrude "Ma" Rainey, Bessie Smith, and Billie Holiday* (New York: Vintage Books, 1998).

12. See, for example, George Yancy, *Reframing the Practice of Philosophy: Bodies of Color, Bodies of Knowledge,* SUNY Series, Philosophy and Race (Albany: State University of New York Press, 2012); Kristie Dotson, "How Is This Paper Philosophy?" *Comparative Philosophy* 3, no. 1 (2012); Kristie Dotson, "Concrete Flowers: Con-

templating the Profession of Philosophy," *Hypatia* 26, no. 2 (2011).

13. Walker, *Anything We Love Can Be Saved,* p. 49.

14. See, for example, William R. Jones, "The Legitimacy and Necessity of Black Philosophy: Some Preliminary Considerations," *Philosophical Forum* 9, no. 2–3 (1977–1978); Lucius Outlaw, *On Race and Philosophy* (New York: Routledge, 1996); Lucius Outlaw and Michael D. Roth, "Is There a Distinctive African-American Philosophy?" *Academic Questions* 10, no. 2 (1997); Leonard Harris, "The Horror of Tradition or How to Burn Babylon and Build Benin While Reading Preface to a Twenty-Volume Suicide Note," in *African-American Perspectives and Philosophical Traditions,* ed. John P. Pittman (New York: Routledge, 1997).

15. The kind of daring it takes to do black philosophy in a professional philosophy context, particularly in the United States, is relatively less severe than when philosophers like William R. Jones, Angela Davis, Lucius Outlaw, Howard McGary, Bernard Boxill, Leonard Harris, and Bill Lawson, for example, began their careers. I would be remiss if I did not mention the debt of gratitude I, as a black professional philosopher in the United States, owe to the many founders of black professional philosophy today for the relative lessening of the pressure of doing black philosophy in a US professional philosophy context. Though the climate for black professional philosophy still is not particularly stellar, it is better than it has been and that did not happen by accident.

16. E. Frances White, *Dark Continent of Our Bodies: Black Feminism and the Politics of Respectability* (Philadelphia: Temple University Press, 2001), p. 37.

17. Kristie Dotson, "Reflections on Academic Passing," *New APPS: Art, Politics, Philosophy, Science* (2012), www.newappsblog.com/2012/03/reflections-on-academic-passing.html; Dotson, "Concrete Flowers."

18. Acontextual critiques of work done responding to prevailing anti-black sentiments in US professional philosophy are already beginning to emerge, as is evidenced in a recent caustic exchange between Lucius Outlaw and Tommy Curry. See Tommy J. Curry, "On Derelict and Method: Methodological Crisis of African-American Philosophy's Study of African-Descended Peoples Under an Integrationist Milieu," *Radical Philosophy Review* 14, no. 2 (2011); Lucius T. Outlaw Jr., "On Tommy Curry's 'On Derelict and Method,'" *Radical Philosophy Review* 14, no. 2 (2011); Tommy J. Curry, "It's Criticism . . . Because 'I' Said So? A Reply to Lucius Outlaw's Defense of Status Quo Disciplinarity," *Radical Philosophy Review* 14, no. 2 (2011).

Africana Philosophy and Philosophy in Black

LEWIS R. GORDON

Black intellectuals face a neurotic situation. On one hand, many critics want to know if there are black thinkers on a par (or beyond) those in the Western canon ranging from Plato and Aristotle to Hegel and Marx and on to recent times such as Sartre and Foucault, and they would like to see black philosophers who aspire to such standards. On the other hand, when black intellectuals take on such a task, one that requires devoting a considerable amount of energy to the proverbial "life of the mind," they receive criticism for being too bookish and for failing to be "in the streets," where "the struggle" is being waged.

This double bind is posed not only by black people but also by white critics who expect black intellectuals to be primarily agents of praxis. It is understandable for familiar reasons: the assault on black humanity makes devoting one's energy to intellectual pursuits seem much like proverbially playing violins while Rome burns.

The unfairness of this situation when posed to black intellectuals, however, is that it fails to account for the importance of intellectual work on its own terms and as a vital part of liberation praxis. To abrogate responsibility for thinking has the consequence of others thinking for one, and where else would that lead but to dependence on others for that which is to be thought—that is, knowledge or epistemic dependency, or, to make it plain, the colonization of the mind?

Such concerns place us on unstable terrain. As I hope will become clear, we find ourselves pursuing what constantly attempts to evade us. As the theme of this special issue is "Black Philosophy," I will devote the rest of this short discussion to some of its challenges, at least as raised through its relative: Africana philosophy.

Africana philosophy refers to an area of philosophy that grew out of intellectual challenges and ideas posed by the African diaspora in the modern world. Although it grew out of what was at times called "black philosophy," it is distinct in important ways. Africana philosophy includes blackness, but it also addresses other problems raised by the intellectual practices, sometimes characterized as colonizing epistemic practices, that led to the emergence of the African diaspora. I will, however, focus here on the converging motif of Africana and black since the problem of intellectual history, especially black European intellectual history, is located there.

Lewis R. Gordon is professor of philosophy, African-American studies, and Judaic studies at the University of Connecticut at Storrs and Nelson Mandela Visiting Professor of Political and International Studies at Rhodes University in South Africa. He is the author of several influential and award-winning books and many articles translated into English, French, Portuguese, Spanish, and Mandarin. Professor Gordon's website, which contains a list of his publications, audio and video presentations, and his blog, is at lewisrgordon. com.

A mistaken view of Africana philosophy and black thought is that they are parasitic of Western philosophy, and that they are so in a way that limits its legitimacy as an area of *thought*. This is one of the idols that must be broken in an effort to articulate Africana philosophy—namely, the tendency to de-intellectualize Africana and black intellectual history. Among the de-intellectualizing practices is the misconception often alluded to, although not intended, by the often-used phrase (see many college catalogs) "philosophy and the black experience" or "philosophy and the Africana experience." This formulation is from a long-standing assumption that Africana and black peoples bring experience to a world whose understanding finds theoretical grounding in European, often read as "white," thought. I mention this to stress the importance of studying Africana philosophy as a constellation of *ideas*. When faced with the task of introducing this field, the problem of articulating it as an *intellectual* endeavor is crucial. It distinguishes the project of the intellectual historian in this field from those in the white normative disciplines, for the legitimacy of those areas of study as intellectual enterprises is often presumed, whereas the Africana and black-oriented fields, which, along with theoretical work in ethnic studies and women's studies is characterized by Nelson Maldonado-Torres as "the decolonial sciences"[1] and by Kenneth Knies as "the post-European sciences,"[2] face constant challenges to their legitimacy.

To understand the difficulty of formulating Africana philosophy as an intellectual project, then, we must take into account the philosophical anthropology that marked the transition from a theological naturalism to a secular, modern scientific one. An ongoing legacy of this period is the category of people who live in the modern world as creatures outside of the properly human domain.

To examine Africana philosophy and black thought as intellectual enterprises requires exploration of the conceptual tools offered by works in the field and the unique problems they formulated and addressed. Among those problems, I have argued, is the meaning of being human in the modern world.[3] Such a task is challenged by the context of its exploration, namely, the impositions of colonialism and racism as leitmotifs of enlightenment and reason. Those hurdles bring W. E. B. Du Bois's observation of black people's problems falling sway to black people *as problems themselves*.[4] This impediment was a function of such people not really being considered people in the first place. Since "real people" are subjects of history, the problem of intellectual history and Africana philosophy's place in it is expanded to asking: How does one offer a history of those or of what is presumed to be "ahistorical"?

Du Bois's response was to present a two-tiered argument on the double standards faced by those whose research avows the humanity of black people. The first was to recognize the general presumptions projected onto such people. The second, which the Antiguan philosopher and sociologist Paget Henry has identified as "potentiated double consciousness," is for intellectual history and philosophy the more important since it involves recognizing the contradictions and falsehoods of such misguided impositions.[5] That latter, dialectical movement expands the researcher's understanding of the overall societal context by particularizing it and revealing its pretensions of achieving universal truth. In *Black Reconstruction* (1935), Du Bois expands this discussion into the problem of historiographical portraits of freedom in a world without guarantees of progressive movement.[6] The *idea* of freedom, in other words, exceeds its material realization, and this expectation collapses back onto the interpretation of events with the mark, whether as success or failure, of their historicity.[7] Du Bois thus, in effect, raised the question of history in the lives of black people in a way that acknowledged and respected the lived-reality of black people and our symbiotic relationship to historical movement. The suppression of freedom in history is, in other words, the repression of black people, especially given the unique relationship black people have to extreme servitude, the radicalized implication of alienated labor, in the modern world: slavery.

In addition to the historicity of African diasporic and black peoples, this dialectical argument of uncovering contradictions also applies to their intellectual life. It calls for examining the value of *ideas* relevant to the plight of such people, and in doing so, reveal what Argentinean philosopher, historian, and theologian Enrique Dussel has described as modernity and humanity's "underside," those repressed and suppressed layers of human existence that offer a more complex, nuanced, and mature portrait of the human condition than the sterilized claims of normative whiteness.[8]

The task of avoiding the pitfall of treating Africana philosophy and black intellectual history as not intellectual or ahistorical requires exploring Africana and black philosophy (and related modes of thought) through at least three themes: (1) philosophical anthropology, (2) philosophy of freedom and liberation, and (3) metacritical reflection on reason.

Philosophical anthropology examines what it means to be human. Unlike empirical anthropology, which presupposes the legitimacy of the human sciences, including their methodologies, philosophical anthropology challenges the methods themselves and the presuppositions of the human offered by each society, and by doing so, offers the transition from method to methodology and methodological critique. That area of research makes sense for Africana and black philosophy from the fact of the challenged humanity of Africana and black people in the modern world. Since many Africana peoples are also black people, and since many black people were enslaved in the modern world, the main thesis of anti-black racism and enslavement supports this turn, for the essence of anti-black racism is the claim that black people are not fully human beings, if human at all. That enslavement involves making human beings into property calls for a response in philosophical anthropology as the theoretical contribution to the ongoing material struggle for freedom.

Developing a philosophy of freedom and liberation is a sensible intellectual response to racism and colonialism, so I will not belabor the second point except to add this. Any theory of freedom with regard to black people must bring along with it more than the unshackling of material chains or the fostering of civil liberties. It must also address the profound alienation of non-belonging in the only world to which such people could possibly belong. The assault on the spirit that constitutes the degradation of freedom in the modern world is for such people marked by a profound homelessness. That displacement connects to the insight of what could be called the exilic consciousness. Exiles, although liberated from immediate persecution, often suffer from the experience of not being free precisely because they are guests of their host countries. As such, their freedom is limited by the ethics of not being in their own home. They lack what the ancient Greeks called *parrhesia* (fearless speech), by which is here meant the ability to reveal themselves not only in the language of nakedness but also *entitled* revelation.[9] It is, in other words, not simply the ability to speak but also having the *right,* if we may use that modern terminology, to speak and to be who and what they are. Africana and black people lack that status in the modern world.

There is, as well, the problem of how reason is used to justify arguments in philosophical anthropology and our discourses of freedom. For example, simply asserting the equality of blacks to whites and demanding recognition of that exemplifies failure by virtue of affirming whites as the initial standard of human assessment. That whiteness was predicated on racism should jeopardize its legitimacy as a standard. It is, in other words, at least in moral terms, a low and regrettable measure of humanity.

The problem cannot be transformed, however, simply by making blacks the standard, especially since that history was not granted the opportunity to be interrogated on terms beyond conditions of white supremacy and anti-black racism. The task, then, is to raise the standard of humanity by going through and beyond black, white,

brown, yellow, and red to the conditions of standards themselves. Standards of the human, it soon becomes evident, are open and incomplete by virtue of depending for their creation on those whom they are supposed to evaluate. The human, in other words, is humanity's project, and we see that in the ever-expanding reach of culture as a condition of possibility of the materially human.

Metacritical reflection on reason is a major aspect of Africana and black philosophy, and the intellectual history of the subject should engage that. Its demand is straightforward: Is what we think justified? How do we even justify justification?

The problem of justification is evident not only with the problem of supporting our philosophical anthropology and discourses of freedom, but also on a recurring question posed to every Africana and black philosopher, especially by those who are postmodernists: Given the abusive use of reason by many great philosophers, such as David Hume, Immanuel Kant, G. W. F. Hegel, and many recent stalwart figures,[10] against black people, why bother with such a discipline for the expansion of freedom and liberation?

Frantz Fanon lamented that reason played cat and mouse with him and had a habit of taking flight whenever he (as *the black*) entered the white intellectual world.[11] Philosophy's love affair with reason suggests that black people do not stand a chance when even it flees blackness. Under such a circumstance, black philosophers encounter embodiments of reason as unreasonable, or, to the point, *unreasonable reason.*

Fanon's response to unreasonable reason was not to *force* reason to become reasonable, which would be *unreasonable* or, as continues often to be the perception toward blacks who attempt to do such, *violent,* but instead to reason with reason.[12] Many Africana and black philosophers, and by extension, intellectuals, exemplify Fanon's situation over the ages. It is a task that is not taken on exclusively by Africana and black philosophers and thinkers, but it is one that presses upon us in a unique way. All philosophers use reason, but only some face the situation of having to reason with reason.

I took up this task, of reasoning with reason, in *An Introduction to Africana Philosophy* as I examined this Promethean struggle throughout the past millennium. The story I wrote is of many communities—tenth-century Afro-Muslims or "Moors" developing arguments for a separation of mosque and sultan and determining their relationship to ideas from antiquity, especially through their efforts to reconcile the thought of Aristotle with Islam; sixteenth-century Catholic priests arguing over who has membership in the human community and the subsequent struggles for freedom in the conflicts between spiritual and materialist utopias; the eighteenth-century Nzeman (Akan from Ghana) Wilhelm Amo, who argued for the equality of the Moors of Europe, challenged Cartesian philosophical anthropology, and who wrote a text on proper reasoning at the University of Halle in the eighteenth century; nineteenth-century work on philosophy of civilization and problems of human study occasioned by the founding of the Negro Academy under the leadership of the Cambridge-educated Alexander Crummell; twentieth-century intellectual movements ranging from the emergence of Negritude in France, prophetic pragmatism and Africana

analytical philosophy in North America and Britain, to Africana existential phenomenology in France, South Africa (among other African nations), and the United States; and, going full circle back to Africa, raising the problem of decolonized reason in a contemporary world of increasingly, supposedly deracialized states but heavily racist and unequal civil societies.

Such an effort is, of course, part of a larger story of recovery and constructing alternative models of intellectual life. The latter are the building blocks by which new ideas and lived relations can be formed and latent, and often invisible, ones can appear. In the meeting place of Africa and Europe on one the hand and the black with history and ideas on the other, the devotion of such energy is no less than part of what is proverbially to be done.

Notes

1. Nelson Maldonado-Torres, "On the Coloniality of Being," *Cultural Studies* 21, no. 2 (2007): 240–270.

2. Kenneth Knies, "The Idea of Post-European Sciences: An Essay on Phenomenology and Africana Studies," in *Not Only the Master's Tools: African-American Studies in Theory and Practice,* eds. Lewis R. Gordon and Jane Anna Gordon (Boulder, CO: Paradigm Publishers, 2006), pp. 85–106.

3. Lewis R. Gordon, *Existentia Africana: Understanding Africana Existential Thought* (New York: Routledge, 2000); Lewis R. Gordon, *An Introduction to Africana Philosophy* (Cambridge: Cambridge University Press, 2008).

4. W. E. B. Du Bois, "The Study of Negro Problems," *Annals of the American Academy of Politi-*

cal and Social Science 11 (January 1898): 1–23. Reprinted in the Annals of the American Academy of Political and Social Science 56 (March 2000): 13–27.

5. Paget Henry, "Africana Phenomenology: Its Philosophical Implications," C. L. R. James Journal 11, no. 1 (Summer 2005): 79–112.

6. W. E. B. Du Bois, Black Reconstruction in America: 1860–1880 (1935; New York: Atheneum, 1992).

7. Susan Searls Giroux, "Reconstructing the Future: Du Bois, Racial Pedagogy and the Post–Civil Rights Era," Social Identities 9, no. 4 (2003): 563–598.

8. Enrique Dussel, The Underside of Modernity: Apel, Ricoeur, Rorty, Taylor, and the Philosophy of Liberation, trans. and ed. Eduardo Mendieta (Atlantic Highlands, NJ: Humanities Press, 1996).

9. Michel Foucault, Fearless Speech, ed. Joseph Pearson., Semiotext(e) (Cambridge, MA: MIT Press, 2001).

10. See Reid (Jerry) Miller, "A Lesson in Moral Spectatorship," Critical Inquiry 34, no. 4 (Summer 2008): 706–728.

11. Frantz Fanon, Black Skin, White Masks, trans. Charles Lam Markman (New York: Grove Press, 1967).

12. See Lewis R. Gordon, "When I Was There, It Was Not: On Secretions Once Lost in the Night," Performance Research 2, no. 3 (September 2007): 8–15; and "When Reason Is in a Bad Mood: A Fanonian Philosophical Portrait," in Philosophy's Moods: The Affective Grounds of Thinking, eds. Hagi Kenaan and Ilit Ferber (Dordrecht, Germany: Springer Press, 2011), pp. 185–198.

The Parrhesiastic Enterprise of Black Philosophy

DEVONYA N. HAVIS

Introduction

Black philosophy, which includes a plethora of divergent viewpoints and competing theoretical frameworks, at its best, is a libertory practice. In its most progressive expressions, Black philosophy is a multi-vocal tradition that seeks to undo the epistemic erasure of Black experience by creating and cultivating philosophical tools that promote social justice. In the context of this journal, *The Black Scholar,* these may not be read as very radical claims. Nevertheless, I want to assert a certain radicality by linking Black philosophy to the exercise of *parrhesia* and note Black philosophy's role in cultivating a parrhesiastic attitude toward traditional philosophy. Such an attitude marks the way in which Black philosophy transgresses traditional Western philosophy by generating a "taxonomy of the different kinds of silences and invisibility"[1] that signal Black folks' epistemic absence.

This essay is not an account of all the instances in which Black philosophy challenges the Western philosophical canon. Such an account exceeds the scope of this essay. My aim, instead, is to explore the ways that Black philosophy promotes the emergence of social justice possibilities that cannot be prefigured or codified. As such, the essay will propose an index for analyzing practices that engage in transgression and resistance as a means of promoting social justice. In short, the essay will argue that where and when parrhesia is exercised it has the effect of promoting social justice—not because of the concrete consequences but because practicing parrhesia invents new modes of subjectivity.

Utilizing parrhesia as an index for resistance becomes especially important when one understands that contemporary power operates through production and not simply prohibition. In this respect, strategic knowledge for effective resistance must account for the productive functions of power and must not see resistance merely as opposition to prohibitions and exclusions. As Foucault has observed, in the contemporary landscape, power's operation is ensured not by law but by normalization. Hence, one might transgress normalizing processes without resisting power's oppressive effects, which are not only prohibitive but also productive.

As a means of establishing a mechanism for analyzing transgression and resistance, let us now turn to an explication of Foucault's notion of parrhesia.

Devonya N. Havis is an assistant professor of philosophy at Canisius College in Buffalo, New York. Her writings include "Blackness Beyond Witness" in *Philosophy and Social Criticism* and "Discipline" in the forthcoming *Cambridge Foucault Lexicon.* She has a long-standing concern with utilizing philosophy to enhance awareness and promote counter-oppressive practices.

Definition of Parrhesia—
Ritualized Practice of Truth-telling

Michel Foucault turns to a practice found in Greek culture called parrhesia. His aim in recuperating the notion is to utilize it as a "tactical point of attack" for approaching a problem in the present. As such, Foucault's account of parrhesia, while attentive to its historical emergence, has a greater concern with the practice's transhistorical significance and effects. Parrhesia in this context becomes a means of exploring the conditions under which persons can engage in the discursive practice of truth-telling even when their very constitution is mitigated by power relations.

In utilizing the notion of parrhesia to think differently about the present, Foucault outlines a number of consistent characteristics for the ritualized practice. He is clear that the truth-telling associated with parrhesia differs from the pursuit of objective, universal truth. Instead, the practice involves action that is indexed to a truth conditioned by a particular setting, context, cast of characters, and time. The exercise of truth-telling, therefore, unfolds in a dramatic scene where a speaker exhibits courage by freely choosing to act and by acting places herself at risk. The speaker assumes a moral duty by offering a critique that draws attention to something that has gone unseen, prompting an awareness that creates the possibility of correcting what is amiss.

While parrhesia involves speaking the truth, its primary function is not simply truth-telling but putting forth a criticism. Hence, the one practicing parrhesia is not focused on indicating the truth to someone else and/or convincing another of this truth. Instead, the speaker offers a criticism, renders a critique, of himself or another. Such a critique "comes from below . . . and is directed towards above. The parrhesiastes risks his privilege to speak freely when he discloses a truth which threatens the majority."[2] He assumes such risk as a matter of moral duty, as obligation because the speaker is not forced to speak and could, in fact, remain silent. As Foucault writes,

> Parrhesia is a kind of verbal activity where the speaker has a specific relation to truth through frankness, a certain relationship to his own life through danger, a certain type of relation to himself or other people through criticism (self-criticism or criticism of other people), and a specific relation to moral law through freedom and duty. More precisely, parrhesia is a verbal activity in which a speaker expresses his personal relationship to truth, and risks his life because he recognizes truth-telling as a duty to improve or help other people (as well as himself). In parrhesia, the speaker uses his freedom and chooses frankness instead of persuasion, truth instead of falsehood or silence, this risk of death instead of life and security, criticism instead of flattery, and moral duty instead of self-interest and moral apathy.[3]

It becomes clear that the practice of truth-telling is a complex process that indexes truth at two levels. There is the statement of truth itself and the fact that the action of enunciating this truth establishes that one is actually committed to what one says. Speaking is not a matter of rhetorical engagement but involves a verbal activity that exposes what one thinks. As such, one seeks to act on others' minds, not through flattery, but by indicating what one actually thinks.

In this account, it becomes evident that critique has a certain relation to power and as a result of this relation may become embroiled with the political. It is in the act of speaking that one is positioned at the axes where ethics, duty, freedom, and identity intersect. In these intersections, it also becomes apparent that parrhesia plays a role in transgression and resistance. More pointedly, parrhesia, in its different manifestations, is necessary for "an ethic of discomfort," an ethic that continually motivates one to think the same things differently, making them live and breathe.[4]

The practice is a catalyst for undefined emerging possibilities, prompting a unique relationship of the self with self, and with others.

The exercise of parrhesia is a site where identity, action, and freedom intersect. These intersecting components denote crucial aspects that constitute parrhesia as a practice. Identity is affected because the speaker's action *effects* the possible modes of being. The action of truth-telling disrupts the familiar and involves the courage to open oneself to risk since one chooses to act even though there is no compulsion forcing one to take ethical action. Nonetheless, one makes the free choice to engage in truth-telling. Let us examine in more detail how the conditions in which parrhesia takes place bring about an intersection between identity, action,

and freedom in a manner that opens new possibilities.

The identity of the subject is implicated when one exercises parrhesia, according to Foucault, because the discursive act effects the subject's mode of being. By acting in this particular way, in the particular dramatic setting, the speaker constitutes herself in the enunciation. She not only states a truth but the action involved in stating the truth makes her someone who tells the truth, has told the truth, and who recognizes herself in telling the truth.[5] She, thus, emerges from the exercise as a subject who is bound to the statement, the act of enunciation, and the risky consequences of both. The act of truth-telling alters the scene and indicates courage on the part of the speaker who willingly opens herself to mortal peril.[6]

Parrhesia disrupts the familiar and usual where it takes place. The introduction of the kind of truth-telling associated with parrhesia causes an irruption that effects an "open situation"—one that cannot be predetermined but is emergent—by creating the possibility of effects that are unknown—namely effects that cannot be proscribed. In this respect, the risk that accompanies parrhesia is unspecified because its introduction "does not produce a codified effect."[7]

The decision to speak, notes Foucault, is an exercise of freedom as well. The speaker is "exposed" and takes up a particular relationship with oneself—a relationship in which one risks death "to tell the truth instead of reposing in the security of a life where the truth goes unspoken."[8] The freedom comes in the speaker's response to a particular circumstance that issues a call to truth-telling. There is also an aspect of freedom associated with the choice and act of enunciation. As Foucault notes, "The parrhesiast is someone who emphasizes his own freedom as an individual speaking." Hence, "parrhesia is the ethics of truth-telling as an action which is risky and free."[9]

The risk opened up by the speaker's verbal act is what defines her utterance as parrhesia. In this respect, parrhesia is a unique form of utterance and can be distinguished from "other formulations of the truth."[10] Moreover, the parrhesiastic process differs from statements of truth that happen under neutral conditions. There is a required relationship between the person making the utterance and the utterance itself.

Parrhesia can also be distinguished from forms of language that command. The aim is not to place others under the yoke of its speech. Parrhesia confronts other discourses, not in an effort to bend others to the will of the speaker but to persuade them by means of truth-telling and the commitment to this truth on the part of the speaker. This means that the speaker's courage rather than her social or institutional status is crucial for parrhesia. Even while asserting this status disclaimer, it is the case that many of the salient examples of parrhesia used by Foucault involve a status differential where someone with less power is addressing an injustice put into motion by someone with greater power. These examples are also the most salient for this essay because they involve the discursive process by which someone weaker reproaches the powerful one and may compel his recognition of the offense committed.[11] With no means of retaliation, nor any means

for revenge, the one in a profoundly unequal situation can do one thing: she can "speak"—engage in a discursive act that calls attention to the offense, that exposes injustice.

Parrhesiastic Attitudes in Black Philosophy

As noted above, one who engages in parrhesia assumes a parrhesiastic attitude by acting and assuming the risk to privilege that accompanies the action associated with disclosing a truth that threatens the majority. In taking up a parrhesiastic attitude, one's actions disrupt the familiar by introducing a critique that calls attention to something that has gone unseen, something that escapes the normal register.

One might argue that Black philosophy's call to transgress Western philosophy's paradigms is in fact a call to parrhesiastic activity. However, in keeping with the fact that parrhesia unfolds at a particular time in a particular dramatic scene, it would be more fitting to talk about some parrhesiastic moments in Black philosophy. Such moments involve criticism, risk, courage, and engagement in truth-telling that "opens" different possibilities.

By publicly challenging the "incongruence" one is made to feel when simultaneously practicing philosophy while embodied in black skin, Black philosophers exercise a kind of parrhesia. George Yancy has characterized philosophy, in particular as it is practiced by people who define themselves as black, as a process of "troublemaking." For Yancy, "troublemaking" involves raising questions about what we take for granted and illuminating positions that might escape visibility. "Troublemaking" presumes discontent with the status quo and its boarders—especially the heavily policed philosophical borders. In this way, Yancy celebrates the role of the troublemaker and indicates the crucial, critical role "troublemaking" plays in expanding our discursive possibilities.[12]

The 1960s civil rights activists' philosophical commitment to nonviolent struggle may also be viewed as an instance of the parrhesiastic attitude. Martin Luther King Jr., for example, characterizes the parrhesiastic process in "Letter from Birmingham Jail," noting that protestors in Birmingham, Alabama, presented their very bodies as a means of "laying [the] case before the conscience of the local and national community." By placing themselves at risk, accepting blows without retaliation, these civil rights activists compelled attention toward the injustice of segregation. Their actions generated the kind of "creative tension" that effected a change increasing people's ability to register segregation as unjust. By invoking a discourse of injustice, the nonviolent witness of the civil rights activists compelled those in a more powerful position to have a confrontation with their complicity in committing injustice.[13]

Defining the concept of "talking back," in her book of the same title, bell hooks notes that "back talk" or "talking back" is an act of speaking to an authority figure, without invitation, as if one is an equal. To the extent that one is talking out of order, not in line with social etiquette, being controversial, and transgressing the established hierarchy,

one could be said to be "talking back." Bell hooks focuses her attention on the ways in which such talking back is courageous and daring.[14] Nonetheless, it is possible to envision discourses in which "talking back" is merely unrestrained speech. In this context, "talking back" would not be courageous because of its confrontation of authority. The confrontation could amount to a punishable transgression but not simultaneously be an act of counter-oppressive resistance. Hooks notes that prohibitions against and punishments for "back talk" were designed to inhibit speech and silence the development of voice. These punishments, consequently, were not necessarily connected to truth-telling even though the aim was to silence what was perceived as unrestrained speech. Unlike talking back, in parrhesia, any penalty for speaking is intimately bound to the impact of the truth-telling.

In his discussions of parrhesia, Foucault provides an illustration of someone from a weaker position compelling the recognition of offense, a form of injustice, from someone in a more powerful position. The example, drawn from the Greek tragedy *Ion,* discusses how Creusa's cry calls the god Apollo to acknowledge an injustice he has committed against her and about which he has remained silent. The cry, notes Foucault, is a "speech act by which someone weak, abandoned, and powerless proclaims an injustice to the powerful person who committed it."[15] The action is an intervention in which the weak person, by invoking a discourse of injustice against the powerful god, challenges and jousts with him by emphasizing the truth of the injustice. Foucault goes on to note that this ritualized practice of truth-telling is practiced in many societies and does not always take place simply as a verbal activity. He writes, "The hunger strike is the ritual act by which someone powerless emphasizes in front of someone powerful that he who can do nothing has suffered the injustice by he who can do anything. For someone who is both the victim of injustice and completely weak [without traditional forms of power], the only means of combat is a discourse which is agonistic but constructed around the unequal structure."[16] It becomes clear that without parrhesia, one is "subject to the madness of the masters." Parrhesia, then, limits the exercise of coercive power by allowing the parrhesiast to "stand up, speak, and tell the truth against the master's foolishness, madness, and blindness, and thereby limit the master's madness."[17]

Conclusion

By discussing the ways that some Black people and some Black philosophers have engaged in parrhesiastic practices, this essay asserts that it is through the exercise of parrhesia that many Black folks have resisted, not by overthrow, but by pivoting obliquely to alter the existing terrain. In this way even the seemingly powerless may engage in counter-oppressive practices. In fact, it is sometimes from this "weak" position that unanticipated occasions for social change emerge. Who could predict that one of W. E. B. Du Bois's most compelling remonstrations would come from his disenfranchised position as an African in the Americas? On

his ninety-first birthday during a speech at Peking University in China, Du Bois made the following statement:

> I speak with no authority; no assumption of age nor rank; I hold no position, I have no wealth. One thing alone I own and that is my own soul. Ownership of that I have even while in my own country for near a century I have been nothing but a "nigger." On this basis and this alone I dare speak, I dare advise.[18]

With this statement, Du Bois speaks to the world by means of his address to the peoples of China and Africa. In doing so, he offers a criticism not from his position as a Harvard-educated scholar but from the "authority" of one who has suffered an offense and who can do no more than cry out against the injustice with the gravity invoked by ritualized truth-telling. Disillusioned by his treatment by other Blacks and by the US government, Du Bois emphasizes an injustice before the world doing "combat" by means of an agonistic structure that draws upon his asymmetry. In short, Du Bois engages parrhesia to promote social change. With this concluding instance, the essay has provided an analytic mechanism for indexing transgressive practices to determine if they are resistant in ways that promote social justice.

Notes

1. Charles Wade Mills, *Blackness Visible: Essays on Philosophy and Race* (Ithaca, NY: Cornell University Press, 1998), p. 3.

2. Michel Foucault, Joseph Pearson, and Joseph Pearson (philosopher), *Fearless Speech* (Semiotext[e], 2001), p. 18.

3. Ibid., pp. 19–20.

4. Michel Foucault, "For an Ethic of Discomfort," in *Power: Essential Works of Foucault 1954–1984*, ed. James D. Faubion, vol. 3 (New York: New Press, 2000), p. 448.

5. Michel Foucault, *The Government of Self and Others: Lectures at the College de France, 1982–1983* (New York: Palgrave Macmillan, 2011), p. 63.

6. Ibid., p. 56.

7. Ibid., pp. 62–63.

8. Foucault, Pearson, and (philosopher), *Fearless Speech,* p. 17.

9. Foucault, *The Government of Self and Others,* pp. 65–66.

10. Ibid., p. 63.

11. Ibid., pp. 133–134.

12. George Yancy, *Philosophy in Multiple Voices* (Lanham, MD: Rowman & Littlefield, 2007), pp. 3–9.

13. Martin Luther King Jr., "Letter from a Birmingham Jail," in *A. J. Muste Memorial Institute Essay Series* (A. J. Muste Memorial Institute, n.d.), pp. 15–17, www.ajmuste.org.

14. Bell hooks, *Talking Back: Thinking Feminist, Thinking Black* (Cambridge, MA: South End Press, 1989), p. 5.

15. Foucault, *The Government of Self and Others,* p. 133.

16. Ibid.

17. Ibid., p. 161.

18. *Black World/Negro Digest* (Johnson Publishing Company, 1972), p. 17.

If You See Something, Say Something

JANINE JONES

The specific role black philosophy plays that I focus on in this piece can be summed up by the dictum: "If you see something, say something."

Engaging black philosophy provides a vantage point for doing philosophy in at least two ways, each related to this adage. First, due to its parrhesiatic attitude, black philosophy encourages a person to *say* what she sees about white supremacy and its relation to various racisms, not least of which is anti-black racism.[1] Second, philosophizing through a lens of black philosophy—that is, the type of lens required for understanding that the relation between historical meanings of blackness and their present ramifications cannot be analyzed away—might stand a person on ground from which she can *see* what she otherwise may not. After all, there is very little chance of someone saying what she cannot see in the first place.

I address both sides of the coin, the first via a brief account illustrating how Simone de Beauvoir, having seen deep structures of white, anti-black racism, as evidenced in her novel *L'Invitée*, neglected to *say* what she had seen in her theory of the radical Other as presented in *The Second Sex,* thereby leaving her account of woman as being more radically Other than the slave untouched by her observations. I approach the flip side of the coin by considering how a feminist theorist has described the South African runner Caster Semenya as *looking* slightly masculine with genitalia that *look* feminine *without stating* that seeing Semenya as looking masculine might just possibly have something to do with blackness, as it has been imagined by a white, Western imaginary.

Both sides—saying what you see and seeing in order to say it—are important to the philosophical endeavor of breaking down epistemologies of ignorance, which, here, I briefly sum up as bodies of belief and "knowledge" actively produced around an issue to engender ignorance around that issue, with such ignorance possibly aiding and abetting exploitation and domination. We might further understand this concept through the lens of an idea formulated by

Janine Jones is associate professor of philosophy at the University of North Carolina at Greensboro. She is interested in philosophical topics and problems where race and gender, philosophy of mind, language, epistemology, and metaphysics intersect. She is the author of "Illusory Possibilities and Imagining Counterparts," *Acta Analytica* (2004); "Cartesian Conceivings," *Metaphysica* 5:1 (2004); "The Impairment of Empathy in Goodwill Whites," in *What White Looks Like,* ed. George Yancy (Routledge, 2004); "Tongue Smell Color black," in *White on White/Black on Black,* ed. George Yancy (Rowman and Littlefield, 2005); and the coeditor of *Pursuing Trayvon Martin: Historical Contexts and Contemporary Manifestations of Racial Dynamics* (Lexington Books, 2012), in which her piece "Can We Imagine *This* Happening to a White Boy?" appears.

Daniel Dennett. Dennett argues that when trying to understand social phenomena we would do well to understand the success of a single-cell organism, such as a bacterium. Among other things, bacteria possess membranes that let in what needs to come in and prohibit anything else from entering. What does the *social* cell need to keep out, according to Dennett?

> The [social] cells' effective operation depends on the relative cluelessness—or innocence—of the participants. The membrane that restricts information flow is just as important as the membrane that restricts entry of outsiders, precisely because inside the barrier there are participants who are capable of understanding that information, information that can quickly transform them into outsiders.[2] (emphasis added)

When considering epistemologies of ignorance we must focus not only on the information the membrane restricts—analogous to that which is seen but not said. We must keep in mind what the membrane ushers in—that said, which excludes what is not seen, thereby delimiting the objects of knowledge for consideration. A social cell devoted to constructing ignorance around an issue as a means of staying alive and thriving erects walls to restrict information that could make insiders into outsiders. But it also specializes in portals for ushering in information that creates and/or nourishes clueless "innocent" participants: information that transforms participants into diehard insiders. One of the advantages of framing this matter in terms of the workings of a successful social cell is that it forestalls a discussion about the intentions of individual silent seers and amaurotic speakers, thus freeing up psychological and philosophical space for considering the structures and modes of operation of the racialized social spaces we are all participants in.

Simone de Beauvoir: The Silent Seer

Due to space limitations, I have selected only a few passages from *L'invitée,* which cannot do justice to all we should consider for grasping just how much Beauvoir had observed. First, I will mention the relation Beauvoir viewed as existing between fiction and philosophy. Second, I will say a few words regarding what her novel is allegedly about.

In "Literature and Philosophy," Edward and Kate Fulbrook claim that for Beauvoir fiction presented experience in such a way that we can and should use it to give meaning to and support for our theories.[3] Following the Fulbrooks, in failing to speak up in *The Second Sex* regarding her findings in *L'invitée,* arguably Beauvoir failed to be true to her own meta-philosophical convictions regarding the symbiotic relationship between theory and literature.

Turning now to *L'invitée,* Edward Fulbrook observed that in her first metaphysical novel, Beauvoir identified three fundamental "procedures" or "attitudes" we may assume with respect to the subjectivity or consciousness of the Other. First, "persons may *seek* to experience themselves as the Other's object"; second, "they may seek to guard their subjectivity by making the Other their object"; and third, "they may seek a reciprocity with the

Other, whereby each treats the other as both subject and object, as equal freedoms of and sources of value."[4] We see these procedures playing out through the relationships of the three main characters, Françoise, Xavière, and Pierre. Nowhere do we see them play out with respect to Beauvoir's black characters—fictional descendants of enslaved and colonized peoples, who are never subjects but, rather, only some white person's object. Indeed, *L'invitée* tells a dramatically different story from that of *The Second Sex* of who should be cast as the more radically Other in terms of who is more radically objectified, who is closer to nature, who is more animal-like.

L'invitée: *au bal nègre*

"Colonial Ball" was written on a door in thick white letters. They entered. A crowd rushed to the cash register—black faces, pale yellow, café au lait. Françoise stood in line to buy two tickets: seven francs for women, nine for men; that rumba on the other side of the partition was fogging up all her ideas.

She remained standing; the orchestra launched into a rumba and a mulatto bowed before her with a ceremonial smile. . . . In this large room . . . one saw almost only colored faces: from ebony black to ochre rose, all the nuances of the skin were to be found. These blacks danced with an unhinged obscenity, but their movements possessed a rhythm so pure that the rumba retained, in its ingenuous rawness, the sacred character of a primitive rite. The whites who mixed in with them were less happy; especially the women, who resembled stiff,

hysterical, mechanical figures in a trance. Only Xavière possessed a grace that defied both obscenity and decency.

-They have a devil in their skin, these nègresses, she said angrily. I'll never be able to dance like them.

-You dance really well, you know, said Françoise.

-Yes, for a civilized person, said Xavière with contempt.

-Oh, Xavière said, I'd give a year of my life to be that negrèsse for an hour.

-She's beautiful, said Françoise. She doesn't have the features of a nègresse. Don't you think she has some Indian blood in her?

-I don't know, said Xavière, as though overwhelmed.

Admiration brought a spark of hatred to her eyes.

Or you have to be wealthy enough to buy her and lock her up, Xavière said. It was Baudelaire who did that, right? Imagine that you could go home and instead of a dog or a cat you find waiting for you this sumptuous creature purring by the fireplace. A naked black body stretched out in front of a wood burning fire . . . Was that what Xavière was dreaming of? How far did her dream go?[5]

Observations on Beauvoir's Observations

1. Beauvoir's narrator makes a *deep* observation when she describes Françoise's thought as obscured by the rumba on *the other side* of the partition. Even before Françoise enters the ball proper, black alterity, represented by all shades of the palette, gets in the way of

thought. Beauvoir could have been writing the musical counterpoint to Fanon's "When the black walks in the door, Reason walks out." But she did not engage what she wrote in such a Fanonian spirit when theorizing the Other in *The Second Sex.* Doing so would have contaminated her perfect man-versus-woman binary. For how could rationality be characterized as masculine with *black* men in the picture . . . unless, of course, they are not really men but something else, perhaps something radically Other?

2. Beauvoir describes Xavière as representing the *middle ground* between the decency of the white world and the world of obscenity, *le monde nègre.* Made by a woman who did not know Fanon or his work at the time she wrote *L'invitée,* the logic of this setup points to another Fanonian point. Namely, *le monde nègre* represents an endpoint; the absolute other end of the spectrum in relation to the white world of civilization.

3. Xavière dreamed of buying the object of her hate-desire, hence, arguably an object of abjection, and of keeping her locked up and naked; waiting and dependent, purring: a pet in lieu of some other animal. Beauvoir does more than give us Xavière—represented via her less than middle-class status and attenuated mastery of dancing—as a midpoint between human civilization and animal savagery. In a different scene altogether that takes place at the Flamenco Club, Françoise and Xavière converse about Spanish women (a type of brown woman?): "They're amazing, these women," said Françoise. "They're wearing layers of make-up on their skin and yet that doesn't give them a look of artificiality; their faces remain vibrant and animal."[6] Unlike a negrèsse these women are *called*

women, with the understanding, nonetheless, that they are located very much near the realm of where the wild things are, somewhere over the rainbow of beautiful negrèsses, who can't really be *pure* negrèsses *if* they are beautiful, since in that case they must possess Indian or some other kind of blood to attenuate onto-aesthetic *laideur.*

Beauvoir, in effect, not only presents a hierarchy of racialized bodies, where an understanding of racialization depends on knowing where the endpoints lie—namely, in whiteness and blackness. She proffers different racialized spaces, thereby offering a racial cartology of the world as she understood it. One might therefore surmise that Beauvoir had observed that social relations constitute the bodies and spaces of whiteness, blackness, and racializations in between the two, and that those bodies and spaces constitute hegemonic white subjects, including middle-class women. I conjecture that it was through her own lived experience that Beauvoir knew that Xavière-like dreams existed in the minds of white women and that she knew basic constituents of those dreams: black females stripped down to meanings projected on to their naked bodies, making it all the easier to Other them as animalistic creatures of sexual servitude to both white men *and* white women. Beauvoir did not, however, tether these everyday dreams and whitely ways of living-through-race wrapped in everyday language to complicate her philosophical theory of radical Otherness in *The Second Sex.* She saw a lot and said nothing. Had she *engaged* black philosophy, she would have been required to say something.[7]

Caster Semenya's Problem According to Brenna Munro

Mariya Savinova, a white Russian track-and-field athlete, was the first to heap scorn upon South African runner Caster Semenya when Semenya won the 800-meter race at the 2009 world championship in Berlin. "Just look at her!" Savinova pronounced.[8] Feminist theorist Brenna Munro seems to agree that if we *just look at* Semenya we can get at the heart of the problem. Thus, she wrote: "The visibility of sex difference, in particular, has been thrown into question for the global audience. Semenya *looks* somewhat masculine, but her genitalia apparently *look* female—inspections of her anatomy usually satisfied her doubters in the past, as many reports have mentioned."[9] She further wrote: "*This* event calls into question how we define sex difference."[10]

Had Munro engaged black philosophy she would have seen a lot more, and *perhaps*, then, said a lot more. First she would have noted that Sojourner Truth, who allegedly looked somewhat masculine, with breasts and genitalia that apparently looked female, had to bear her breasts to a white public to "prove" that she was a female and a woman. Althea Gibson, who allegedly looked somewhat masculine with genitalia that apparently looked female, was forced to take a sex verification test to play in the US National Tennis Championship in 1957. Serena Williams's femininity is constantly called into question. With one blogger calling Semenya the lost Williams sister, I suppose it would not be far-fetched to suppose that she, too, looks somewhat masculine

with genitalia that apparently look female. Finally, the research findings of Goff et al. showed that "when participants [a sample of white students on the northeastern seaboard of the United States] 'guessed' the gender of target faces, they were more often wrong about the gender of Black women than about any other race/gender intersection. That is, participants guessed that Black women were actually men a higher percentage of the time than they miscategorized any other group by gender."[11]

Had Munro engaged black philosophy, specifically the topic of the black female body and how it has been troped as masculine since the advent of modern slavery—precisely in an attempt to undermine black women's femininity—my guess is that she could have and would have seen that *this* event—the Semenya event—wasn't the big event that called into question how we define sex difference. *That* event has been playing out over the centuries in various forms and contexts, some of which may be used to conceptualize some understandings of intersex people. Further, Munro may have been led to conjecture what Goff et al. concluded from their study. Namely, "it may be the case that perceiving race and perceiving gender are not isolated processes. *Rather, intersectional identities may sometimes be the 'basic category' of person perception.*"[12]

Blackness dropped out of sight in Munro's initial considerations. Therefore, it could not but go missing from her report of the problem. Engaging race in the form of black philosophy may have allowed Munro to see the visible in invisible blackness, and to find the words to say it.

Notes

1. For a discussion of the parrhesiatic attitude, see Devonya Havis's piece, "The Parrhesiastic Enterprise of Black Philosophy," in this issue.

2. Daniel Dennett, "What Do Debutant Balls, the Japanese Tea Ceremony, Ponzi Schemes, and Doubting Clergy All Have in Common?" ase. tufts.edu/cogstud/papers/socialcell.pdf, accessed March 22, 2013.

3. Edward and Kate Fulbrook, *Simone de Beauvoir: A Critical Introduction* (Cambridge, UK: Polity Press, 1998).

4. Edward Fulbrook, "Being and Nothingness," in *The Philosophy of Simone de Beauvoir: Critical Essays,* ed. Margaret A. Simons (Bloomington: Indiana University Press, 2006), pp. 42–64.

5. Simone de Beauvoir, *L'invitée,* my translation (Paris: Gallimard, 1943/1972), pp. 308–315.

6. Ibid., p. 351.

7. To my knowledge, very little has been said in the literature about these passages, suggesting that by many Beauvoirian feminist theorists— these passages have been *overlooked.*

8. David Epstein, "Inside Track and Field." sportsillustrated.cnn.com/2012/olympics/2012/ writers/david_epstein/08/11/caster-semenya-800-meters/index.html, accessed October 16, 2012.

9. B. Munro, "Caster Semenya: 'Of Gods and Monsters,'" *Safundi* 11, no. 4 (2010): 383–396.

10. Ibid.

11. Phillip Atiba Goff, Margaret A. Thomas, and Matthew Christian Jackson, "'Ain't I a Woman?': Towards an Intersectional Approach to Person Perception and Group-based Harms," in *Sex Roles* 59, no. 5–6 (2008): 400.

12. Ibid., pp. 402 (emphasis added).

Marxism, Philosophy, and the Africana World

A Philosophical Commentary

STEPHEN C. FERGUSON II

African-American Philosophy in the Bourgeois Academy: The Crisis in Black and White

The philosophical marketplace is ensnared in a scandal of sorts. The general rule of thumb in far too many philosophy departments is that one "Negro" philosopher is more than enough. African-American philosophy in its totality is still not seen as worthy of sitting at the proverbial table of professional philosophy. Within the halls of academia, African-American philosophy and the concrete history of African-American philosophers is reduced to a rather minor subfield—the philosophy of race. This is an unwonted occurrence in philosophy departments because knowledge of the history of philosophy is a necessary condition for competency as a philosopher. One's philosophical competence, for example, would undoubtedly be called into question if you did not know the English philosopher John Locke. But knowledge of the philosophical work of the African-American "gadfly" Alain Locke is not required to be a competent philosopher in the academy today. As the late William R. Jones astutely notes, more than forty years ago, African-American philosophy still stands as a "bastard philosophy" and a "semantic monstrosity."[1] To make this observation does not necessarily imply that some African-American philosophers have not made inroads in professional philosophy. Yet, both *ontological* and *conceptual* tokenism remains the *rule,* not the *exception.* This is the smoke and mirrors of the new multiculturalism.

The professionalization of philosophy—not unlike other disciplines in the white academy—is firmly rooted in institutional racism. The virtual absence of African Americans from the history of philosophy, and the philosophical canon, in the United States is due to a history of neglect and exclusion deeply rooted in academic racism.[2] The institutional character of racism gives priority to the behaviors and institutions that give material support to the racist attitudes and beliefs by the actual suppression of the supposed inferior groups. Thus, academic racism is rooted in material practices associated with the complex matrix of institutions including colleges and universities in addition to professional associations such as the American Philosophical Association (APA). This matrix of institutions exerts a considerable amount of institutional power by establishing standards of professionalization that are historically racist in nature and continue to be racist today.[3]

Stephen C. Ferguson II is an associate professor in liberal studies at North Carolina A & T State University. He is coauthor of *Beyond the White Shadow: Philosophy, Sports and the African American Experience* (Kendall Hunt, 2012) with John H. McClendon III.

What Is African-American Philosophy?

Philosophical inquiry is preeminently conceptual rather than empirical in nature. It involves taking ideas and inquiring about the nature of our basic presuppositions and assumptions. Philosophical inquiry involves subjecting these presuppositions and assumptions to the tribunal of reason. Philosophical inquiry as such is concerned with the rational justifications that ground our presuppositions and assumptions. One of the critical functions of philosophy is the justification of our beliefs via rational arguments.[4]

In the case of religion and mythology, in contrast to philosophy, we don't question our basic presumptions and presuppositions. This is important to understand in the case of religion and mythology because we accept what is habitual or traditional based on the principle of authority. The tribunal of reason is sacrificed on the basis of the authority of the gods. In the case of religion, the authority of a given individual (e.g., Jesus or Muhammad), institution (e.g., the Roman Catholic Church), or a given religious text (e.g., the Quran or biblical texts) gives authority to our claims, which we then accept primarily on the basis of faith, or unjustified belief. So, while religion and mythology are forms of social consciousness, all forms of social consciousness are not philosophical consciousness.

What exactly is African-American philosophy? A host of African-American philosophers have tried to engage metaphilosophical questions such as, "What does it mean to be a philosopher of African descent in the American empire?"[5] I strongly disagree with the notion that philosophy is a system of collective thought, spontaneous, implicit, and unchanging, to which all Black people adhere.[6] In reaction to the false universalism of Western philosophy, proponents of Afrocentrism (the American cousins of African ethnophilosophy) such as Molefi Asante and Marimba Ani have argued along these lines.[7] Asante states in unequivocal terms,

> We have one African Cultural System manifested in diversity. Nevertheless to speak of the Arab in Algeria as my brother is quite different from speaking so of the African-Brazilian, Cuban or Nigerian. We respond to the same rhythms of the universe, the same cosmological sensibilities, the same general historical reality as the African descended people.[8]

We should take note that Asante's claim is presented as a matter of fact. But rather than grant truth to his claim, a philosopher has the obligation to challenge its factual merits. Is it the case that the experience of African Americans in the United States has the "same general historical reality" of Africans in Nigeria or Afro-Brazilians? The real answer to this question would mandate an empirical investigation into concrete (material) history. However, Asante and his band of merry Afrocentrists would only require that we make a leap of faith and accept this assertion on grounds of intuition rather than reason and empirical verification. At the end of the day, Asante rejects any rational basis in logic for his claim about the substance of this universal African identity and relies instead on the mysterious, irrational notion of collective "cosmological sensibilities" that are adjoined to "the same rhythms of the universe."[9]

Asante's speculative idealism stands opposed to a scientific (materialist) comprehension of the world. Hence, from Asante's perspective, we can infer that there is no qualitative difference between Condeleezza Rice and Lucy Parsons, Jonas Savimbi and Chris Hani, or Barack Obama and Malcolm X. As Barbara Ransby brings to our attention, it is easy to view continental Africans as one "monolithic mass" without regard to class or politics, when one is concerned primarily with the "rhythms of the universe" and "cosmological sensibilities." A dialectical materialist philosophical perspective demands that we examine the nitty-gritty material realities of people's day-to-day lives—in all their dialectical complexities.[10] In the context of political struggle, it is very important to understand the determinate difference between Chris Hani of South Africa and Jonas Savimbi of Angola. Hani was a socialist freedom fighter committed to the liberation of African people; Savimbi was responsible for the massacre of thousands of African people in the service of imperialism. Both men are African, but they respond to very different rhythms and sensibilities.[11]

It is imperative that we "cuss and discuss" the metaphilosophy of William R. Jones. He argued that African-American philosophy should not be taken to mean a collective worldview or community with a shared metaphysics, philosophical vocabulary, or orientation. After all, there are philosophers of African descent who are Marxists, existentialists, phenomenologists, and pragmatists who conceptually dwell within different and conflicting discourse communities. In addition, there are philosophers who are of various political orientations such as liberalism, conservatism, left-radicalism, and Marxism.

Black philosophy is another instance of the concrete particularity that in fact grounds the universality of philosophy. The concept of "black" in Black philosophy, Jones argues, should not be thought of as exclusively a *racial* designation. Accordingly, race is not the necessary organizing principle of a black philosophy. On the contrary, Jones argues, "The experience, history, and culture are the controlling categories for a black philosophy—not chromosomes."[12] The concept of "black" in Black philosophy refers to such factors as author, audience, ancestry, accent, and antagonist.[13] Hence, on this view, which I agree with, black philosophy is simply philosophy that engages the Black experience and condition rather than a case of representing a unitary philosophical perspective, which is shared by all or even most Black people. So, I do not have a Black philosophical perspective, but I do engage in the *philosophical comprehension of the Black experience*. Blackness in all of its dialectical complexity is my motivation for doing philosophy, but it does not determine the limitations of my philosophical orientation. It is not an issue of thinking in Black philosophical terms; rather it is an imperative to think philosophically about the Black experience.[14] So, I am quite critical of the reactionary retrograde Afrocentric notion that one must think in Black or African modes of philosophizing.

On the Significance of Militant Materialism: Ideology, Critique, and Science

I am a Marxist-Leninist philosopher. My interest in philosophy was aroused by my passion for political struggle and the critical function of philosophical materialism. My passion for politics was inspired by the revolutionary courage of working-class people, particularly Black people throughout the world, against the juggernaut of capitalism. Marxism is a distinctive social theory and political movement that made its entrance on the world historical stage not only with its dialectical critique of capitalism founded on the law of value and the theory of surplus value, but also the materialist conception of history, the materialist ontology of dialectical materialism, the theory of class struggle, and the dictatorship of the proletariat.

What are the tasks of Marxist philosophy? Marxist philosophy in its function as the ideology of the working-class gives expression to the political interest of the "grave-diggers" of capitalism. There is no Chinese wall that separates philosophy from ideology. David Hume's fork, therefore, has no place at the Marxist dinner table. Giving attention to the ideological character of philosophy, however, does not mean limiting the content and significance of philosophy to its ideological function. The real power of Marxist philosophy rests in being a "theory of scientific practice," which plays a seminal role in advancing scientific knowledge.[15] When we conceive of philosophy as involved in advancing scientific knowledge, then we see that it is not able to solve the transcendental problems in which traditional speculative metaphysics engages in. Nor can it replace the empirical work of the social and natural sciences.[16]

Few African-American philosophers have traveled down the road of Marxism in the academy. Of this small coterie of philosophers, we could mention Eugene C. Holmes, C. L. R. James, Angela Davis, John H. McClendon, and me as individuals who have sought to advance a dialectical materialist philosophical perspective on the Black experience in the academy.[17] McClendon and I, most recently, have written a Marxist contribution to the philosophy of sports titled *Beyond the White Shadow: Philosophy, Sports and the African American Experience* (Kendall Hunt, 2012). In the tradition of cricket's philosopher king C. L. R. James, we argue that sports, as a subfield of African-American popular culture, must be examined within the matrix of the political economy of capitalism. Sport, from our standpoint, is fundamentally a class institution totally integrated into the mechanism of capitalist production relations and class relations. In its organization and system of competitive selection, promotion, and social advancement, sport is a reflection of the logic of capitalism. The sports spectacle presents to us a microcosm of the bourgeois world. The wide world of sports feeds off of the exploitation of athletic labor; capital is vampire-like whose continued existence is grounded on sucking more and more living labor.[18]

Special note should be made of the groundbreaking work by Holmes, who made significant progress in developing a materialist conception of space and time.[19] Now, perhaps more than ever, there is a need for a materialist interpretation and critique of the latest developments in science. Throughout US history, African-American scholars and thinkers from Frederick Douglass to Malcolm X have sought to provide an intellectual rebuttal to the authority of scientific racism.[20] Yet, in the hands of rightist demagogues like Tyler Perry, Cleflo Dollar, and T. D. Jakes, Black religious ideology has continued to foster political quietism and distrust of scientific knowledge. Despite the "dubious blessings of Christianity," the pernicious onslaught of capitalist exploitation continues to bring forth the "sorrow songs" from the Black working class, who are overwhelmingly unemployed or underemployed. While some Black public intellectuals have screamed that the "Black church is dead," there is no denying the powerful influence of religious ideology on African Americans in the sphere of ideas.[21] As Hubert Harrison noted, "Show me a population that is deeply religious, and I will show you a servile population, content with whips and chains, contumely and the gibbet, content to eat the bread of sorrow and drink the waters of affliction."[22]

There is a continuing need for a materialist critique of rightist political efforts to attack science in the name of pseudoscience such as creationism and the intelligent design movement, or creationism redux, and the assault on the validity and veracity of evolution.[23] We should keep in mind the words of the renowned African-American astrophysicist Neil deGrasse Tyson, who wrote, "I have yet to see a successful prediction about the physical world that was inferred or extrapolated from the content of any religious document. . . . Whenever people have used religious documents to make detailed predictions about the physical world they have been famously wrong."[24] There is no scientific validity, objectivity, or predictive truth to biblical prophecy.

If Black philosophers are to be militant materialists, they are obligated to view the philosophy of dialectical and historical materialism as indispensable theoretical weapons in the class struggle of working-class and oppressed people. In the short amount of space that I have, I am not going to tackle the difficult problem of Marxism's right to sit at the philosophical table. Nor will I end with any platitudes about the importance of reading and studying Marx's *Capital* or Lenin's *Materialism and Empirio-Criticism*. Yet, it is important to refer to Marx's famous eleventh thesis on Feuerbach: philosophers have only sought to interpret the world, but the point, however, is to change the world.[25]

Notes

1. William R. Jones, "The Legitimacy and Necessity of Black Philosophy: Some Preliminary Considerations," *Philosophical Forum* 9, no. 2–3 (Winter–Spring 1977–1978): 149–160.

2. Given this brief discussion of the beginnings of African-American philosophy, it should come as little surprise that many African-American philosophers are excluded from works that treat the philosophical canon. Bruce Kuklick's recent book, *A History of Philosophy in America, 1720–2000* (New York: Oxford University Press, 2001), includes only one African-American philosopher in passing, namely, W. E. B. Du Bois. On academic racism in professional philosophy, see Robert Bernasconi and Sybol Cook, eds., *Race and Racism in Continental Philosophy* (Bloomington: Indiana University Press, 2003); Leonard

Harris, "'Believe It or Not' or the Ku Klux Klan and American Philosophy Exposed," *American Philosophical Association Newsletter on Philosophy and the Black Experience* 68, no. 5 (1995): 133–137; J. K. Ward and T. Lott, eds., *Philosophers On Race: Critical Essays* (Malden, MA: Blackwell, 2002); and Andrew Valls, ed., *Race and Racism in Modern Philosophy* (Ithaca, NY: Cornell University Press, 2005).

3. Michael R. Winston, "Through the Back Door: Academic Racism and the Negro Scholar in Historical Perspective," *Daedalus* 100, no. 3 (1971): 678–719.

4. Oftentimes philosophy is seen as any activity in which we engage in introspection, contemplation, and speculation. I want to submit that this is not necessary philosophy. Philosophers do engage in such activities; however, these activities are not a necessary and sufficient condition for being classified as a philosopher. In folklore, proverbs, and wives' tales we find, for example, gems of wisdom, but this does not necessarily constitute philosophical labor.

5. See Cornel West, "The Black Underclass and Black Philosophers," in *I Am Because We Are: Reading in Black Philosophy,* eds. Fred Lee Hord (Mzee Lasana Okpara) and Jonathan Scott Lee (Amherst: University of Massachusetts Press, 1995), p. 356. One of the early African-American efforts in metaphilosophy is William D. Johnson, "Philosophy," in *Afro-American Encyclopedia,* ed. James T. Haley (Nashville, TN: Haley and Florida, 1895). For a work in the metaphilosophy of African philosophy, see Paulin Hountondji, *African Philosophy: Myth and Reality* (Bloomington: Indiana University Press, 1983). As much as philosophical inquiry in Africa and the African diaspora has been concerned with the traditional subdisciplines in philosophy, arguably its primary focus has been what I have termed the philosophy of the Black experience. By drawing on a broad range of philosophical areas such as the history of philosophy, metaphilosophy, aesthet-

ics, metaphysics, epistemology, philosophy of science, and social and political philosophy, contemporary Africana philosophers have attempted to address a range of philosophical issues related to the Black experience. For example, Africana philosophers have been greatly concerned with the origins of philosophy. As the traditional narrative goes, philosophical thought has its origins in Greece. However, the groundbreaking works of George G. M. James, Theophile Obenga, Cheikh Anta Diop, and Martin Bernal offer a different conception of the origin of philosophy, locating it instead in Africa. The most significant contribution to the ongoing debate about the African origins of philosophy is James's *Stolen Legacy.* The Guyanese-born philosopher presents a historico-philosophical interpretation of the African origins of philosophy. According to James, Greek philosophy was largely taken from classical African/Egyptian philosophy. Obenga—in the tradition of James—has done important work detailing the nature of classical African philosophy. See George G. M. James, *The Stolen Legacy* (New York: Philosophical Library, 1954); William Leo Hansberry, "Stolen Legacy," *Journal of Negro Education* 24, no. 2 (Spring 1955): 127–129; and Théophile Obenga, *African Philosophy: The Pharaonic Period, 2780–330 B.C.* (Popenguine, Senegal: Per Ankh, 2004). See also Yosef ben-Jochannan, "In Pursuit of George G. M. James' Study of African Origins of Western Civilization," *Yosef ben-Jochannan Virtual Museum,* www.nbufront.org/html/MastersMuseums/DocBen/GGJames/OnGGJamesContent.html, accessed March 10, 2013.

6. I capitalize the word "Black" when making reference to people of African descent. For a number of years, it was customary to use this in regard to the word "Negro." Over a number of generations, there was a consistent fight to capitalize the word "Negro" as a way of establishing racial respect and dignity. Since the word "Black" has now come to replace "Negro" as the contempo-

rary convention, I follow in that tradition with the capitalization of "Black." For a further discussion of this issue, see Richard B. Moore, "The Name 'Negro'—Its Origin and Evil Use," in *Richard B. Moore, Caribbean Militant in Harlem: Collected Writings, 1920–1972,* eds. W. Burghardt Turner and Joyce Moore Turner (Bloomington: Indiana University Press, 1988), pp. 223–239. See also John H. McClendon, "Black/Blackness: Philosophical Considerations," in *Encyclopedia of the African Diaspora: Origins, Experiences, and Culture,* ed. Carol Boyce Davies, vol. 3 (Santa Barbara, CA: ABC-CLIO, 2008), pp. 198–203.

7. Marimba Ani's *Yurugu* is considered to be an "underground Bible" for the Afrocentric movement. For hordes of excited acolytes to the cult of Afrocentrism it offers a systematic outline of the African-centered critique of Eurocentrism. Ani seeks to formulate a counter-hegemonic discourse in the tradition of Leopold Senghor's Negritude. See Ani, *Yurugu: An African-Centered Critique of European Cultural Thought and Behavior* (Trenton, NJ: Africa World Press, 1994). For a critique of ethnophilosophy, see Hountondji, *African Philosophy.* For a leftist critique of Negritude, see Marcien Towa, *Léopold Sédar Senghor, Négritude ou servitude?* (Yaounde, Cameroon: Editions CLE, 1971).

8. Molefi Asante, *Afrocentricity* (Trenton, NJ: Africa World Press, 1989), p. 2.

9. For a Marxist critique of Afrocentrism, see Ferguson, "The Utopian Worldview of Afrocentricity: Critical Comments on a Reactionary Philosophy," *Socialism and Democracy* 25, no. 1 (2011): 44–70.

10. Barbara Ransby, "Afrocentrism and Cultural Nationalism," in *Dispatches from the Ebony Tower,* ed. Manning Marable (New York: Columbia University Press, 2000), p. 219.

11. Chris Hani was the general-secretary of the South African Communist Party, taking over from Joe Slovo in 1991. He also served as chief of staff of Umkhonto we Sizwe, the armed wing

of the African National Congress (ANC). He fought against apartheid in South Africa until he was assassinated on April 10, 1993, outside his home, by Polish anti-Communist immigrant Janusz Waluś, who shot him in the head and at the back as Hani stepped out of his car. Waluś had close links to far Right groups, Afrikaner Weerstandsbewging (AWB) (or Afrikaner Resistance Movement), and the Conservative Party. See Janet Smith and Beauregard Tromp, *Hani: A Life Too Short: A Biography* (Johannesburg: Jonathan Ball, 2009). Jonas Savimbi was the leader of an Angolan anti-Communist political organization, the National Union for the Total Independence of Angola (UNITA), that was in opposition to the leftist People's Movement for the Liberation of Angola (MPLA) during the Angolan civil war of 1975–2002. He was supported by the United States and its ally Apartheid South Africa. Most recently, he has been featured in the video game *Call of Duty: Black Ops II* (2012). In January 1986, Savimbi met with Ronald Reagan and in turn received $15 million in military aid from the Reagan administration. Therefore, given Savimbi's anti-Communism, Reagan feted him as a freedom fighter. For a definitive account of Savimbi's reactionary role in the Angola's war of independence, see Piero Gleijeses, *Conflicting Missions: Havana, Washington, and Africa, 1959–1976* (Chapel Hill: University of North Carolina Press, 2002). See also Terence Hunt, "Reagan Tells Savimbi He Wants to Be Very Helpful," *Associated Press News Archive,* January 30, 1986, www.apnewsarchive.com/1986/Reagan-Tells-Savimbi-He-Wants-to-Be-Very-Helpful/id-aac4344cb87abdb200515823dcf2b712, accessed March 10, 2013.

12. Jones, "The Legitimacy and Necessity of Black Philosophy: Some Preliminary Considerations," p. 152.

13. Jones explains, "The intent appears to be one or more of the following: to identify that the author is black, i.e. a member of a particular ethnic community, that his primary, though not

exclusive, audience is the black community, that the point of departure for his philosophizing or the tradition from which he speaks or the worldview he seeks to articulate can be called in some sense the black experience. . . . Special attention must be to 'black' as a designation of the antagonist. . . . Accordingly, to call for a black philosophy, from this perspective, is to launch an implicit attack on racism in philosophy, especially in its conceptual, research, curricular, and institutional expressions." Ibid., p. 153.

14. McClendon, "Act Your Age and Not Your Color: Blackness as Material Conditions, Presumptive Context, and Social Category," in *White on White, Black on Black,* ed. George Yancy (Lanham, MD: Rowman & Littlefield, 2005), p. 284.

15. Paulin Hountondji, "What Philosophy Can Do," *Quest* 1, no. 2 (1987): 18.

16. See R. Andrew Sayer, *Method in Social Science: A Realist Approach* (London: Routledge, 1992); and Patrick Murray, *Marx's Theory of Scientific Knowledge* (Atlantic Highlands, NJ: Humanities Press International, 1988).

17. The Marxist philosopher and historian C. L. R. James embarked on an investigation of the role of dialectics in political struggle in his magnum opus, *Notes on Dialectics: Hegel-Marx-Lenin.* Angela Davis, one of the most widely known among past Communists of African-American descent, has a distinguished career in activism and scholarship challenging racism and sexism, and supporting black political prisoners. For a groundbreaking study of James's *Notes on Dialectics,* see McClendon, *C. L. R. James's* Notes on Dialectics: *Left-Hegelianism or Marxism-Leninism?* (Lanham, MD: Lexington Books, 2005).

18. Karl Marx, *Capital: A Critique of Political Economy,* Vol. 1 (New York: International Publishers, 1967), p. 224.

19. Holmes also did work in the general area of the philosophy of the black experience, writing essays on African-American sociopolitical philosophy, the aesthetics of black art, and thinkers

such as W. E. B. Du Bois, Langston Hughes, and Alain Locke. See John H. McClendon, "The Philosopher, Rebel," *Freedomways* 22, no. 1 (1982); McClendon, "Eugene Clay Holmes: Black Marxist Philosopher," in *Philosophy Born of Struggle,* ed. Leonard Harris (Dubuque, IA: Kendall Hunt, 1983), pp. 36–50; Percy E. Johnson, *Phenomenology of Space and Time: An Examination of Eugene Clay Holmes' Studies in the Philosophy of Space and Time* (New York: Dasein Literary Society, 1976).

20. The racist arguments clothed in the methods of science during the nineteenth century were based primarily on craniometry, the measurement of human skulls. While the scientific credibility of craniometry was severely attacked and discredited by African-American intellectuals, the eugenics movement has continued to be spurred on by "data" supporting the view that IQ tests adequately measure something we call "intelligence." In journals like *The Black Scholar* and *Sage Race Relations Abstracts,* the bourgeois (class) character of the racist arguments of Richard J. Herrnstein and Charles Murray's *The Bell Curve: Intelligence and Class Structure in American Life* and the political dangers of psychometrics was exposed. See Ned Joel Block and Gerald Dworkin, *The I.Q. Controversy: Critical Readings* (New York: Pantheon Books, 1976); Ashley Montagu, *Race and IQ* (New York: Oxford University Press, 1975); Stephen Jay Gould, *The Mismeasure of Man* (New York: Norton, 1981); Richard C. Lewontin, Steven P. R. Rose, and Leon J. Kamin, *Not In Our Genes: Biology, Ideology, and Human Nature* (New York: Pantheon Books, 1984). For an excellent discussion of the historical development of Marxist philosophy of science, see Helena Sheehan, *Marxism and the Philosophy of Science: A Critical History* (Atlantic Highlands, NJ: Humanities Press, 1985). For an idealist approach to the philosophy of science by an African-American philosopher, see Roy Dennis Morrison, *Science, Theology, and the Tran-*

scendental Horizon: Einstein, Kant, and Tillich (Atlanta: Scholars Press, 1994).

21. Eddie Claude Jr., "The Black Church Is Dead," *Huffington Post,* February 24, 2010.

22. Hubert Harrison, "The Negro a Conservative: Christianity Still Enslaves he Minds of Those Whose Bodies It Has Long Held Bound," in Hubert H. Harrison, *A Hubert Harrison Reader,* ed. Jeffrey B. Perry (Middletown, CT: Wesleyan University Press, 2001), p. 44.

23. Today's proponents of intelligent design like William Dembski are not just opposed to Darwinian evolutionary theory. Their critique is aimed at philosophical materialism, the view that the world is explained in terms of itself, by reference to material conditions, natural laws and contingent, emergent phenomena, and not by invoking the supernatural or the gods. See John Bellamy Foster, Brett Clark, and Richard York, *Critique of Intelligent Design: Materialism Versus Creationism from Antiquity to the Present* (New York: Monthly Review Press, 2008); Ashley Montagu and Isaac Asimov, *Science and Creationism* (New York: Oxford University Press, 1984); and Robert T. Pennock, *Tower of Babel: The Evidence Against the New Creationism* (Cambridge, MA: MIT Press, 1999).

24. Tyson, "Holy Wars: An Astrophysicist Ponders the God Question," in *Death by Black Hole: And Other Cosmic Quandaries* (New York: W. W. Norton, 2007), p. 348.

25. Marx is not objecting to the need for philosophical interpretation and inquiry. Yet, he is condemning philosophical speculation that limits itself to the mere task of interpreting what exists. See T. I. Oizerman, *The Making of the Marxist Philosophy* (Moscow: Progress Publishers, 1981), pp. 344–355.

Black Philosophy and the Erotic

ANIKA MAAZA SIMPSON

"Black love is dead," bemoaned a friend at a dinner party I hosted recently for a diverse group of black friends. Fully expecting a spirited debate to ensue, I was disheartened when his declaration was met with little opposition from the guests gathered around my dining room table. The tacit acceptance of this fallacious remark by my dinner guests, I believe, is demonstrative of the pernicious representations of black love and sexuality that continue to be perpetuated in the media, popular culture, and academia. Academics and non-academics alike have become accustomed to troubling, yet familiar, refrains about black love and sexual intimacy. To the detriment of our psychosexual well-being, black sexuality studies remains undertheorized in the humanities.[1] This lack of scholarship is markedly evident within the canon of black philosophy as our contributions to the philosophy of love and sex are woefully inadequate. The intricacies of our sexual identities, our sexual experiences, and our concomitant family structures are inextricably tied to central themes in black philosophy. I contend that black philosophers must engage rigorously our sexuality and love relationships because philosophical explorations of the black experience are incomplete without a full articulation of our embodied, erotic selves.

In the following, I will examine briefly several arguments pertaining to marriage in an effort to illustrate possible threads of philosophical inquiry into black eros, especially within black feminist philosophy. The institution of marriage is befitting for this purpose because it serves as a site in which state interests converge with private intimate relationships and where assumptions of sex, gender, and sexual orientation are questioned. Mainstream philosophical literature on the subject of marriage explores the aforementioned issues without sufficiently addressing the particularity of our experiences with the institution. Marriage has functioned historically for black people, and expressly for black women, not only as a nexus for romantic and familial love but also as a necessary component of racial uplift, a marker of personhood, and a sign of sexual chastity in the face of stereotypes of sexual deviance.[2] As black women, our belonging to, or alienation from, the controlling categories of personhood that emanate from the marital institution, such as "wife" and "mother," have significant implications for black feminist philosophers' work in ethics, epistemology, and political theories of justice.

In "Interracial Marriage: Folk Ethics in Contemporary Philosophy," Anita L. Allen

Anika Maaza Simpson is an associate professor in philosophy and religious studies at Morgan State University. She is the founding coordinator of MSU's women's and gender studies program. Her publications have primarily focused upon black feminism and African-American philosophy. Her current research explores the morality of black women's sexuality and marriage.

offers a moral defense of interracial marriage through a careful consideration of objections that are commonly raised by blacks who reject the practice.[3] My purpose here is not to debate the merits of Allen's conclusion but rather to gesture toward two aspects of her position that are germane to black feminism. First, Allen asserts that limitations within mainstream moral philosophy have impeded sustained engagement of ethical topics that are salient to particular ethnic groups, for example, interracial marriage. She notes that "there may be a relationship between the openness of philosophy to explorations of ethical perspectives that not all groups share and the racial diversification of the field."[4] Allen laments the limited number of black philosophers within the discipline who frustrate attempts to expand the breadth of moral philosophy. I agree wholeheartedly with Allen's assessment of the intellectual perils of persistent racial exclusivity within mainstream moral philosophy. I would make the further claim, however, that the predominance of heterosexual black men within the discipline, coupled with the dearth of black women philosophers and black LGBTQ philosophers, may also serve to impede research efforts concerning the patriarchal and heteronormative institution of marriage.

Second, Allen's argument underscores dimensions of the marital institution that are specific to the lived experience of black women. She writes, "For blacks, the ban on interracial marriage had been seen as a powerful symbol of exclusion and inequality, particularly in the South where interracial sex was commonplace despite the ban on interracial marriage."[5] She asserts that prior to the *Loving v. Virginia* (1967) decision,

black women felt shame for desiring and engaging in sexual relationships with white men outside the confines of marriage.[6] We have yet to untangle fully the thorny knots intertwining the morality of black women's sexual choices in relation to their marital status. This investigation should be undertaken by black philosophers and should not be left primarily to historians, sociologists, and literary scholars.[7]

Allen also frames the moral question of interracial marriage as one that is of notable concern to black women. According to Allen, the moral objections that she critiques have been voiced by many "ordinary men and women, but especially women, of all social and economic classes."[8] She is not alone in feminizing the issue of interracial marriage. Charles Mills, in his essay "Do Black Men Have a Moral Duty to Marry Black Women?", also claims that hostility toward interracial marriage within the black community is notably acute among black women.[9] Mills reconstructs "somewhat presumptuously" black women's arguments in support of this presumed moral imperative with the intent of exposing the invalidity of their claims.[10] While I agree with both Allen and Mills that romantic and sexual intimacy between interracial partners is neither immoral nor counterproductive to black solidarity, I believe the most intriguing facets of their respective arguments are the underlying and unchallenged assumptions that motivate the tendency to depict the promotion of endogamous relationships, or matrimony itself, as primarily a black women's issue. Furthermore, I caution against these authors' uncritical acceptance of the merits of the marital institution. Before asking if there is an ethical duty to encourage intraracial marriages, we need to ask whether black people indeed have a moral obligation to marry at all? Are there exigent moral and/or ontological reasons for black feminists to argue in favor of perpetuating this institution?

The evolving marriage debate within mainstream philosophy would be enriched immeasurably by a significant black feminist philosophical intervention. Through a cursory examination of Debra B. Bergoffen's essay "Marriage, Autonomy, and the Feminine Protest," I endeavor to show how the inclusion of black feminist resources can advance current philosophical investigations.[11] Bergoffen offers a defense of marriage in opposition to feminist calls to abolish the institution. She aims to provide a positive feminist account of marriage that departs from the discourse promulgated by marriage defenders on the political right, who appeal to divinity or nature in support of their beliefs. Such appeals are problematic, for they are often interpreted as reinscribing patriarchal norms and continuing the subordination of women. While I am sympathetic to the feminist commitments that motivate Bergoffen's argument, I believe that the force of her claims is undermined by the absence of explicit attention to the manner in which racial identity can influence our marriage experiences. Her focus upon the nexus of heterosexual erotic desire, patriarchy, and the state obscures queer and straight black women's engagement with marriage and hinders the development of a racially inclusive marriage defense. This obfuscation is most evident in her discussion of state authority and its valuation of the married couple's erotic bond.

Bergoffen describes the institution of marriage as a reflection of the relationship between the erotic, the ethical, and the political. She seeks to show that there is a "direct relationship between a state's ability to pursue justice and its understanding of marriage such that when a state sanctions marriage traditions that betray the meaning of marriage it forecloses the possibility of justice."[12] The state's structural and material misunderstandings of marriage, according to Bergoffen, disclose a patriarchal system's erasure of the ethical meanings and political implications of the erotic. She makes the case that marriage should be conceived by the state as an ethical-erotic event between the desiring couple devoid of sexual subordination. For Bergoffen, marriage—properly understood—is a political project that stabilizes the erotic and preserves the place of the ethical-erotic event. Upon entering the political institution of marriage, the heterosexual couple chooses to accept state authority and their union serves to remind the state of the limitations of its authority over its subjects.

Acknowledging that the relationship between blacks and the state historically has been tenuous at best, and lethal at its worst, an argument in defense of marriage that aims to incorporate racially diverse couplings must delve beyond racially neutral characterizations of "misunderstandings of the state" or "marks of a patriarchal system." Bergoffen aptly describes how women's bodies are abused and misused within marital relationships. However, she does not consider the deleterious consequences that state-sanctioned violence inflicted upon generations of black women has wrought upon our relationship with the government and its legal system. The adoption of Bergoffen's optimistic view of the state's potential requires an overestimation of our trust in state authority and an underestimation of the state's diminished value of black bodies. Furthermore, we must be careful not to critique a patriarchal system when there are, in fact, racially, ethnically, and culturally divergent systems of patriarchy. On two separate occasions in her essay, Bergoffen cites the reactionary discourses of the Promise Keepers and the Million Man March as exemplars of patriarchal misunderstandings of matrimony. The conflation of these disparate events neglects the specificity of black masculinities, black feminists' varied and nuanced responses to black patriarchal discourses, and ultimately, the distinctiveness of black erotic relationships.

Drawing on Simone de Beauvoir's discussion of intentionality in *The Ethics of Ambiguity*, Bergoffen writes, "As an erotic relationship, marriage is the ethical site of the gifting couple. It embodies the ethical intentionality of letting be."[13] Bergoffen claims that the institution of marriage is worth preserving to support the value of the gifting couple's ethical-erotic bond. Her insightful phenomenological description of the gifting couple has the unfortunate, and I believe unintended, consequence of devaluing the ethical-erotic bond between couples who choose not to, or who have been legally barred from, entering into a state-sanctioned marriage contract. Counter to Bergoffen's sanguine vision of heterosexual marriage, Claudia Card asserts that the institution of marriage is "so

deeply flawed" that it is unworthy of "emulation and reproduction" by lesbian and gay partners.[14] Card insists that the laws regulating marriage will never be just.[15] She states that she "would rather see the state deregulate heterosexual marriage than see it begin to regulate same-sex marriage."[16] Card thus rejects ceding authority to the state to define the legitimacy of intimate relationships between consenting adults.

What role, if any, should the state have in the legitimization, or regulation, of our intimate relationships? Can the laws governing our erotic relationships ever be just? The provocative questions raised by the rival positions of Bergoffen and Card merit further review with the voices of black philosophers at the fore. In crafting her argument against marriage, Card, like Bergoffen, uncritically draws upon the life experiences of black people. For example, in her essay "Against Marriage and Motherhood," Card casually states that the institution of marriage for women is analogous to black chattel slavery. While this rather dubious claim is ripe for critique, I believe, more interestingly, that it underscores conjoining lines of inquiry between the subfields of black philosophy and the philosophy of love and sex. Black philosophers, such as Bernard Boxill, Angela Davis, Bill Lawson, and Howard McGary, to name a few, have explored black chattel slavery to answer philosophical questions pertaining to freedom, personhood, self-respect, and morally justifiable acts of violence. How might these explorations inform current research on love, sexuality, and marriage?

Frances Smith Foster, in *'Til Death or Distance Do Us Part: Love and Marriage in*

African America, offers a historical account of marriages between antebellum blacks that illuminates possibilities for such philosophical inquiry.[17] The narratives and historical records uncovered by Foster reveal how black couples remained bound together through love under extraordinary and horrific conditions. She states that blacks often chose to remain enslaved with their partners rather than be separated from them in freedom. Historical records, according to Foster, indicate that the marriage vows between antebellum blacks "were sincere and lasting testaments of desire" even in those instances where couples forcibly separated.[18] Although marriage is considered primarily as a legal contract in the twenty-first century, Foster states that "laws can say what they will, but African Americans have long insisted on their own definitions and recognitions of marriage."[19] The legacy of our novel definitions of marriage provide a wellspring for future analysis.

In keeping with Socrates's declaration in *The Apology* that an unexamined life is not worth living, I believe that the role of black philosophy is to offer thoughtful examinations of the multifarious dimensions of black life. To that end, I encourage black philosophers to commit to a sustained study of black eros. As a black feminist philosopher, I consider this area of study to be a particularly worthy theoretical enterprise. The persistent efforts of black women to cultivate affirming erotic identities and to negotiate collective and personal sexual freedoms in light of our devastating historical experiences deserve our intellectual attention. I remain hopeful that black philosophers will produce bodies of work that cut through the cacophonous noise of the media and popular culture so that unfortunate utterances like "black love is dead" are no longer met with sullen and uncontested nods of agreement.

Notes

1. Stacey Patton, "Who's Afraid of Black Sexuality?" *Chronicle of Higher Education,* December 3, 2012, chronicle.com/article/Whos-Afraid-of-Black/135960.

2. According to historian Anastasia Curwood, "At the turn of the twentieth century . . . African American public culture presented female chastity and morality as the cornerstones of a respectable middle-class marriage." Anastasia Curwood, *Stormy Weather: Middle-Class African-American Marriages Between the Two World Wars* (Chapel Hill: University of North Carolina Press, 2010), p. 13.

3. Anita L. Allen, "Interracial Marriage: Folk Ethics in Contemporary Philosophy," in *Women of Color and Philosophy,* ed. Naomi Zack (Malden, MA: Blackwell Publishers, 2000).

4. Ibid., p. 197.

5. Ibid., p. 186.

6. *Loving v. Virginia,* 388 US 1 (1967). In this landmark civil rights case, the Supreme Court voted unanimously to legalize interracial marriage.

7. See bell hooks, *Salvation: Black People and Love* (New York: HarperCollins, 2001); Tricia Rose, *Longing to Tell: Black Women Talk About Sexuality and Intimacy* (New York: Farrar, Strauss and Giroux, 2003); Robert Staples, *Exploring Black Sexuality* (Lanham, MD: Rowman & Littlefield, 2006).

8. Allen, "Interracial Marriage," p. 183.

9. Charles Mills, "Do Black Men Have a Moral Duty to Marry Black Women?" *Journal of Social Philosophy* 25, Supplement s1 (1994): 131–153.

10. Ibid., p. 134.

11. Debra B. Bergoffen, "Marriage, Autonomy, and the Feminine Protest," *Hypatia* 14, no. 4 (1999): 18–35.

12. Ibid., p. 19.

13. Ibid., p. 24.

14. Claudia Card, "Against Marriage and Motherhood," *Hypatia* 11, no. 3 (1996): 2.

15. Claudia Card, "Gay Divorce: Thoughts on the Legal Regulation of Marriage," *Hypatia* 22, no. 1 (2007): 27.

16. Card, "Against Marriage," p. 6.

17. Frances Smith Foster, *'Til Death or Distance Do Us Part* (New York: Oxford University Press, 2010).

18. Ibid., p. 15.

19. Ibid., p. 56.

Are You My People?

The Surprising Places This Black Woman Philosopher Did Not Find Community

DESIRÉE H. MELTON

No one can accuse philosophy of being diverse. White men dominate the discipline, what counts as mainstream philosophy is often the sort of philosophy that has been traditionally done by white men, and the most well-regarded publications are filled with the works of white men. Feminist philosophy and critical race theory—the kinds of philosophy traditionally done by women and nonwhite philosophers—are marginalized as not being rigorous enough to count as "real" philosophy or not being concerned with matters that are universal in scope. Breaking into the white-boys' club of mainstream philosophy has not been easy. Still, our exclusion has spurred the creation of wonderful organizations, conferences, and workshops, where we can discuss our ideas in a welcoming environment and offer support and community to one another.

In my experience, however, exclusionary behavior in philosophy is not limited to white males. Nonwhite and women philosophers do well at organizing conference panels that address racial, gender, and ideology domination. We publish essays and books devoted to increasing inclusion in the world of philosophy and in the real world beyond it. We have not done so well, however, in recognizing our own privilege and the ways

in which it impairs our ability to see how we have excluded one another.

This essay, my personal account of moving about the world of academic philosophy looking for community—my people—and not quite finding it, was a long time coming. Anecdotally, I am not the only one who has felt squeezed out of or not welcomed into communities that should welcome us. If we are not having difficult conversations around this issue already, my hope is that this essay will encourage us to begin a meaningful discourse. If we are, then this essay will hopefully add to the dialogue.

Looking for Community

I was recently invited to participate in a philosophy roundtable on a local radio show that included another minority philosopher and Hamid Dabashi, who is a minority and a professor of Iranian studies and comparative literature. We were to discuss Dabashi's article "Can Non-Europeans Think?"[1] The article takes up the question of why African and Indian philosophy is often characterized as ethnophilosophy rather than just simply as philosophy. Our roundtable discussion began with some history about colonialism and slavery and the exclusion of blacks

Desirée H. Melton is an associate professor of philosophy at the Notre Dame of Maryland University. She specializes in critical race theory, social and political philosophy, and existentialism.

and other people of color from rationality. Eventually I remarked that for these works to be considered philosophy they must be *treated* as philosophy. We must assign such works on our syllabi, minority philosophers must be included in the main program of the American Philosophical Association—the mainstream philosophy organization—and minority philosophers must be published in mainstream journals. Dabashi had joined us by phone and at times the poor sound quality made it difficult to hear him, but toward the end of the discussion his frustration was clearly audible. He thought that we had strayed from the topic and that his question had gone unanswered.

I left the discussion feeling unsettled and confused but it wasn't until later that I was able to articulate what had troubled me. First, perhaps my answer did not cover all of the ways in which we can bring philosophy done by Indians and Africans (as well as women, I insisted on adding) into the mainstream, but I had certainly answered his question. And I was not the first one, either. Feminist and minority philosophers have repeatedly asked and answered this very question.[2] Second, all of the white male moderator's questions about the classroom and pedagogy were directed at me: How do I treat marginalized works in the classroom, and what do I teach my students? The other panelists teach courses, too, but it is clear that their role was to speak from their positions as researchers, academicians, and thinkers, while my role was to speak as the educator.[3] So, in a conversation between minorities *about* marginalization of minorities, I was relegated to the margins and not

heard. Can my views and the views of other black women philosophers ever assume the lofty place of the universal if we cannot count on being heard by those who should be sympathetic to our efforts at inclusion?

I was disappointed with them and with myself. I was disappointed with myself for making the old mistake of assuming that the common ground we shared as racial and ethnic minorities would put us on equal footing. Somehow, at that roundtable, this feminist had forgotten about gender.

Referring to Eurocentrism, Dabashi says, "There is thus a direct and unmitigated structural link between an empire, or an imperial frame of reference, and the presumed universality of a thinker thinking in the bosoms of that empire."[4] The same can be said for gender domination. I had forgotten that in the bosom of the gender domination empire, I am at the bottom of the hierarchy, and the imperial male frame of reference—white and nonwhite—seems committed to keeping me there. Or perhaps I had not forgotten about gender completely. Perhaps I had been seduced into thinking that race can be an immediate source of understanding and connection, even as I know the literature and my own experiences say that is not the case. I should have known better; I have been seduced before.

A couple years ago I was a member of a workshop panel for undergraduates in philosophy from underrepresented groups. The workshop was to provide an opportunity for students considering graduate study in philosophy to interact with other minority students and faculty. Faculty presenters were free to structure their presentation in any way they chose. I discussed an article I had previously published, which they had been assigned to read before my arrival, and then move into a discussion on a work in progress that builds on the ideas from the article. The presentation went well, but something troubling happened during the question-and-answer period: the room became divided by gender. The women (white, black, brown) understood, welcomed, and engaged with my work on its own terms while the men (black, brown) were concerned with challenging and poking holes in my argument and presenting me with an endless string of "what ifs" capped off by the exasperating but all too familiar question: "I know this isn't at all what you're talking about, but can you comment on it anyway?" The article we were discussing was about the importance of openness and vulnerability as a requirement to understanding others who come from a different perspective than one's own. Ironically, in the article I propose that minorities will be less resistant to vulnerability than whites since they are not invested in obscuring reality. Afterward, several women (black, brown, and white) approached me to discuss my ideas further and to share with me their concerns about studying philosophy in a field that is often hostile to women. I had no such interaction with any of the male students or the male faculty. These experiences—and others I do not have space to discuss here—have led me to conclude that while minority male philosophers do offer more community to nonwhite women than white male philosophers do, those minority men at the roundtable and at the workshop were a false community; they were not my people.

The earliest experience of false community I had was early in my graduate career at a conference of feminist philosophers. I was excited to be there, having read a lot of feminist philosophy in my courses and riding high on the expectation of a diverse and welcoming group of women with whom to interact. Yet, almost immediately I was disappointed. I'm fairly certain I was the only black woman there, but that was not what disappointed me.[5]

I was disappointed in the snatches of conversation I overheard at a cocktail gathering before the conference began; conversations about who wore heels, and who wore lipstick, who shaved their legs, and who brought husbands along (and called them by the term "husband" rather than "partner"). The women who did not measure up, including me, found it difficult to enter conversations and have the kinds of interactions that drew us to the conference in the first place. At a particularly low point, I actually entertained the idea of working my bisexuality into a conversation to earn a bit of cred. But then I remembered that in some circles bisexuality isn't a "real" sexual orientation, often treated with disdain or outright disbelief. I'm fairly certain that this conference was in one of those circles. Again, I was disappointed with them, but I was also disappointed with myself for even thinking of trying to put some part of myself on display to appease someone else's narrow ideology. There I was, seduced into thinking that I could find community—this time among my gender—but no, these white feminist women were not my people either.

Feeling the Intersectionality of Race and Gender Domination

When I reflect on these experiences I am reminded of Charles Mills's description of the interplay of race and gender domination among white men, white women, nonwhite men, and nonwhite women.[6] It is no surprise that white men, invested in retaining their race and gender privilege over everyone, will have to work the hardest to see racial and gender discrimination. The disregard that so many white women, nonwhite men, and nonwhite women experience as we try to make our way into philosophy, that bastion of white male rationality par excellence, bears this out.

Mills holds that white women, invested in preserving their racial privilege, are often blind to the ways in which they dominate nonwhite women and men. This should come as no surprise either, but my experience at conferences points to ideological domination in addition to racial domination. My experience tells me, along with anecdotes from others, that women—white or nonwhite—who do not ascribe to a particular interpretation of feminism, or who comport themselves in a manner that does not fit the dominant ideology, are not welcomed into the community. I do not see a difference between that kind of ideological domination and the ideological white male domination of philosophy that we are fighting against.

Nonwhite men are not privileged by race but they are privileged by gender. Invested in preserving gender domination, they will be blind to the patriarchy that positions them above nonwhite women.[7] Nonwhite women will look to their brothers for community and find that the sights of those men are not on their sisters but instead on getting to the top of the hierarchy alongside their brothers in gender domination, white men.

And nonwhite women? We get it from all sides—racial domination from white men and women, and gender domination from white, brown, and black men. While white women are invested in getting their full share of privilege by virtue of their race, and nonwhite men are invested in getting their full share of privilege by virtue of their gender, nonwhite women are invested in getting out from under.

The way I see things, white women and nonwhite men have some work to do if they do not want to inadvertently ally themselves with white men and reproduce the gender and racial domination that minority women already experience. Nonwhite feminist philosophers have well emphasized the importance of treating race and gender as intersectional rather than separate and unconnected.[8] Still, there are times in academic environments when race shifts into stark focus while gender assumes the background and vice versa, thus leaving minority women struggling mightily to remain whole in the awkward position of being cleaved into parts. And as much as we may want to believe that only a white male philosopher would victimize us in this way, there are times when the person wielding the blade is one of our own. As we try to carve out a niche for ourselves in philosophy while pushing philosophy to be more inclusive, we slip into reproducing the very domination we are rallying against. I wonder: Will white women and black men have to work as hard at seeing their privilege as white men do because they *assume* that by virtue of their own gender or racial subordination they do not have to work at all?

Conclusion

Dabashi says, "It is precisely that self-confidence, that self-consciousness, that audacity to think yourself the agent of history that enables a thinker to think his particular thinking is 'Thinking' in universal terms, and his philosophy 'Philosophy' and his city square 'The Public Space.'"[9]

In the quest to become audacious enough to think themselves agents of history, gaining self-confidence, and self-consciousness to be universal, are white women philosophers and nonwhite male philosophers stepping on the backs of nonwhite women?

Seduced by the promise of community from my would-be people, I was disappointed at every turn.

For now, an occasional gathering with a group of black women philosophers and the university where I teach is where I feel most at home in academia. I am one member of a four-member department, three of whom are women, and we have a good working relationship. My students are all women, most of them are of color, and a good many of them are bisexual or lesbian. It is not a tier-one school and the teaching load is heavy, but I do not have to fight for respect when I enter the classroom on the first day of class, no one questions that the work I do is anything less than philosophy, no one looks at me sideways when I wear heels and lipstick

(which I do regularly), and it would not occur to them to think that I am an educator only and not also a scholar. And when I came out as a bisexual in a committed relationship with a woman, I was applauded. I find it disheartening, sadly regressive, and yet comforting that my people are the people who are most like me in most ways.

Notes

I want to thank Paul Breines for giving me extensive feedback on the earliest draft of this article, and Maeve O'Donovan and Laurie Wilks for their supportive comments on later drafts.

Terra, your love has given me the courage to write from my heart. Thank you.

1. Dabashi Hamid, "Can Non-Europeans Think?" www.aljazeera.com/indepth/opinion/2013/01/2013114142638797542.html.

2. See Sally Haslanger, "Changing the Ideology and Culture of Philosophy: Not by Reason (Alone)," *Hypatia* 23, no. 2: 210–233; Charles W. Mills, *The Racial Contract* (Ithaca, NY: Cornell University Press, 1997); Charles W. Mills and Carole Pateman, *Contract and Domination* (Cambridge, UK: Polity Press, 2007); and various articles. Anita Superson, "Strategies for Making Feminist Philosophy Mainstream Philosophy," *Hypatia* 26, no. 2: 410–418.

3. I embrace my role as an educator. I know I am needed at my university that has a minority student population of 40 percent and where I am one of maybe five black women faculty out of about one hundred total.

4. Hamid, "Can Non-Europeans Think?"

5. There just are not many of us to go around. At last count, there are only about thirty black

women philosophers in the United States and there were even fewer years ago when I attended the conference.

6. Mills and Pateman, *Contract and Domination.*

7. Ibid., p. 184. In general, racial domination has historically trumped gender domination positioning nonwhite men beneath white women.

8. For just a few, see Angela Davis (1981), Maria Lugones (1994), Kimberle Crenshaw (1989), Gloria Anzuldua (2001).

9. Hamid, "Can Non-Europeans Think?"

Philosophical Blacknuss

American Philosophy and the Particular

BILL LAWSON

WE is gathahed hyeah, my brothahs, In dis howlin' wildaness, Fu' to speak some words of comfo't To each othah in distress.[1]

—**Paul Laurence Dunbar,**
An Ante-Bellum Sermon

Teaching philosophy from within the African-American social historical context has always been important to me. I want to explore the particulars of the black experience with the skills of a philosopher. As a graduate student, I was trained to think of philosophy as the discipline that disregards the particulars of an individual's life and to focus on the aspects that were both "universal" and "impartial." In graduate school, any discussion of racism or sexism was too partial and better suited for academic exploration in the disciplines of sociology, criminology, or political science. In this regard, questions concerning social justice and blacks or women were not philosophical questions. This was disheartening given that I wanted to write a dissertation that drew on the experiences of black people in the United States. I was told that if I chose to write about race and race-related issues, I would not have a job as a philosopher in the United States and probably nowhere in the world. Undaunted, I took on this challenge and have attempted to address in a philosophical manner concerns that I think are rooted in the black American social, political, and historical experience.[2] *I knew that I must take the black experience seriously as an area of research and as a source of philosophical insight as my starting point for my work in philosophy.*[3]

I had to take a position because I knew that the black experience was not given a high level of regard and respect as a lived experience by philosophers, and I wanted to do philosophy.[4] I knew that the discipline's unwillingness to take seriously the lived experiences of black people has a significant effect on the research projects and career opportunities for those philosophers that Kristie Dotson calls diverse practitioners of philosophy.[5]

The challenge is to do philosophy in a society and profession that devalues black life experiences and expects black philosophers to revel in the lived experiences of others. As diverse practitioners of philosophy, taking the black experience seriously means

Bill E. Lawson is distinguished professor of philosophy at the University of Memphis in Tennessee. His areas of specialization are African-American philosophy and social and political philosophy. His published works include *Pragmatism and the Problem of Race* (Indiana University Press, 2004), edited with Donald Koch; *Faces of Environmental Racism,* 2nd ed. (Rowman & Littlefield, 2001), edited with Laura Westra; *Frederick Douglass: A Critical Reader* (Blackwell, 1999), edited with Frank Kirkland. He has testified before a US congressional subcommittee on welfare reform. He was a 2011–2012 University of Liverpool Fulbright Fellow at the University of Liverpool in the UK.

that we must start with the view that our task is to challenge and counter the "deforming mirror of truth."[6]

The Master Narrative and Race

Before his death in 1989, historian Nathan Huggins added a new introduction, "The Deforming Mirror of Truth," to his important book, *Black Odyssey*. Huggins's basic thesis was that historians helped to foster the national belief in what he called a "master narrative" regarding race, racism, and slavery in the United States that deformed historical truth. This narrative was etched into the Constitution and had become the mantra for thinking about the role of slavery and race in the United States. Huggins writes:

> American historians have conspired with the founding fathers to create a national history, teleologically bound to the Founders' ideals rather than their reality. They have chosen to see American history from even before the Revolution as an inexorable development of free institutions and the expansion of political liberty to the broadest possible public. Like the framers of the Constitution, they have treated racial slavery and oppression as curious abnormalities–aberrations–historical accidents to be corrected in the progressive upward reach of the nation's destiny.[7]

In this narrative, the United States is a country founded on and dedicated to the proposition that all men were created equal or one day will be. "The holy nation thus acquired a holy history. A conspiracy of myth, history, and chauvinism served to create an ideology as the dominating historical motif against which all history would resonate."[8] The story had no place for racial slavery or the racial caste system that followed emancipation. It is a sanitized account of race and racism that the United States tells and sells about its founding and its aims. This narrative becomes the foundational script for what it means to be an American and to be in America.[9] This fable supports, among many others, two themes: The first is to glorify the white presence in the United States. The second is to ignore the meaningful presence of nonwhites, in particular enslaved Africans. It is this myth that deforms truth.

I think that there are ample examples of the prevalence of these themes in our reading of American history. What Huggins forcefully argues is that this telling of the creation and aims of the United States reinforced the positioning of blacks as inferior beings and the black experience as having no positive value. While Huggins focuses on historians, it is clear that he could include philosophers, sociologists, theologians, and a host of others as purveyors of the myth of black inferiority. It is through the retelling and reinforcing of this narrative that black females, males, and children are devalued as members of the society.[10]

It is the marginalization of blacks as full human beings that becomes the focus of racial consciousness in the United States. As Clarence S. Johnson notes, in a quote worth repeating:

> An individual's consciousness about racial categories in this transgressive, counter-hegemonic sense consists in her or his

awareness of the fact that to be black (in terms of a person's pigmentation) automatically translates into occupying a subordinate social position in society. By contrast, to be white (in terms of a person's skin pigmentation) automatically translates into occupying a position of power. The significant point here concerns the individual's awareness of "whiteness" and "blackness" as terms for racial categories that represent and reflect distinct and unequal social locations in society, wherein the criterion for membership into a racial category, and hence for entry into a given social location, is skin color.[11]

The use of racist practices and policies has helped to create a heightened racial consciousness in this country and also has helped to form the belief that blacks are a stable racial group both in physical and psychological terms. The social practices, laws, and educational and religious teachings have all worked to marginalize the social standing of blacks.[12]

The main point here is that the social and political history and practices of this country have fostered views (1) of blacks as morally and intellectually inferior to whites and (2) that the black experience has no redeeming value.[13] This shaping of the status of blacks in the United States has been four hundred years in the making. The idea to subjugate blacks was formed early in the development of the country. A. Leon Higginbotham Jr. writes in his book *In the Matter of Color*:

In treating the first 200 years of black presence in America, this book will demonstrate how the entire legal apparatus was used by those with the power to do so established a solid legal tradition for the absolute enslavement of blacks. It will be an effort to look at this history primarily through the special focus of a legal lens, to examine the pathology of the law, its creation, it sanctioning, its tolerance, and its occasional eradication of the racist practices that caused one group of human beings to receive such special, harsh, disparate treatment.[14]

These practices and customs devalued both black people and the black experience. This positioning of black people can help explain why the black experience has no value in the discipline of philosophy; the people who have these experiences have no value.

It was this problematic framing of the black American experience that I hoped philosophy would help me find answers to. I hoped that philosophy would help me find answers about, if not solutions to, liberty, justice, and freedom that would help me counter and correct these misconceptions about the black experience. I was wrong about both. Philosophy and many of the philosophers I encountered had no interest intellectually, politically, or academically about the manner in which philosophy could address concerns rooted in the African-American lived experience.[15]

I realized that the history and the wider social understanding of the social status of blacks shaped how we think about what it means to know, how we distribute social goods, how we understand beauty, how we understand what it means to be human. Race affected how groups value their female members and the quality of respect and regard given to women who are members of the "other." It affected the manner in which black men viewed black women and how black women viewed black men. In this regard, race and racial practices have shaped the social practices and customs of the United States in that race and racist ideology have been in play from the cradle to the grave for black Americans. Race affects where we are born, who our parents are, the type of prenatal treatment our mothers received, where our parents could work, where they could live, where they could be treated when ill, where they could be buried when they died. Race and racism affected what they valued and whom they valued.[16] Race and racist practices also affected the manner in which whites saw and thought about blacks as persons and the black experience. It is not a pretty image.[17] Professional academic philosophers are not immune to societal racism and sexism.

What often shocks new graduate students of color is that those people who are supposed to be rational and reflective about life and life experiences are not particularly welcoming to the life experiences of others. These students realize that these are the people teaching them and recommending them for jobs to other persons who have little regard for black people or the black experience. This is the harsh reality of life in the philosophy game.[18]

What does it mean to be a philosopher and to do philosophy in a society that has devalued you and the group to which you can be identified as socially, morally, and intellectually inferior? How do you work from within your lived experience in a discipline that has no respect or regard for your experiences? These are difficult questions. To be steadfast requires courage and fortitude. Indeed, we find ourselves working in a discipline that devalues black people and the black experience. For many of these "scholars" in philosophy, in regards to positive values, the black experience is a null set. Confronting these negative evaluations is the challenge of the diverse practitioner of philosophy.

Let me note that black women professional philosophers have their own particular issues and concerns that arise out of the racist/sexist reading of the black experience. These issues and concerns are related to and connected to those of black male professional philosophers. While both groups challenge the strength and vitality of the master narrative regarding race and sex, their challenges are different. Challenging the master narrative does not mean replacing it with one that uses *race* as a catchall for the experiences of black men and women. We each have our own particular issues and concerns and we have some that overlap and connect. If we as diverse practitioners of philosophy are going to take the black experience seriously, we must seriously respect the experiences of black women and men.[19]

What is the point? The point is that working on issues and concerns that arise out of lived experience within the tradition of Anglo-American philosophy is difficult. Philosophers are not immune to racism and sexism. It is not as if the ability to formulate a complicated argument is a vaccination against racism and sexism. Reason and sound arguments have not dislodged the view of the black experience as having no value.[20]

When Howard McGary and I cowrote *Between Slavery and Freedom,* we had to grapple with using the American slavery experience as the focal point of the book. We had to answer the charge that our work was too partial. We wrote:

> We think that a philosopher might aspire to universalist criteria in some sense and still be committed to taking account of matters that are essentially perspectival, such as the American slave experience. Often the moral issues one focuses on depend on one's sensitivity to the actual experience of those involved. When one takes the slave experience seriously, issues like oppression and forgiveness come to the fore. But thinking seriously and reflectively about these issues, taking full account of the slave's experience, does not, so far as we can see, preclude aiming at universality or impartiality (or, for that matter, objectivity). It would be limiting if one were interested solely in how things seem from that perspective, but one can hardly appreciate the moral issues involved in American slavery without examining, inter alia, how things seemed from the slave's point of view.[21]

Many years later I still think it is true that we can do philosophy from within our own lived experience and bring out important philosophical insights. However, we must first respect and be sensitive to our lived experiences. Unfortunately, the discipline of philosophy has not shown respect or sensitivity to the experiences of its diverse practitioners. To have the courage to research with the knowledge that our work may not get acclaim or regard because it is about our lived experience is a difficult choice. I am not suggesting that anyone make this choice, but it was my choice.

With all of this said, I contend that philosophers of color have been faithful to philosophy even when philosophy has not been faithful to them. We still recruit young scholars of color to attend graduate school to study philosophy and to one day teach philosophy, even though we know there are academic "haters."[22] One can liken these times to the early years of school desegregation when blacks sent their children into hostile schools even with the knowledge that the trek would be full of haters (persons who had no respect for blacks). We still send our children out to integrate schools, only this time it is in philosophy programs as graduate students and into hostile philosophy departments as new professors. Just like the black students who integrated elementary and high schools in the 1960s, we are integrating philosophy departments in the new millennium. The struggle continues. It is my contention that to take the black experience seriously is to appreciate the manner in which racism and sexism affects our role as diverse practitioners of philosophy and what it means to do philosophy in a society that devalues our experiences and then still do it.

The title of this essay, "Philosophical Blacknuss," draws on the composition by Rahsaan Roland Kirk: "Blacknuss." The track is entirely built on and performed with the thirty-six black keys of the piano.[23] Kirk states at the beginning of the composition: "We don't mean to eliminate nothin,' but we're gonna just hear the black notes, if you don't mind." In this regard, this essay is like the Rahsaan Roland Kirk song that postulates that sometimes we must focus our work from within our own lived experience. This essay is dedicated to the memories of William R. Jones and Paul Laurence Dunbar, who understood the value of both black people and the black experience, and Shelton Howden, who did not.[24] Blacknuss!

Notes

1. Paul Laurence Dunbar, *An Ante-Bellum Sermon,* www.dunbarsite.org, accessed April 6, 2013.

2. I was fortunate to come to philosophy after having been a grunt in Vietnam, a hustler on the block, and a menial laborer. These life experiences have affected how I do philosophy. Since I came to philosophy after my time in 'Nam, working in philosophy was a career choice, not a spiritual calling. I was also fortunate to meet and interact in graduate school and early in my career with other like-minded diverse practitioners, such as Williams R. Jones, Angela Davis, Lucius Outlaw, Howard McGary, Bernard Boxill, Leonard Harris, Tommy Lott, Cornel West, Frank Kirkland, and Laurence Thomas.

3. John Hope Franklin noted that the black scholar has to prove that he or she is a scholar and, if he or she wants to do academic research on the African-American experience, show that that experience is worth studying. John Hope Franklin, "The Dilemma of the American Negro Scholar," in *Soon, One Morning; New Writing by American Negroes, 1940–1962* (New York: Knopf, 1963), pp. 60–76.

4. I met some black philosophers who thought that my obsession with the black experience was academically misguided and thought that as philosophers we must transcend race. The experience of those diverse practitioners of philosophy who have attempted to show that their work can do so have done no better than those who have worked to make the black experience a part of the larger philosophical landscape. In some cases the frustration and disappointment felt when the race-transcending person's work is not given the respect and regard of the average white philosopher is crushing. Who wants to be crushed morally and spiritually? That's why I placed my bet on black.

5. Kristie Dotson, "How Is This Paper Philosophy?" *Comparative Philosophy* 3, no. 1 (2012): 4.

6. I take Dotson's use of diverse practitioners of philosophy seriously because I agree with her concern that much of black/Africana philosophy has been black male philosophy; see note 16.

7. Nathan Irvin Huggins, *Black Odyssey: The African-American Ordeal in Slavery* (New York: Vintage Books, 1990), Kindle edition.

8. Ibid.

9. It must be remembered that there has been a great deal of literature and scholarship that has supported the master narrative. The text *Problems of Citizenship* is an interesting read. It was an attempt to provide a problems course for introductory social sciences at Dartmouth College. It has a section on the Negro and notes that it will address the woman question, which was noted but not discussed in many textbooks. It may be argued that it is not representative of the racist diatribe that has been used to disparage blacks, but its attempt to be even-handed makes it worth considering. Hayes Baker-Crothers, *Problems of Citizenship* (New York: Holt, 1924).

10. Avril Fuller, "Black Rue: The Hunger Games and Rhetorics of Innocence," unpublished manuscript.

11. Clarence S. Johnson, "(Re) Conceptualizing Blackness and Making Race Obsolescent," in *White on White/Black on Black,* ed. George Yancy (Lanham, MD: Rowman & Littlefield, 2005), p. 178.

12. Bill E. Lawson, "Social Disappointment and the Black Sense of Self," in *Existence in*

Black: An Anthology of Black Existential Philosophy (New York: Routledge, 1997), pp. 149–156.

13. Derrick Bell has the best analysis of way in which laws and social practices are able to self-correct for whiteness. See, for example, Derrick A. Bell, *Silent Covenants: Brown vs. Board of Education and the Elusive Quest for Racial Justice* (New York: Oxford University Press, 2004); Derrick A. Bell, Richard Delgado, and Jean Stefancic, *The Derrick Bell Reader* (New York: New York University Press, 2005); and Derrick A. Bell, *Faces at the Bottom of the Well: The Permanence of Racism* (New York: Basic Books, 1992).

14. A. Leon Higginbotham Jr., *In the Matter of Color: Race & The American Legal Process: The Colonial Period* (New York: Oxford University Press, 1978), p. 14.

15. John H. McClendon, "On the Politics of Professional Philosophy: The Plight of the African American Philosopher," in *Reframing the Practice of Philosophy: Bodies of Color, Bodies of Knowledge,* ed. George Yancy (Albany: State University of New York Press, 2012).

16. See, for example, Paul C. Taylor, "Pragmatism and Race," in *Pragmatism and the Problem of Race* (Bloomington: Indiana University Press, 2004); Charles W. Mills, "Do Black Men Have a Moral Duty to Marry Black Women?" *Journal of Social Philosophy* 25, no. S1 (1994); George Yancy, *Black Bodies, White Gazes: The Continuing Significance of Race* (Lanham, MD: Rowman & Littlefield, 2008); Bernard R. Boxill, *Blacks and Social Justice* (Totowa, NJ: Rowman & Allanheld, 1984); Howard McGary, *Race and Social Justice* (Malden, MA: Blackwell, 1999); Laurence Thomas, *Vessels of Evil: American Slavery and the Holocaust* (Philadelphia: Temple University Press, 1993); Leonard Harris, *Philosophy Born of Struggle: Anthology of Afro-American Philosophy from 1917* (Dubuque, IA: Kendall Hunt Publishing, 1983).

17. George M. Fredrickson, *The Black Image in the White Mind: The Debate on Afro-American Character and Destiny, 1817–1914* (Hanover, NH: Wesleyan University Press, 1987).

18. "Philosophical Playa Hatin' Race, Respect and the Philosophy Game," in *Reframing the Practice of Philosophy: Bodies of Color, Bodies of Knowledge,* ed. George Yancy (Albany: State University of New York Press, 2012).

19. See also Patricia Hill Collins, "The Social Construction of Black Feminist Thought," *Signs* 14, no. 4 (1989); Valerie Smith, "Black Feminist Theory and the Representation of the 'Other,'" in *Changing Our Own Words: Essays on Criticism, Theory and Writing by Black Women,* ed. Cheryl Wall (New Brunswick, NJ: Rutgers University Press, 1989); Michele Wallace, *Invisibility Blues: From Pop to Theory* (New York: Verso, 1990); Gloria T. Hull and Patricia Bell Scott, eds., *All the Women Are White, All the Blacks Are Men, but Some of Us Are Brave: Black Women's Studies* (Old Westbury, NY: Feminist Press, 1982); Rebecca Wanzo, *The Suffering Will Not Be Televised: African American Women and Sentimental Political Storytelling* (Albany: SUNY Press, 2009); Melissa Harris-Perry, *Sister Citizen: Shame, Stereotypes, and Black Women in America* (New Haven, CT: Yale University Press, 2011); Anna Julia Cooper, "Our Raison D'etre," in *The Voice of Anna Julia Cooper: Including a Voice from the South and Other Important Essays, Papers, and Letters,* ed. Charles Lemert and Esme Bhan (Lanham, MD: Rowman & Littlefield, 1992).

20. Laurence Thomas, "Moral Equality and Natural Inferiority," *Social Theory and Practice,* 31, no. 3 (July 2005): 379–404.

21. Howard McGary and Bill E. Lawson, *Between Slavery and Freedom: Philosophy and American Slavery* (Bloomington: Indiana University Press, 1992), p. xviii

22. This bit is cribbed from my paper "Philosophical Playa Hatin' Race, Respect and the Philosophy Game."

23. Rahsaan Roland Kirk, *Blacknuss,* Atlantic Records, 1972. Songs on the pentatonic scale:

"Ol' Man River," "Amazing Grace," "New World Symphony"—Dvorak, "Deep River," "Swing Low, Sweet Chariot," "Sometimes I Feel Like a Motherless Child," and "My Girl"—The Temptations.

24. William R. Jones, "The Legitimacy and Necessity of Black Philosophy: Some Prelimi-nary Considerations," *Philosophical Forum* 9, no. 2–3 (Winter–Spring 1977–1978); J. Saunders Redding, *Stranger and Alone: A Novel* (Boston: Northeastern University Press, 1989).

From *Logos* to *Sarx*

Black Philosophy and the Philosophy of Religion

TIM GOLDEN

The righteousness of God is not an abstract quality in the being of God, as with Greek philosophy. It is rather God's active involvement in history, making right what human beings have made wrong.

—James Cone,
A Black Theology of Liberation

I.

Black philosophy, as I conceive of it in this essay (there are other ways to conceive of black philosophy), is a sort of critical reflection on the experiences of African Americans, Africans, and Afro-Caribbeans in Western modernity.[1] This sort of critical reflection arises from within epistemologically motivated and oppressive axiological, political, and religious conceptual schemes that maintain white supremacy. Black philosophy succeeds in turning such oppressive conceptual schemes against themselves by holding them accountable with rigorous standards of authentic moral, religious, and political praxis; standards that the epistemic motivations of oppressive axiological, political, and religious conceptual schemes ignore altogether. That there could be such a thing as black philosophy in Western modernity, given Western modernity's anti-black racism, is remarkable. For Western modernity and its attendant white supremacy, as

manifested through the horrors of chattel slavery, Jim Crow, lynching, colonialism, and mass incarceration, has demonstrated such dehumanizing behavior toward blacks that one would reasonably think it impossible for philosophical reflection to occur under such hostile conditions. But the resiliency of philosophical reflection is quite remarkable; for philosophical reflection on the experiences of blacks in the West has flourished in a dehumanizing environment. Black philosophy thus originates—indeed, thrives—in a hostile environment that purported to undermine its possibility. And black philosophy's function is as interesting as its origin; for black philosophy functions as both sentinel and savior. As sentinel, black philosophy stands watch over against the very same hostile environment that denied its possibility, providing powerful moral, religious, and political critiques of that same hostile environment that at once both—almost paradoxically—suppressed and birthed it, demanding justice. And as I

Timothy Joseph Golden, JD, PhD, is associate professor of philosophy and director of the Frederick Douglass Institute at West Chester University of Pennsylvania. He is the author of *And the Word Was Made Flesh: Frederick Douglass and the Philosophy of Religion* (Lexington Books, under contract), and "Epistemic Addiction: Reading 'Sonny's Blues' with Levinas, Kierkegaard, and Nietzsche," published in the *Journal of Speculative Philosophy*, and he is editor of *Racism and Resistance: Essays on Derrick Bell* (SUNY Press, under contract).

will argue below, as savior, black philosophy saves the philosophy of religion from its moral disorder of epistemic addiction, giving both voice and face to the abstractions that ignore moral and political praxis, thus making the move from *logos* to *sarx,* or, to put it another way, making the word flesh.

There are many manifestations of anti-black racism in Western modernity—too many to enumerate here. So I emphasize a serious moral problem at work in Western modernity that both denies the humanity of blacks and also helps give rise to black philosophy: the moral problem of epistemic addiction. I have written of this moral problem elsewhere,[2] and I provide a brief definition of this moral problem here. Epistemic addiction is the Aristotelian "desire to know" run amok; it is the quest for knowledge without regard for ethics; the incessant intellectual gesticulation that is so preoccupied with rational justifications for beliefs, that it ignores pressing moral and political concerns. Perhaps nowhere is this phenomenon seen more clearly than in the philosophical subfield that professional philosophers call the "philosophy of religion," where it manifests itself in what Martin Heidegger termed the "onto-theological" constitution of metaphysics; the demand for the Deity to enter into philosophy only upon the conditions of rationality.[3] Narrowly construed here to refer to the hyper-analytic and overly conceptual accounts of God and his attributes, the problem of evil, theodicy, and proofs for God's existence, the philosophy of religion is so focused on conceptual analysis that it ignores moral and political praxis. And as Charles Mills has argued in his critique of John Rawls, the same hyper-theorizations

and abstractions that are impotent against injustice will likely perpetuate injustice.[4] As it is with political philosophy, so it is with the philosophy of religion: the philosophy of religion, because of its epistemic addiction, not only omits pressing moral and political concerns at the level of praxis, but such omissions perpetuate the injustices that cause the moral and political concerns in the first place. Hence, the need for black philosophy to be a sentinel; to stand watch over against the very environment that denied its possibility; and to critique that very same environment on practical, moral, political, and religious grounds.

Since I deal with the philosophy of religion here, it is appropriate to employ a framework from the Judeo-Christian tradition in making my argument. I argue that black philosophy performs its function of sentinel of an epistemologically addicted philosophy of religion by demanding that the philosophy of religion make the word (*logos*) flesh (*sarx*). Whereas the epistemic addiction of the philosophy of religion uses abstraction to attain disembodiment for the sake of conceptual analysis, thus making the flesh into a word, black philosophy employs a critique of abstraction to make the word flesh. In section two, I frame my argument in terms of the biblical distinction between word and flesh, aligning philosophy of religion with *logos,* and black philosophy with *sarx.* In section three, I draw from Frederick Douglass's *Narrative of the Life of Frederick Douglass: An American Slave* (*Narrative*), and David Walker's *Appeal to the Coloured Citizens of the World, but in particular, and very expressly, to those of the United States of America* (*Appeal*), to show how black philosophy performs its functions of sentinel and savior, of making the word flesh, and of addressing deep and abiding moral, religious, and political concerns at the level of moral praxis through an embodied and concrete liberation hermeneutic, and also through aesthetics. I conclude in section four.

II.

Since much of the philosophy of religion, as I conceive of it here, arises from the Judeo-Christian theological framework of scholasticism,[5] it is appropriate to make a biblical allusion to the distinction between word and flesh. *Logos* and *sarx* are the Greek terms for word and flesh, respectively. What is their relevance here? These terms are important because they establish a framework for my account of black philosophy and its relationship to the philosophy of religion. In Greek, the term *logos* implies word, reason, or language. Since the philosophy of religion suffers from epistemic addiction, its preoccupation with epistemic justification and hyper-theorization puts it squarely within the network of meaning implied by the term *logos*. A good example of this sort of epistemic addiction is Alvin Plantinga's essay "The Free Will Defense," where Plantinga, through a vast array of thought experiments and appeals to the abstractions of set theory, purports to refute John Mackie's claim that religious beliefs are "positively irrational."[6] Completely inattentive to moral praxis, the thought experiments and logical rigor occlude abiding moral and political problems like anti-black racism. One may object here

and argue that Plantinga and other philosophers of religion, in addressing the problem of evil and theodicy, are addressing moral concerns. My response to this objection is that although philosophers of religion do address moral concerns as they relate to theodicy and the problem of evil, those concerns are still addressed from an overly theoretical standpoint for the purposes of rational thematization and epistemic justification, rather than for moral action at the level of human praxis. God exists, on their accounts, as an onto-theological construct of rationality, utterly disconnected from the concrete experiences of human beings. I do not mean to suggest that logical rigor and epistemic justification are somehow expendable. I do not believe that they are. I do believe, however, that they cannot, standing alone, address the deep and abiding religious, social, political, and economic manifestations of anti-black racism. So the philosophy of religion, as epistemologically addicted, uses the *logos* for almost exclusively epistemological purposes.

Now according to the Christian theological narrative, if the word is never made flesh, there can be no salvation.[7] The same is true of the philosophy of religion: its epistemic addiction puts it in serious need of a savior, and it cannot be saved unless its epistemic addiction is cured, and it is given, to use Ralph Ellison's description, "flesh and bone, fiber and liquids."[8] Enter black philosophy.

The black experience in Western modernity exposes the abstraction of the philosophy of religion at the level of moral and religious praxis for what it is: an epistemologically driven, oppressive methodology that not only ignores anti-black racism—an obvious moral, religious, and political problem—but also perpetuates it through its glaring omission of the moral problem of anti-black racism. But in the midst of anti-black racism, there arise powerful voices of moral and religious condemnation; voices that reveal that religious profession and epistemic justification mean very little except when accompanied by authentic moral and religious practice; voices that transform the abstractions of the philosophy of religion into living, breathing, and doing, concrete human beings. These voices remind us that the epistemic justifications of *logos* count for nothing except that they are embodied in the practices of the flesh. They remind us that philosophy of religion needs a savior. I now turn to two of these black voices: David Walker and Frederick Douglass.

III.

David Walker's *Appeal* makes the word flesh through its extensive biblical references and its identification of the black experience of oppression in the United States during chattel slavery with the experiences of the children of Israel in Pharaoh's Egypt. In contrast to Plantinga's thought experiments and appeals to set theory that abstract all flesh and bone from religious and theological reflection, David Walker puts religion solidly within the realm of moral and political praxis, restoring flesh, bone, and perhaps most important, *faces* to the theorizations of religious belief. Walker's methodology in the *Appeal* can hardly be done justice here, so I focus on only a small portion of that magnificent work. In a footnote to Article I of *Appeal,* after articulating the plight of blacks and comparing it to the children of Israel, Walker, exhibiting a hermeneutic of suspicion as it relates to Christian missionary work, writes of the profound shortcomings of Christianity as whites practice it, and as blacks experience it:

> If ever the world becomes Christianized . . . it will be through the means, under the God of the Blacks, who are now held in wretchedness, and degradation, by the white Christians of the world, who before they learn to do justice to us before our Maker—and be reconciled to us, and reconcile us to them, and by that means have clear consciences before God and man . . . they must learn to do justice at home . . . when they learn to do justice, God will accept their offering.[9]

In this passage, Walker makes the word flesh by reflecting on the hypocrisy of white slave-holding Christians; those who profess religion with their tongues yet deny it with their actions; a corrupt religious community that adheres to the letter of the law while denying its spirit. The theology of Christianity moved nineteenth-century white Christians to believe in its doctrines, but the word has never been made flesh in their lives.[10] White Christians thus never make the move to embodiment, and possess a form of godliness, but deny the actual power of godliness.[11] Black philosophy thus functions in David Walker's *Appeal* to critique oppressive philosophical doctrines and conceptual schemes because of their failed practical applications. Walker reminds us that the absence of moral and political praxis is itself profoundly immoral, as it encourages form over matter; the appearance of religion without real moral and political commitments; and a hypocritical, corrupt religious community—in short, a community in which the word is never made flesh.

Frederick Douglass is likewise an example of how black philosophy makes the word flesh. Douglass's *Narrative* shows us how the experiences of those in chattel slavery, through art, breathed life into what can become stale philosophical and theological doctrine devoid of flesh and bone, as is the case with the philosophy of religion. Douglass recognized the importance of art in terms of its ability to shed light on the human condition in a way that theory alone cannot. In his *Narrative,* he wrote of the slaves and their use of song that:

> They would sing, as a chorus, to words which to many would seem unmeaning jargon, but which, nevertheless, were full of meaning to themselves. I have sometimes thought that the mere hearing of those songs would do more to impress some minds with the horrible character of slavery, than the reading of whole volumes of philosophy on the subject could do.[12]

"Volumes of philosophy," as Douglass uses that term here, refers to the hyper-theoretical moral and religious reflections that I associate with the philosophy of religion. No amount of theoretical musings—for example, theodicy and the problem of evil—could impress minds with the horrible character of slavery quite like a song. Nietzsche echoes Douglass nearly thirty years later in *The Birth of Tragedy* when he condemns

the naive Socratic optimism of the quest for knowledge for its forgetfulness of Dionysian tragedy in music, and nearly forty years later in *The Gay Science,* where the madman pronounces the death of God; the end of theology; the utter uselessness of theoretical abstractions to grapple with the problem of suffering.[13] Douglass understood that the suffering of the slaves was beautifully captured, not as "evil" in a theoretical, dialectical relationship to good, but rather as an aesthetic production in music that gave the word flesh.

IV.

As fallen humanity is in need of salvation from sin, according to the Christian narrative, the philosophy of religion is in need of salvation from its "sin" of epistemic addiction. And as there can be no salvation in the Christian tradition except that the word be made flesh, there can be no salvation for the philosophy of religion, except that the *logos* of the philosophy of religion is transformed into the *sarx* of black bodies as the sight of oppression, and white bodies as the sight of the oppressor. If we conceive of sin as moral evil, then we might say that the philosophy of religion is in need of a savior from the moral evil—the sin—of epistemic addiction. Through black philosophy as portrayed in David Walker's *Appeal,* and Frederick Douglass's *Narrative,* we see black philosophy functioning as both sentinel and savior: as sentinel, black philosophy stands watch to critique oppressive methodologies that exalt form over substance, and as savior, black philosophy gives voice, flesh, bone, and face to epistemologically driven, axi-ological, political, and religious oppression. Black philosophy thus makes the word flesh.

Notes

1. I qualify my definition of black philosophy with the notion of "Western modernity" because Eastern religions, too, have been interpreted as having elements of anti-black racism. For example, William R. Jones describes Thomas Gossett's account of the *Rig Veda,* the Hindu scriptures of ancient India, where Indra, the god of the Aryans, hates black skin. Jones refers to the Hindu scriptures here as a "concrete" example of the "highly visible" phenomenon of "divine racism." See William R. Jones, *Is God a White Racist?* (Boston: Beacon Press, 1998), p. 3.

2. See my essay "Epistemic Addiction: Reading 'Sonny's Blues' with Levinas, Kierkegaard, and Nietzsche," *Journal of Speculative Philosophy* 26, no. 12 (2012): 554–571, where I reimagine the fall of humanity from the book of Genesis as a mistaken belief that good and evil can be "known" without being practiced. Eve was deceived in that she thought that she could simply "know" good and evil without doing them; it is this deception that caused Eve to "fall," for as she sought the "knowledge" of "good and evil," she did so in direct violation of an ethical command not to do so. Such is the nature of what I termed "epistemic addiction": it ignores ethics for the sake of knowledge.

And in "Two Forms of Transcendence: Justice and the Problem of Knowledge," in *Pursuing Trayvon Martin: Historical Contexts and Contemporary Manifestations of Racial Dynamics,* ed. George Yancy and Janine Jones (Lanham, MD: Lexington Books, 2012), I tried to show how the racist imaginary transforms the semiotic structure of divine transcendence into a pernicious semiotic formation that facilitates the racist imaginary's violence against African Americans. Such was the case for George Zimmerman, who employed his overly aggressive, self-appointed neighborhood-watch tactics against a historical backdrop of a racist ontological and semiotic field that helps him to "know" Trayvon Martin prior to ever even seeing him.

These two essays show the trajectory of my research as moving, in part, in the direction of critiques of epistemological preoccupations and hyper-theorizations that occlude moral and political concerns; especially in the philosophy of religion as it relates to the treatment of African Americans. I first address such dangers in my essay "From Epistemology to Ethics: Theoretical and Practical Reason in Kant and Douglass," *Journal of Religious Ethics* 40, no. 4 (December 2012): 603–628, where I argue that Reverend Godwin's argument for Negro baptism was rooted in an overly theoretical Cartesian metaphysical dualism that renders Christian theology compatible with chattel slavery and also with white supremacy at the expense of African Americans. The end result of this "compatibility" is an onto-theological, ersatz version of the Christian Gospel that is fused into a thoroughly anti-black—and thus thoroughly racist—epistemological framework of oppression. Douglass cannot tolerate such hyper-theorizations; hence his rejection of Godwin's solution to the "problem" of Negro baptism and his turn toward a view of the soul that is less theoretical and more attentive to one's moral development.

3. Martin Heidegger, "The Onto-Theological Constitution of Metaphysics," in *Identity and Difference,* trans. Joan Stambaugh (Chicago: University of Chicago Press, 2002), pp. 71–72.

4. Charles Mills, "Rawls on Race/Race in Rawls," *Southern Journal of Philosophy* 47 (2009): 161–184.

5. That much of the epistemic justifications for God's existence, his attributes, theodicy, free will, etc., arise from the writings of Augustine and

Saint Thomas Aquinas is undeniable. I do not intend to diminish the thought of either Augustine or Aquinas, but one can argue that the papacy demanded these sorts of epistemic justifications as part of its own program of oppression of those poor and illiterate persons within the jurisdiction of its coercive politics. Interestingly, however, the transformation of the word into flesh occurs even in this oppressive context, as Marsilius of Padua's *Defensor Pacis* affirms poverty—as contrasted with the wealth of the papal totalitarian regime—as a central Christological feature. Marsilius, then, in the *Defensor Pacis,* serves as a precursor to contemporary liberation theology in some of its various forms (i.e., black liberation theology, and Latin American liberation theology). See especially Chapter 13 of Discourse Two titled, "On the Status of Supreme Poverty, Which Is Usually Called Evangelical Perfection; And that This Status Was Held by Christ and His Apostles," Marsilius of Padua, *Defensor Pacis,* trans. Alan Gerwith (New York: Columbia University Press, 2001), pp. 196–215.

6. Alvin Plantinga, *God, Freedom, and Evil* (New York: Harper & Row, 1974).

7. See *Holy Bible,* John 1:14.

8. Ralph Ellison, *Invisible Man* (New York: Random House, 1995).

9. David Walker, *Appeal to the Coloured Citizens of the World, but in particular, and very expressly, to those of the United States of America* (*Appeal*) (New York: Straus and Giroux, 1995), p. 18.

10. See my analysis of the defect in the ecclesial formation of the slave-holding church in "From Epistemology to Ethics," pp. 608–620.

11. See *Holy Bible,* II Tim. 3:5.

12. Frederick Douglass, *Narrative of the Life of Frederick Douglass: An American Slave* (New York: Penguin, 1997), p. 29.

13. See my discussion of Nietzsche in "Epistemic Addiction."

The Terrifying Tale of the Philosophical Mammy

JEANINE WEEKES SCHROER

Recently I've been reflecting on the possibility that choices I've made and commitments I've accepted—choices and commitments like being part of the academy and treating philosophy as a productive way to pursue truths about race and racism—have made me into a Philosophical Mammy.[1] In short, as a Black Feminist Philosopher, I have been thinking about *my* role in philosophy. Despite the worrisome evidence, I hold fast to the belief that my intellectual identity can be defended to include *all* of my intellectual ancestors: both those in the canon of Western philosophy and intellectual forebears such as Audre Lorde, Cherrie Moraga, and Patricia Hill Collins, among others.[2] Some of those to whom I owe an intellectual debt are more like cousins; alongside a small but growing number of black female philosophers, I occupy a unique position.[3] It is to them that I most owe an account of myself. I believe I have one to give, an earnest defense that is not simply self-serving but one that is also not a concession.

The goal of this essay is to investigate and answer the challenge posed by the possibility of a Philosophical Mammy. What is revealed is not just the personal, social, and professional location of one particular philosopher, but a surprising and valuable stage in the ongoing progress of both black feminism and philosophy.

How Does One Get the Job "Philosophical Mammy"?

Like other black female archetypes, the Mammy first emerged in ideological service to slavery. Depicted as happy, she challenged "critics who argued that slavery was hard and demeaning."[4] The "happiness" of the Mammy relies on her having a very specific character:

> Mammy had no personal needs or desires. She was a trusted adviser and confidante whose skills were used exclusively in service of the white families to which she was attached. . . . She represented a maternal ideal, but not in caring for her own children. Her love, doting, advice, correction, and supervision were reserved exclusively for white[s].[5]

The Mammy survives into Reconstruction as a symbol of unification: from loyal Southern slave to loyal Northern servant. For the black community, however, the Mammy is a race traitor. "Whatever [the Mammy] had . . . she surrendered to those who lived to lynch her sons and ravish her daughters."[6] She survives

Jeanine Weekes Schroer is an assistant professor of philosophy at the University of Minnesota Duluth. Her recent research investigates the cognitive underpinnings of racism and sexism and uses traditional and experimental philosophical methods to explore agency and morality in the context of social oppression.

into current popular culture in various films and television shows as sassy, as little seen, as a wise black friend who appears briefly to magically solve the problems of white heroines and disappear just as quickly.

What does it mean to be a Philosophical Mammy? The central charge against the Mammy is that she sacrifices her own interests and those of her kindred to serve an Other who oppresses her. The charge against me is that I have struggled to defend, protect, and prop up the Anglo-American philosophical tradition—and by extension its institutional manifestations—despite its apparent woeful disregard for both my social peers and my intellectual interests and methods. The Philosophical Mammy is the black woman carefully promoting and protecting the traditions—both institutional and methodological—of Anglo-American philosophy while it disregards and suppresses her and her kindred. She does this despite the fact that little has been done to improve the representation of women or blacks in the profession.[7] She does this despite the fact that while *some* room has been made in the profession for *discussions* of methodological approaches to philosophy that aren't commensurate with analytic and other Western traditions, very few philosophers are successfully integrating those approaches into the profession. Although we are allowed to sometimes *talk* about the possibilities of such approaches, because the proof is in the publications, hard questions remain: Is it possible to publish enough to maintain one's place in the profession when these different methodologies are *applied*? Will philosophy allow one to build a career if that career's *central* focus is on work that will improve the social and material circumstances of blacks and other minorities?

My unique material and social circumstance—numbering among the zero percent of philosophers in the United States who are black, female, and fortunate enough to enjoy paid employment in the profession for which earning a doctorate in philosophy is commonly an apprenticeship[8]—necessarily changes my relationship to academic philosophy. My presence in the profession—in its physical spaces like departments, conferences, and in its conceptual spaces like committees and editorial boards—is controversial and a problem.[9] My *intellectual* identity—as a Black Philosopher, a Feminist Philosopher, and a Black Feminist—reframes that already contested relationship as a bind: Does choosing academic philosophy position me to ignore my kindred in favor of securing the well-being of those who are (ideologically and otherwise) indifferent to me or worse?

I Was Warned . . . Repeatedly

Weeks away from my first semester of philosophy in graduate school, a once-removed cousin asked me a smart question that I thought was dumb. He said, "Are you going to study *their* philosophy or *our* philosophy?" I tried to look wise and nodded condescendingly as if I was pretending to understand a story told by a toddler, then patiently replied that there was no "us" and no "them" in philosophy. The worst part is that I knew better.[10] Long before I began my apprenticeship into professional philosophy, I had already been warned.

While enrolled in a specialized liberal arts program that was especially concerned with critical engagement, I first encountered Audre Lorde's worry that "the master's tools will never dismantle the master's house."[11] While I take Lorde to have been worried about a very specific set of tendencies that she believed white feminism to have borrowed from patriarchy, the worry about the master's tools seemed to demand an interrogation of all of my disciplinary practices. Philosophy, a discipline that still struggles to incorporate and benefit from the critical feminism and critical race theory that has had considerably more success in other disciplines, seems especially worthy of such scrutiny.

Lorde was, in fact, worried about the way that marginalized women's resources are spread thin by the requirement that those women make sense of themselves, their needs, and their oppression *for* their oppressors:

> To stretch across the gap of [privileged] ignorance and to educate [the privileged] as to our existence and our needs. This is an old and primary tool of all oppressors to keep the oppressed occupied with the master's concerns.[12]

The same worry is expressed in Donna Kate Rushkin's "The Bridge Poem": "I've had enough / I'm sick of seeing and touching / Both sides of things / Sick of being the damn bridge for everybody." This worry is spread throughout the namesake collection of essays—*This Bridge Called My Back*—that Rushkin's poem opens.[13] In these texts, Lorde, Moraga, and Anzaldua, alongside other women of color, called forth the Third Wave of Feminism. This next stage of feminism endeavored to learn from, rather than silence, the discordant voices within the feminist movement. These feminists also heralded a feminism centered on women of color. In order for feminists of color to do the hard work of understanding and interpreting themselves, they had to put down the burden of interpreting Others.

I was warned again in graduate school. My graduate training immersed me in the Western canon of philosophy and feminist philosophy, and I was torn between optimism and pessimism. Feminist thought was slowly influencing the way people read and understood canonical philosophical thought; I hoped black feminist thought would as well. On the other hand, research that didn't locate me in that Western canon—that did not clearly build the bridge from there—seemed ill-advised, even dangerous. I struggled to understand what an earnest commitment to my black feminist heritage would look like. I became especially worried about Derrick Bell's "Third Rule of Racial Standing":

> The black person who publicly disparages or criticizes other blacks who are speaking or acting in ways that upset whites [is] granted "enhanced standing" even when the speaker has no special expertise or experience in the subject he or she is criticizing.[14]

When I dedicated my efforts to better understandings of Kant and even feminist criticisms of Kant, did I tacitly endorse those thinkers and their methodologies over black feminist ones? Was I succumbing to "pressure to . . . legitimate a system that devalue[d] and exclude[d] the majority of black women"?[15] Was I "trading up" by reallocating my resources to the care and concern of a perspective that wasn't truly mine?

As I have passed through the trial of apprenticeship into the crucible of professionalism, the worries provoked by Lorde, Bell, and Collins have ceased to be anxious conjectures and have become genuine predicaments. My work concerns gender, race, racism, sexism, and moral agency and is informed by several intellectual traditions including black philosophy, feminist philosophy, and black feminism. I struggle to understand the intersections of racism and sexism in ways that will reveal and undermine the systematic oppression to which black folk, particularly black women, are still subject and by extension promote black flourishing.

This pursuit has taken me in some surprising directions both in terms of some of my chosen methodologies—cognitive science and experimental philosophy, for example[16]—and in terms of the ideas to which I've committed. As I've earnestly struggled to understand the social construction of race and the consequences of the complicated ways race and gender identities are constructed and privileges distributed, I have found myself making what at least appear to be worrisome commitments both in writing and in public. A number of experiences blend into an amalgam containing these shared particulars: me smiling broadly, nodding encouragingly at a room full of white faces (often white male faces), reassuring them of the certainty of *my* privilege. That I have class privilege (as well as privilege related to age, ability, and sexuality) and that it shapes other social dimensions of my life—like race and gender—is not a particularly controversial idea. However, this image—a black woman standing up in a room full of white folk, testifying to her privilege, in a way that smacks of the effort to bridge some gap, in a way that could be understood by those present as a concession or criticism of theories articulating the problems of white and male privilege—has worried me. This is the danger of the Philosophical Mammy.

A closer look, however, reveals that my worries have focused too much on how the content of my ideas—the thinkers I read and criticize, the positions I occupy relative to those thinkers—might constitute a betrayal of my intellectual heritage. They have failed to see my dedication to the *methods* of black feminism.

The Bridge I Must Be

> I must be the bridge to nowhere
> But my true self
> And then
> I will be useful.[17]

Fundamental to black feminist thought, argues Patricia Hill Collins, are the alternative methods black women employ to produce and validate knowledge. Detached researchers, producing objective generalizations, absent emotional or even ethical investment in their subject, are required to legitimate black women's knowledge claims in the "Eurocentric, masculinist knowledge-validation process."[18] However, even after substantial mastery of white masculinist epistemologies, many black women scholars invoke their own concrete experiences and those of other black women in selecting topics for investigation and methodologies used. . . . Such women felt that . . . the best way of understanding another person's ideas was to try to share the experiences that led the person to form those ideas. At the heart of the procedures used by connected knowers is the capacity for empathy.[19]

There are two features of the black feminist epistemology that Collins describes here that I am interested in highlighting: (1) the elevation of concrete experience as both a source of intellectual concern and a criterion for critical analysis, and (2) the import of empathetic extension to the employment and function of that method. Armed with this reconsideration, I am finally able to articulate why, appearances to the contrary, the Philosophical Mammy is an illusion.

Before Joyce Mitchell Cook earned a doctorate from Yale in 1965, in an important sense, there were no black women philosophers (professional or otherwise).[20] I say that in no way to discount the incredible intellectual contributions that black women and Black Feminists have made to a multitude of disciplines, including philosophy. My point, rather, is that the arrival of the *first* black woman philosopher is a requisite step in the path leading to the hundredth. Moreover, it is a practically and socially necessary stage before the possibility of a Black Feminist Philosopher. The struggle to interpret black feminism for philosophy and integrate its

concerns and methods is possible only because of the unique location occupied by particular women enamored with both black feminism and philosophy.

Nearly fifty years later, though our numbers still haven't risen to statistical significance, evidence suggests that there are more and more black women committing to philosophy. Our rising numbers will lead to the development of distinct intellectual voices and perspectives. The lessons taught by black feminism—that we should resist the urge to silence dissenting or controversial voices; that concrete experience is a valuable resource for a richer and deeper understanding of our social lives; that empathy is a necessary tool for harnessing the value of concrete experience through discourse and sharing— apply here. Though the philosopher in me might be inclined to seek objective universal claims, the black feminist sees the virtue in starting my analysis from my precise social location—with all the complexities of privileges granted and withheld entailed therein. I must give an honest appraisal of the world viewed through my eyes. I must tell my true story—controversial, threatening, self-critical, and complicated—if I have any hope of ever being useful. The claim is not that my story is a universal one or even correct in some epistemological "absolutist" sense; it is, however, a starting place—the one deeply available to me—and valuable as such.

In the end, the Mammy is merely an illusion. To see the Mammy is, as it always has been, a willful failure to see the flesh-and-blood woman. Historically, the Mammy was a rewriting of the identity of slave and paid domestic workers. As confidants, loyal companions, and "almost members of the family," they did not need time off to care for their own family's needs, overtime pay, benefits, or evening a living wage.[21] The Philosophical Mammy is no different. She is a phantom disrupting the unity and suppressing the complication, variation, and expansion of black female voices in philosophy. I am not a Philosophical Mammy; I, alongside others, am a stage in the evolution of philosophy and black feminism. I am a Black Feminist Philosopher.

Notes

1. Throughout this essay, I will discuss both ordinary social groups, like members of racial groups or professions, and intellectual canons—sets of texts, authors, and practitioners unified by common ideas and practices—using the same or extremely similar language. To distinguish black philosophers, professional philosophers who happen to be identified as of African descent, from Black Philosophers, people committed to particular sets of intellectual traditions, I will treat the latter as proper nouns and capitalize accordingly.

2. My intellectual debts extend far beyond this short list and include a variety of philosophers living and dead, black and white, women and men. I have focused on the intellectual lineage that I believe is most relevant to issue being explored in this essay: Black Feminists and Black Feminist Philosophers.

3. I owe a multitude of debts to all the women in the Collegium of Black Women Philosophers (and to Kathryn T. Gines) for founding that organization. They, especially, share this fascinating journey with me.

4. K. Sue Jewell, *From Mammy to Miss America and Beyond: Cultural Images and the Shaping of US Social Policy* (New York: Routledge, 1993), p. 38, quoted in Melissa V. Harris-Perry, *Sister Citizen: Shame, Stereotypes, and Black Women in America* (New Haven, CT: Yale University Press, Kindle Edition, 2011), pp. 1063–1065.

5. Harris-Perry, *Sister Citizen,* pp. 1070–1073.

6. W. E. B. Du Bois as recorded by Micki McElya, *Clinging to Mammy: The Faithful Slave in Twentieth-Century America* (Cambridge, MA: Harvard University Press, 2007), n.d., quoted in Harris-Perry, *Sister Citizen,* pp. 1157–1159.

7. Cf. Katherine T. Gines, "Being a Black Woman Philosopher: Reflections on Founding the Collegium of Black Women Philosophers," *Hypatia* 26 (2011): 429–437; Robin Wilson, "Black Women Seek a Role in Philosophy," *Chronicle of Higher Education* (September 28, 2007), http://chronicle.com/article/Black-Women-Seek-a-Role-in/24971 for insights into a striking exception, accessed March 15, 2013.

8. I have chosen this construal for the express purpose of capturing the incredible and disappointing absence of black women among the ranks of professional philosophers. Cf. National Center for Education Statistics, *2009 Digest of Education Statistics,* http://nces.ed.gov/programs/digest/d09/tables/dt09_256.asp?referrer=list, accessed March 15, 2012. We fail—in virtue of numbers—to meet reporting standards for full-time faculty in philosophy and represent possibly 0.5 percent of part-time faculty and instructional staff. A generous estimate, however, makes black women about 0.3 percent of the 26,000 professional philosophers in the United States.

9. Cf. *The Feminist Philosophers Blog; "*Gendered Conference Campaign," blog entry, December 10, 2009; *What Is It Like to Be a Woman in Philosophy?* http://beingawomaninphilosophy.wordpress.com, accessed March 15, 2013; *What We're Doing About What It's Like,* whatwere

doingaboutwhatitslike.wordpress.com, accessed March 15, 2013.

10. Uncle Rudy, please forgive me. You were right; folks like us have to watch where we step.

11. Audre Lorde. "The Master's Tools Will Never Dismantle the Master's House," in *Sister Outsider: Essays and Speeches* (Freedom, CA: Crossing Press, 1984), p. 112.

12. Ibid., p. 113.

13. Donna Kate Rushkin, "The Bridge Poem" in *This Bridge Called My Back: Writings by Radical Women of Color,* eds. Cherrie Moraga and Gloria Anzaldua, 2nd ed. (New York: Kitchen Table: Women of Color Press of New York, 1983), p. xxi.

14. Derrick Bell, *Faces at the Bottom of the Well: The Permanence Of Racism* (New York: Perseus Books Group, Kindle Edition, 1993), p. 114.

15. Patricia Hill Collins, "The Social Construction of Black Feminist Thought," in Joy James and T. Denean Sharpley-Whiting, *The Black Feminist Reader* (Malden, MA: Blackwell Publishing, 2000), p. 188.

16. I am interested, for example, in racial cognition and its importance to the moral understanding of racism. Experimental philosophy has features that can be used to analyze implicit racial attitudes and their relationship to racist action.

17. Rushkin, "The Bridge Poem," p. xxii.

18. Collins, "The Social Construction of Black Feminist Thought," p. 187.

19. Ibid., pp. 193–194.

20. Gines, "Being a Black Woman Philosopher," p. 434.

21. Harris-Perry, *Sister Citizen,* pp. 1122–1125.

On the Dialectical Relationship of Philosophy to African-American Studies

A Materialist Assessment on *The Black Scholar* and Its Intellectual Legacy

JOHN H. MCCLENDON III

Given the intellectual and academic legacy of *The Black Scholar*—since its advent in November 1969—I think it is saliently apropos that this historic journal now devote its pages to a special issue on the examination of how philosophy is related to the African-American experience with the objective of clarifying the road to African-American liberation. Born in the dialectical conflict of the Black liberation movement and the ancillary struggles for radical transformation of the conditions surrounding African-American education, *The Black Scholar,* in my view, became a beacon light for scholars, students, and activists in consistently forging a link between the struggles within different Black (internationally focused) communities.[1] Through its various special topics, *The Black Scholar* facilitated, for instance, connecting African-American movements such as Black Power and the myriad of student struggles for Black Studies—on US campuses—to the African diaspora and also with the liberation movements in Africa.[2]

For example, in its first issue devoted to "Black Studies" (September 1970), *The Black Scholar* featured an interview with the West Indian Marxist and Pan-Africanist C. L. R. James. James offers a number of critical suggestions about the content and method of Black Studies in the United States. James actually went against the grain of the prevailing trend—inclusive of previously published articles in *The Black Scholar*—which articulated the need for formulating a distinctively Black ideological perspective as foundational to Black Studies and African-American liberation.[3]

James opposed the notion that there was something akin to "The Ideology of a Black Social Science" wherein scientific inquiry was subordinated to Black ideology or that we must by some means forge "The Way to a Black Ideology" as articulated by Abdul Alkalimat and Floyd B. McKissick, for instance. Philosophically a materialist, James understood that scientific inquiry was grounded on the objective foundation of philosophical materialism, dialectically conceived. James rejected the view that Black Studies required a uniquely formulated Black perspective (Black ideological viewpoint) on the world or that the study of the Black experience was in principle mutually exclusive of the scien-

John H. McClendon III is a professor of philosophy at Michigan State University. He is the author of *C. L. R. James's Notes on Dialectics: Left Hegelianism or Marxism-Leninism* (Lexington Books, 2005) and the coauthor with Dr. Stephen Ferguson of *Beyond the White Shadow: Philosophy, Sports and the African American Experience* (Kendall Hunt, 2012).

tific analysis of white/European ideology/ history. James argued:

> When I give classes on history I use certain books, and I always use Du Bois' Black Reconstruction. Not because it deals with black history or because he is a black man, but because that is one of the finest history books ever written by anybody. To this day, I don't know any book which deals with the history of the Civil War in the way that Du Bois' book does. That is black studies. Otherwise, black studies is a lot of nonsense.

James further stated:

> And I should like to say that I don't believe in race as a basis for intellectual dissension. But I believe that it is black men, black men who live in the black community, who are connected with it and have the black experience and are sensitive to it, who are best able to do the kind of studies the black race needs. They are not the only ones able to make such studies, but they are best able to do an analysis, not only of black people, but of white people who were concerned with the black experience.[4]

Although his arguments were counter to the subjectivist notions of Black racialist/nationalist ideology, James was not solitary in his efforts at a critical summation of Black Studies. Hence we have a plethora of articles (from varied academic and ideological positions) on education and Black Studies, penned in the pages of The Black Scholar.[5]

Not only did The Black Scholar signal the Pan-Africanist scope of Black liberation, but we also discover persistent critical analysis of the elements affixed to the materialist underpinnings of Black oppression. Namely, we uncover The Black Scholar's unyielding opposition to the scourge of white supremacy, racism, colonialism, and neocolonialism, and this was often brought to the fore by highlighting the adjoining role of material (political economic) forms of international finance monopoly capitalism. The critique of African, Caribbean, and African-American class exploitation and national oppression with its adjoining connections to capitalism and imperialism was not lost on a number of its early contributors.[6]

During its formative years (when the institutionalization of programs in the field of African-American studies was prominent) The Black Scholar arguably proved to be one of the pioneering and foremost journals in creating a deeply needed outlet for an intellectual culture of critical discourse. Hence, at this early juncture, The Black Scholar provided a rather fruitful and dynamic scholarly channel for meaningful dialogue, erudite discussion, and rigorous debate as well as ongoing substantive theoretical inquiry into this burgeoning area of inquiry.[7]

In addition to Pan-Africanism, the very first issue of The Black Scholar addressed topics such as Black culture, education, and revolution as well as the significance of Black Studies curriculum.[8] In the same year as this inaugural issue, Robert L. Allen published his Black Awakening in Capitalist America, which offers an insightful documentation about the role of corporate capitalist financing of certain elements of the Black Power movement. Shortly thereafter,

Allen would join *The Black Scholar* editorial board and currently is senior editor. The inclusion of Allen amplified the leftist anti-capitalist orientation of *The Black Scholar*.[9]

I still own the inaugural issue, "The Culture of Revolution." I contend that President Sékou Touré's profoundly insightful philosophical essay, "A Dialectical Approach to Culture," stands out as one of the premier contributions and formidable introductions to the presentation of the dialectical materialist philosophical analysis of African culture, particularly in the throes of the anti-imperialist struggle. Within the context of the Black Studies movement in the United States, concerns about the nature of Black culture, at that time, were pivotal in the ranks of the black liberation movement. The clarion call for idealist forms of cultural nationalism, both as an ideological perspective for Black liberation and as the philosophical bedrock of Black Studies, was hotly debated in the pages of *The Black Scholar*.[10] Touré's essay gave us penetrating insights into how culture was dialectically adjoined to a materialist philosophical approach. Touré argues:

> The creation of material values, the creation of spiritual values, the creation and development of this global culture progresses continuously despite momentary slowing-down, stagnation and setbacks. Material culture production and spiritual cultural production are dialectically linked and exercise a reciprocal influence on each other. But the absolute priority rests with material production, which itself participates directly in man's concrete action.

Touré further comments:

> To meet the needs of all, material action must have tactics, and strategies, and intellectual effort to action, a certain degree of planning, both criticism and self-criticism in light of the results, and a methodology bringing into play a whole series of intellectual operations. Culture is a material and spiritual acquisition, both the product and price of action.[11]

As with C. L. R. James's commentary on Black Studies, Touré's materialist dialectical treatment of culture would open the philosophical door to a vision of Black Studies that would go beyond the confinement of a narrow Black cultural nationalism. The critical commentary of Touré was a refreshing outlook not only on African culture but also on how to explicate the general principles for outlining a materialist inquiry into the substance of culture as affixed to social and political development, especially in the material transformation of nature and relations of production, albeit fettered by the yoke of imperialism and class struggle. Within the contours of class struggle and the fight to overcome imperialist hegemony, the dialectics of the creation of material and spiritual values, Touré informs us, cannot be sustained without giving priority to material conditions and material values. Hence, according to Touré, the idealist concept of erecting "A Black Value System," as represented by Maulana Karenga and Amiri Baraka, remained a purely utopian and reactionary project.[12] Ultimately Baraka would reach similar political conclusions and adopt the same philosophical perspective as Touré.[13]

On the Value of a Materialist Critique and Theory and Method in African-American Studies

In terms of method of inquiry, Touré presents to us some valuable gems of philosophical thought, which we can immediately transfer to our discussion on African-American studies. It is precisely the problem of "intellectual effort to action" that dynamically and concretely connects philosophy to African-American studies, that is to say, in the particular fashion of a materialist philosophical project; for this project seeks to attach theory and practice with the practical (political) aim of Black liberation. Given the material locus and critical function of "intellectual effort to action," it follows that such effort toward "action" draws us immediately into the material/practical realm or what Touré identifies as "the creation of material values." Thus "action" as the "creation of material values" cannot be removed from the pressing ideological concerns and political objectives linked to the practical tasks of liberation as an objective interest, which in turn is the upshot of our stance in advocating the dialectical materialist philosophical analysis.[14]

Concomitantly, we must insist—in conjunction with Touré—that the context of "both criticism and self-criticism in light of the results, and a methodology bringing into play a whole series of intellectual operations," is at the core of the philosophical question of how *theory* and *method* must function to frame the contours of African-American studies. Ideological criticism or critique along with theory and method are decisive conceptual issues for anchoring the framework of African-American studies. Moreover, I submit they are keys to establishing, from a materialist perspective, how we actually define what constitutes African-American studies. Of import to our discussion is the looming philosophical task and need for locating where a critique originates vis-à-vis empirical, conceptual, and ideological levels of criticism.[15]

By ideological critique, I mean a level of criticism that aims to disclose the worldview attached to a given set of formulations, theses, paradigms, or theoretical frameworks. Ideological critiques are therefore directed at the fundamental presuppositions, assumptions, and presumptions shaping and grounding one's formulations, theses, paradigms, or theoretical frameworks. If and only if the fundamental presuppositions, assumptions, and presumptions engaged are foundationally different than those informing the critique, then what results is an external criticism. Consequently, by external criticism I mean a critique, which is foundationally different from the ideology under review. Here by definition external criticism is synonymous with ideological critique.

In contrast, if the critic shares the same ideological commitments with the one under scrutiny, what occurs is an internal criticism and de facto we do not have an ideological critique. Instead the criticism is either an *empirical* critique, at the level of observation and factual matters, and/or it is a *conceptual* critique calling into question the issues relating to logical reasoning, theoretical consistency, systemic conceptual contradictions, and interpretative evaluations adjoined to given formulations, theses, paradigms, or theoretical frameworks. In African-American studies (AAS), William R. Jones imparts to us one of the first scholarly efforts in utilizing this method of internal criticism. Jones's powerful text *Is God a White Racist?* is an illuminating (internal) critique of Black liberation theology.[16]

Ideological critique, however, need not be devoid of empirical or conceptual criticism. The only qualification is that in the case of ideological critique, we discover all conceptual criticism follows from an external vantage point. Matters of logical reasoning, theoretical consistency, systemic conceptual contradictions, and interpretive evaluations affixed to and adjoined with given formulations, theses, paradigms, or theoretical frameworks derive ultimately from ideological differences or fundamental divergences in worldview.

There is also another instance of *internal criticism*, which does not rely upon the prima facie exclusive utilization of empirical and/or conceptual critique. The key concept here is the caveat, prima facie. If it is assumed one is engaged in ideological critique or external criticism, and yet, for whatever reason, the critic overlooks or fails to comprehend there are in fact shared ideological commitments, with the ideology under investigation, then this putative ideological critique is *objectively* an internal criticism. The prior bi-conditional stipulation (if and only if the fundamental presuppositions, assumptions, and presumptions engaged are foundationally different than those informing the critique) cohesively outlines the conditions for ideological critique. Given we operate with a bi-conditional stipulation, then such requirements are both objectively and absolutely mandatory.[17]

What we have in this second instance of internal criticism is a contradiction between *intended* ideological *functions* and *objectively* rendered ideological *practices*. This is what I designate as the *dialectics* of ideological critique in AAS. The dialectical contradiction of intended ideological critique and de facto ideological commitment of racial/racialist ideologues to bourgeois ideology is the substance that forms the basis for this essay. The racial/racialist critique is constituted in a kind of dichotomized theoretical modus operandi, wherein Black intellectual/cultural paradigms stand contra white intellectual/cultural paradigms.[18] Subsequently, despite all intended purposes, this modus operandi undermines the critique of white supremacy and racism when understood as forms of bourgeois ideology. Hence, this kind of critique defaults in its attempt to be specifically *ideological* in character.[19]

Over the years, since its founding, the pages of *The Black Scholar* have allowed various thinkers to demonstrate how Marxism-Leninism is concretely a philosophy of liberation. Thus, from the philosophical standpoint of Marxism-Leninism, People's College, "A Study Program: Imperialism and Black Liberation," Wilber Haddock's "Black Workers Lead the Way," and Amiri Baraka in "Needed: A Revolutionary Strategy" point us to strategies for Black liberation in the United States. Additionally, Frank Wright's "The National Question: A Marxist Critique" accents how African-American national liberation is theoretically rooted in a Marxist analysis of African-American national oppression. Amilcar Cabral's "The Guinean Revolution: The Struggle Has Taken Root" and Julia Hervé in her "Kwame Nkrumah: His Last Views of African Struggle" explicate via Marxist philosophical analysis the course of African liberation. Marxist philosopher Angela Davis's "Rape, Racism and the Capitalist Setting" accents the nature of Black women's triple oppression and the road toward revolutionary transformation and liberation. For all of the aforementioned (along with Walter Rodney, C. L. R. James, and Sékou Touré), Marxist dialectical materialist philosophy has the practical aims of concrete struggle for social transformation and liberation from oppression and exploitation.

In conclusion, the philosophical task we face today in AAS is to uproot the dangerous ideological weed of idealism. How can we do this? We must use as our theoretical instrument the philosophy of dialectical materialism. Furthermore, issuing from this instrument will be the understanding that the real nature of ideological critique rests not in the putative Black/white antithesis. Instead we will see that politically the contradiction is the *left* in opposition to the *right*. More concretely, this mandates an ideological critique from the standpoint of Marxism-Leninism as our scientific world outlook.

Notes

1. I capitalize the word "Black" when making reference to people of African descent. For a number of years, it was customary to use this in regard to the word "Negro." Over a number of generations, there was a consistent fight to capitalize the word "Negro" as a way of establishing racial respect and dignity. Since the word "Black" has now come to replace "Negro" as the contemporary convention, I follow in that tradition with the capitalization of "Black." For a further discussion of this issue, see Richard B. Moore, "The Name 'Negro'—Its Origin and Evil Use," in *Richard B. Moore, Caribbean Militant in Harlem: Collected Writings, 1920–1972*, eds. W. Burghardt Turner and Joyce Moore Turner (Bloomington: Indiana University Press, 1988): pp. 223–239. See also John H. McClendon, "Black/Blackness: Philosophical Considerations," in *Encyclopedia of the African Diaspora: Origins, Experiences, and Culture*, ed. Carol Boyce Davies, vol. 3 (Santa Barbara, CA: ABC-CLIO, 2008): pp. 198–203.

2. For an overview of the themes and debates in *The Black Scholar,* see John H. McClendon III, coauthor of "The Changing Tone of Three Black Periodicals" in Faustine C. Jones, *The Changing Mood in America* (Washington, DC: Howard University Press, 1977). See, for example, Nathan Hare, "The Challenge of a Black Scholar," *The Black Scholar,* 1, no. 2 (1969): 58–63; Nathan Hare, "From the Publisher: A Torch to Burn Down a Decadent World," *The Black Scholar* 2, no. 1 (1970): 2–5.

3. Floyd B. McKissick, "The Way to a Black Ideology," *The Black Scholar* 1, no. 2 (1969): 14–17; C. L. R. James, "The Black Scholar Interviews: C. L. R. James," *The Black Scholar* 2, no. 1 (1970): 35–43; Abd-l Hakimu Ibn Alkalimat, "The Ideology of Black Social Science," *The Black Scholar* 1, no. 2 (1969): 28–35.

4. C. L. R. James, "*The Black Scholar* Interviews: C.L.R. James," *The Black Scholar* 2, no. 1 (1970): 35–43.

5. Robert Allen, "Politics of the Attacks on Black Studies," *The Black Scholar* 6, no. 1 (1974): 2–7; Phil Hutchins, "Report of the ALSC Conference," *The Black Scholar* 5, no. 10 (1974): 48–53;

Darlene Clark Hine, "The Black Studies Movement: Afrocentric-Traditionalist-Feminist Paradigms for the Next Stage," *The Black Scholar* 22, no. 3 (1992): 11–18; Roosevelt Johnson, "Black Administrators and Higher Education," *The Black Scholar* 1, no. 1 (1969): 66–76; William H. McClendon, "Black Studies: Education for Liberation," *The Black Scholar* 6, no. 1 (1974): 15—25; Robert Staples, "Racial Ideology and Intellectual Racism: Blacks in Academia," *The Black Scholar* 15, no. 2 (1984): 2–17; Luke Tripp, "The Political Views of Black Students During the Reagan Era," *The Black Scholar* 22, no. 3 (1992): 45–52; Alvin Poussaint, "The Black Administrator in the White University," *The Black Scholar* 6, no. 1 (1974): 8–14; Bobby Seal, "An Appeal from Prison: Revolutionary Action on Campus and Community," *The Black Scholar* 1, no. 2 (1969): 4–7.

6. Amilcar Cabral, "The Guinean Revolution: The Struggle Has Taken Root," *The Black Scholar* 4, no. 10 (1973): 28–31; Eldridge Cleaver, "Education and Revolution," *The Black Scholar* 1, no. 1 (1969): 44–52; C. L. R. James, "*The Black Scholar* Interviews: C. L. R. James," *The Black Scholar* 2, no. 1 (1970): 35–43; Stokely Carmichael, "Marxism-Leninism and Nkrumahism," *The Black Scholar* 4, no. 5: (1973): 41–43; Angela Y. Davis, "Rape, Racism and the Capitalist Setting," *The Black Scholar* 9, no. 7 (1978): 24–30; Wilbur Haddock, "Black Workers Lead the Way," *The Black Scholar* 5, no. 3 (1973): 43–48; Julia Hervé, "Kwame Nkrumah: His Last Views of African Struggle," *The Black Scholar* 4, no. 10 (1973): 24–27; Phil Hutchins, "Report of the ALSC Conference," *The Black Scholar* 5, no. 10 (1974): 48–53; Cheddi Jaggan, "Guyana at the Crossroads," *The Black Scholar* 5, no. 10 (1974): 43–47; Clarence J. Munford, "The Fallacy of Lumpen Ideology," *The Black Scholar* 4, no. 3 (July/August 1973): 47–51; Clarence J. Munford, "Imperialism and Third World Economics: Part One of Two Parts," *The Black Scholar* 6, no. 7 (1975): 15–25; Earl Ofari, "A Critical Review of the Pan-African Congress," *The Black Scholar* 5, no. 10 (1974): 12–15; People's College, "A Study Program: Imperialism and Black Liberation," *The Black Scholar* 6, no. 1 (1974): 38–42; Walter Rodney, "Contemporary Political Trends in the English-speaking Caribbean," *The Black Scholar* 7, no. 1 (1975): 15–21; Frank M. Wright, "The National Question: A Marxist Critique," *The Black Scholar* 5, no. 5 (1974): 45–53.

7. Gerald A. McWorter, and Ronald Bailey, "Black Studies Curriculum Development in the 1980s: Its Patterns and History," *The Black Scholar* 15, no. 2 (1984): 18–31; Robert Allen, "Politics of the Attacks on Black Studies," *The Black Scholar* 6, no. 1 (1974): 2–7; Molife Kete Asante, "African American Studies: The Future of the Discipline," *The Black Scholar* 22, no. 3 (1992): 20–29; "Black Studies: A Review of the Literature," *The Black Scholar* 2, no. 1 (1970): 52–55; Melba Joyce Boyd, "The Legacy of Darwin T. Turner and the Struggle for African American Studies," *The Black Scholar* 41, no. 4 (2011): 11–16; Eldridge Cleaver, "Education and Revolution," *The Black Scholar* 1, no. 1 (1969): 44–52; Angela Davis, "Reflections on the Black Woman's Role in the Community of Slaves," *The Black Scholar* 3, no. 4 (1971): 2–15; Darlene Clark Hine, "The Black Studies Movement: Afro-centric-Traditionalist-Feminist Paradigms for the Next Stage," *The Black Scholar* 22, no. 3 (1992): 11–18; Manning Marable, "Blueprint for Black Studies and Multiculturalism," *The Black Scholar* 22, no. 3 (1992): 30–35; McClendon, "Black Studies: Education for Liberation"; and Sydney Walton, "Black Studies and Affirmative Action," *The Black Scholar* 6, no. 1 (1974): 21–28.

8. Stokely Carmichael, "Pan-Africanism—Land and Power," *The Black Scholar* 1, no. 1 (1969): 36–43; Eldridge Cleaver, "Education and Revolution," *The Black Scholar* 1, no. 1 (1969): 44–52; Nathan Hare, "The Challenge of a Black Scholar," *The Black Scholar* 1, no. 2 (1969): 58–63; Sidney Walton, *The Black Curriculum: Developing a Program in Afro-American Studies* (East

Palo Alto, CA: Black Liberation Publishers, 1969); Preston Wilcox, "The Black Curriculum: Developing a Program in Afro-American Studies by Sidney F Walton (review by)," *The Black Scholar* 1, no. 1 (1969): 85–86.

9. Robert L Allen, *Black Awakening in Capitalist America* (Garden City, NY: Doubleday, 1969); "Nathan Hare Resigns from *The Black Scholar*: Charges Black Marxist Takeover," *The Black Panther* 13 (1975): 12; Robert L. Allen, "Forty Years Later: Reflections on the Writing of 'Black Awakening in Capitalist America," *The Black Scholar* 40, no. 2 (2010): 2–10.

10. Amiri Baraka (LeRoi Jones), "A Black Value System," *The Black Scholar* 1, no. 1 (1969): 54–60; Eldridge Cleaver, "Education and Revolution," *The Black Scholar* 1, no. 1 (1969): 44–52. For an overview, see John H. McClendon III, coauthor of "The Changing Tone of Three Black Periodicals" in Faustine C. Jones, *The Changing Mood in America* (Washington, DC: Howard University Press, 1977), .

11. Sékou Touré, "A Dialectical Approach to Culture," *The Black Scholar* 1, no. 1 (1969): 11–26.

12. Ibid., pp. 11–26. See also Touré, "Sekou Touré's Speech to the Congress," *The Black Scholar* 5, no. 10 (1974): 23–29. For a similar argument, see Stephen C. Ferguson II, "The Utopian Worldview of Afrocentricity: Critical Comments on a Reactionary Philosophy," *Socialism and Democracy* 25, no. 1 (2011): 44–70.

13. See, for example, Amiri Baraka, "Black Liberation Is a Struggle for Socialism," *Unity and Struggle* 4, no. 2 (1975).

Amiri Baraka, "Some Questions About the Sixth Pan-African Congress," *The Black Scholar* 6, no. 2 (1974): 42–46.

14. For a materialist analysis within African-American studies, see Angela Y. Davis, "Women and Capitalism: Dialectics of Oppression and Liberation," in *The Angela Y. Davis Reader,* ed. Joy James (Malden, MA: Blackwell, 1998); Stephen C. Ferguson II, "The Utopian Worldview of Afrocentricity: Critical Comments on a Reactionary Philosophy," *Socialism and Democracy* 25, no. 1 (2011): 44–70; Eugene C. Holmes, "A Philosophical Approach to the Study of Minority Problems," *Journal of Negro Education* 38, no. 3 (1969): 196–203; John H. McClendon III, "On the Nature of Whiteness and the Ontology of Race: Toward a Dialectical Materialist Analysis," in *What White Looks Like: African American Philosophers On the Whiteness Question,* ed. George Yancy (New York: Routledge, 2004); Clarence J. Munford, *Production Relations, Class and Black Liberation: A Marxist Perspective in Afro-American Studies* (Amsterdam: B. R. Gruner, 1978); Robert Young, "Putting Materialism Back into Race Theory: Toward a Transformative Theory of Race," *Red Critique* 11 (Winter/Spring 2006), redcritique.org/WinterSpring2006/index.html.

15. For a more in-depth discussion of this issue, see McClendon, "Black and White or Left and Right? Ideological Critique in African American Studies," *American Philosophical Association Newsletter on Philosophy and the Black Experience* 2, no. 1 (2002): 47–56.

16. See Jones, *Is God a White Racist?* I should add that in more general terms, my notion of critique falls within the philosophical tradition of German dialectical criticism. With his three *Critiques,* Kant initiates this conception of critique, on an idealist basis. Hegel offers a seminal and even more advanced contribution to this dialectical practice, albeit while remaining within the confines of idealism. It is, of course, Karl Marx's materialist conception of history and dialectics that represents the apogee of dialectical critique, viz. we have the advent of a scientific mode of analysis for social relations and history. And it should not be lost on the reader how this idea of critique is prominently part of the subtitle to Marx's magnum opus, *Capital.* See V. I. Lenin, "What the 'Friends of the People' Are and How They Fight Social Democrats," in *Collected Works*

(Moscow: Progress Publishers, 1973); and Paul Murray, *Marx's Theory of Scientific Knowledge* (Atlantic Highlands, NJ: Humanities Press International, 1990). See also McClendon, "Black and White or Left and Right?"; and McClendon, "Materialist Philosophical Inquiry and African American Studies," *Socialism and Democracy* 25, no. 1 (2011): 71–92.

17. Charles W. Mills is a more recent exemplar of how internal criticism masquerades as ideological critique. Mills fervently argues that his political theory of *The Racial Contract* is in "the best tradition of oppositional materialist critique of hegemonic idealist social theory." Nevertheless, Mills states that he "criticizes the social contract from a normative base that does not see the ideals of contractarianism themselves as necessarily problematic but shows how they have been betrayed by white contractarians." For Mills, the problem is not that contractarianism is, more fundamentally, a form of bourgeois ideology; his concern is only that contractarianism has been corrupted by "white contractarians." What becomes immediately transparent is that Mills undermines his own claim to "oppositional materialist critique." Mills's assumption is simply that contractarianism is formally a credible political theory; and with the injection of a black perspective as content, the path is paved for the ideological critique of white supremacy. Mills's black philosophical perspective of contractarianism or his racial contract theory thus assaults white supremacy from, nevertheless, within the confines of contractarianism. I argue, along with Marx, contractarianism is a form of bourgeois ideology. Charles W. Mills, *The Racial Contract* (Ithaca, NY: Cornell University Press, 1997), pp. 129–130.

18. See, for example, Molefi Asante, *The Afrocentric Idea* (Philadelphia: Temple University Press, 1987); M. Karenga, "Black Studies and the Problematic of Paradigm: The Philosophical Dimension," *Journal of Black Studies* 18, no. 4 (1988): 395–414.

19. For a critique of Asante's Afrocentricity as a distinctive form of idealism rooted in religious mythology, read James Palermo, "Reading Asante's Myth of Afrocentricity: An Ideological Critique," www.edu/PES/97_pre/palerno.html. See also McClendon, "The Afrocentric Project: The Quest for Particularity and the Negation of Objectivity," *Explorations in Ethnic Studies* 18, no. 1 (1995).

The Violence of Presence

Metaphysics in a Blackened World

**PATRICE DOUGLASS AND
FRANK WILDERSON**

Over the past fifteen to twenty years, black philosophy has enhanced its explanatory power by way of a deliberate engagement with critical theory. One of the most notable examples of this turn is found in Lewis Gordon's extended readings of Frantz Fanon and Jean-Paul Sartre—the dialogues Gordon has staged between Fanon's blackened psychoanalysis and Sartre's Marxist existentialism.[1] We contend that black philosophy should continue to pursue this kind of juxtaposition: an irreverent clash between ensembles of questions dedicated to the status of the subject as a relational being and ensembles of questions dedicated to what are more often thought of as general and fundamental problems, such as those connected with reality, existence, reason, and mind; in the form, specifically, of a clash between questions concerning the always already deracination of blackness and questions, for example, of metaphysics—rather than pursue a line of inquiry that assumes a stable and coherent philosophical vantage point from which a black metaphysics can be imagined. This is because, as we argue below, for blacks no such vantage point exists. Such a project could stand the assumptive logic of philosophy on its metaphysical and ethical head; just as a similarly blackened project has turned the assumptive logic of critical theory (specifically, its start-ing point, which assumes subjectivity) on its relational head.[2]

A focus on violence should be at the center of this project because violence not only makes thought possible, but it makes black metaphysical being and black relationality impossible, while simultaneously giving rise to the philosophical contemplation of metaphysics and the thick description of human relations. Without violence, critical theory and pure philosophy would be impossible. Marx and others have intimated as much. But what is often left unexamined is that this violence is peculiar in that, whereas some groups of people might be the recipients of violence, after they have been constituted *as people,* violence is a structural necessity to the constitution of blacks. Ideally, philosophers (studying metaphysics) and critical theorists (studying the relational status of the subject) should not be able to labor without contemplating the violence that

Patrice Douglass is a PhD candidate in the Culture and Theory Program at the University of California, Irvine. Her work explores the relationship between sexual violence and black subjection under slavery as a theoretical framework to think through the position of blackness within contemporary political theory.

Frank B. Wilderson III is a professor of African-American studies and drama at the University of California, Irvine. He is the author of *Red, White & Black: Cinema and the Structure of U.S. Antagonisms* (2010) and *Incognegro: A Memoir of Exile and Apartheid* (2008).

enables black (non)being; but, in fact, the evasion of blackness-qua-violence is what gives these disciplines their presumed coherence. This *unthought* dynamic is a best-case scenario, as will be seen below with a critique of Elaine Scarry's *The Body in Pain: The Making and Unmaking of the World*.[3] A worst-case scenario ensues when the critical theorist deploys anti-black violence in her/his critique—and restricting of subjectivities and genres, as will be seen with a critique of Jasbir K. Puar's *Terrorist Assemblages: Homonationalism in Queer Times*.[4]

Jasbir Puar frames *Terrorist Assemblages* by taking further the underwriting assumptive logics of critical theory and cultural criticisms, the fields the text both draws on and contributes to. The text foregrounds theories of subject resistance in relation to violence by atomizing the logic of analysis down to the level of genre distinctions.[5] This framework posits a critical interrogation of how subject categories are incorporated by the state. The terrorist assemblage is a theoretic that resists subsumption into the war machine of the homonationalist nation-state formation, by contesting, refusing, morphing, and acting against classifications in a manner that suggests an incomprehensibility rather than legibility. This increases the possibility to apprehend the ontological and affective possibilities that resonate in queer futurity.

By situating two genres of subjectivity, race and sexuality, in tension with one another, *Terrorist Assemblages* maneuvers to mark an investment in upholding the underlying structures upon which these terms are constituted. Puar argues,

It is precisely within the interstices of life and death that we find the differences between queer subjects who are being folded (back) into life and the racialized queerness that emerges through the naming of populations, thus fueling the oscillation between the disciplining of subjects and the control of populations. . . . We can complicate, for instance, the centrality of biopolitical reproductive biologism by expanding the terrain of who reproduces and what is reproduced . . . rather than being predominately understood as implicitly or explicitly targeted for death.[6]

While this argument unhinges many protocols for thinking subjectivity in the humanities, it does not contest the grounds upon which genres, as subcategories of the subject, are produced and enacted. That is to say, the gesture to think outside of the constrictors and binds of race and sexuality as distinctive orientations by assessing the mergers, overlaps, and divergences of their competing and coalescing concerns, does not interrogate the parameters that suture race and sexuality as categories, and life and death as legible modes of existing and suffering within those categories. Instead it demands a more suitable relationship to genre and while the forms of relationality may at times be unnamable for Puar, this assessment still maintains that existing in the world is in fact a possibility.

Also what is apparent in the formation of the terrorist assemblage as an inhabitance of resistance is the assumption of the state as the predominating force of violence and it furthermore asserts that all violence has the potential to be definitively recognized as such, violence. Metaphysics, in this context, is wholly unattended to, yet present in its absent consideration. Violence is assumed as the constitution of a singular, refracted, and namable predominating force, the state and its extension, and is blind to considerations of violence located at the constitution of being itself and present prior to the arrival of the state.

In *Scenes of Subjection: Terror, Slavery, and Self-Making in Nineteenth-Century America,* Saidiya Hartman provides a critical collapsing of the analysis put forth by Puar by placing the legibility of resistance in question when explicitly considering the status of the female slave. What is brought to bear in Hartman's analysis of the case, *Missouri v. Celia* (the slave), and countless other legal (non)accounts of sexual violence involving both female and male gendered slaves, is a mediation on metaphysical violence that asks first under what conditions of existence can injury become legible.[7]

> In the case of slave women, the law's circumscribed recognition of consent and will occurred only in order to intensify and secure the subordination of the enslaved, repress the crime, and deny injury, for it asserted that the captive female was both will-less and always willing. Moreover, the utter negation of the captive's will required to secure absolute submission was identified as willful submission to the master in the topsy-turvy scenario of onerous passions. Within this scenario, the constraints of sentiments were no less severe than those of violence.[8]

Critical theory's questions are silenced in the face of the evidence presented by Hartman. While Puar places concern on the formation of the terrorist assemblage as "a queer praxis of assemblage [which] allows for a scrambling of sides that is illegible to state practices of surveillance, control, banishment, and extermination,"[9] Hartman places in peril the assumption that such a choice alignment of being is in fact a sustaining resistance to violence for all.

The anxious intent to sidestep blackness, which is wholly apparent in *Terrorist Assemblages,* cannot underwrite the reality of an existence for which space and time do not shift. Through an intentional mediation on black existence, *Scenes of Subjection* brings to bear a witnessing that cannot be witnessed in the precarious existence of a being that is simultaneously injured and injurious, harmed and harmful, resistant and complicit, willful and unwilling, at the level of its constitution. That is to say, blackness is not deformed by slavery but quite the contrary. Slavery as an ancient political system finds itself disfigured by blackness, as its structural components proliferate the constraints and definitive power of the master's gaze beyond the reach of actual physical property status and proximity. Black philosophical inquiries push introspections to shift concerns beyond thinking direct relations of violence as a tractable force by instead engaging the infinite refractions of violence at the level of being and existence within the world. What Hartman uncovers in her world-shifting theoretical engagement with slavery is the question of exactly whose agency and suffering is revealed through an engagement with a blackened existence. Is it the suffering of the black, or is the status of something else altogether revealed?

In her groundbreaking book, *The Body in Pain: The Making and Unmaking of the World,* Elaine Scarry made a series of interventions that advanced critical theory's conceptual framework regarding the status of the subject. The ground zero of her assumptive logic assumes the universality of metaphysical presence in all victims of torture; and it is this metaphysical presence that torture seeks to undo.[10] Scarry offered new pronouncements that were arrived at in ways that scholars in the humanities were often unaccustomed. Her arguments were not built on, for example, the positive protocols of hybridity (though she did not set out to interrogate those protocols, as Puar would do a generation later); nor on what would later be called the politics of difference; nor were they arrived at through psychoanalytic protocols grounded in semiotics and language.[11] Instead of cathedralizing the subject's potential, Scarry worked at the site of deracination: the injured body, the tortured body, the body in pain, pain beyond words—pain as that phenomenon for which there are no words. For Scarry, the violence deployed in acts of mutilation and the infliction of pain not only attempt to annihilate metaphysical presence, but it also attempts to disguise its purpose in "fictions" that evade the central issue: that torture involves attempts to undo *being* at the subject's core. The torturer's goal, she asserted,

> is to make . . . the body . . . emphatically and crushingly present by destroying it. It is in part this combination that makes torture, like any experience of great physical pain, mimetic of death for in death the body is emphatically present while that more elusive part represented by the voice is so alarmingly absent that heavens are created to explain its whereabouts. . . . Through his ability to project words and sounds out into his environment, a human being inhabits, humanizes, and makes his own a space much larger than that occupied by his body alone. This space, always contracted under repressive regimes, is in torture almost wholly eliminated. The "it" in "Get it out of him" refers not just to a piece of information but to the capacity for speech itself[12] (italics added).

Torture's assault on metaphysical presence is compounded by its assault on ethics, its inevitable bad faith in which (a) the victim must, necessarily, produce a "fiction" to fill the void of her world as it is unmade and (b) the torturer is empowered to produce a "fiction," which ratchets down the scale of abstraction by asserting that the purpose of torture is to extract information; when, in point of fact, Scarry argues, the purpose is to extract "existence, objects and their properties, space and time, cause and effect, and possibility"[13]—torture is an assault on the victim's metaphysical capacity.

Scarry argues, correctly, that the violence of torture destroys (provisionally if not altogether) the torture victim's capacity to know herself as a relational being; but she assumes, *incorrectly,* that all sentient beings who are tortured are relational beings; and that all victims of torture enter the chamber with the capacity for psychic integration.

By way of contrast, John Murillo describes the psychic life of black people as *no life at all*.[14] In other words, for Murillo, neither torture nor the havoc wreaked by war qualifies as an event that affects the metaphysical plentitude of black life because blackness is constituted by an injunction against metaphysics, against, that is, black people's attempts to clarify the fundamental notions by which people understand the world, for example, existence, objects and their properties, space and time, cause and effect, and above all possibility.

At a glance, the black psyche is homologous with the "unmade" (Scarry) world of the torture victim. Institutional violence (the slave trade and its subsequent iterations, i.e., Jim Crow and lynching) enables the performative moment of "Dirty Nigger," just as institutional violence (a repressive political regime) precedes and anticipates the performative moment of torture. The torture victim, in the event of being tortured, has no recourse, cannot reciprocate as long as s/he is bound to the chair; and black fantasies of lynching white people (or, "Look, a honky!") have no "objective value" because the law is white.[15] Both victims have been dissected; both (it seems) must be made whole again; and until that piecing together again happens, they both will exist as "fragments . . . split from and yet internal to" (Murillo) themselves. But this is a ruse, there is no homology.

To draw out the ruse, Murillo reflects on Fanon's "Look, a Negro!" and "Dirty Nigger!" recollections. He argues that Fanon, the author who recollects the incidents, does not have (in the process of recalling), nor did he have (prior to the episodes) an unniggarized vantage point from which to see the world or be *seen* by the world.[16] There

can be no temporal or spatial coordinates that mark metaphysical plenitude; no space and time of memory; no life to remember. Fanon's "recollection," Murillo writes, "will be told and dissected as a piecing together of fragments, performed by another Fanon, one that is split and yet internal to Fanon."[17]

Murillo argues that the fragmenting process the black psyche undergoes is beyond "the event horizon," unlike Scarry's subject whose event horizon is the episode(s) of torture. For Murillo, the event horizon is not a narrative moment, or a moment that can be narrated, but *being* itself.

> Being black, or . . . black(ened) being . . . submits my being to the perpetuity of political ontological breaking with and by inescapable gravity and absolute darkness, such that, on orders of time and space both macro and micro—being, life, existence, knowledge, ethics, as they are framed by the permanence promised by capital "D" Death (social death) and the temporariness inherent in lower-case "d" death (corporeal death)—I, we, break. Blackness breaches, is breach impervious to breaching.[18]

In other words, the black arrives at the torture chamber in a psychic state too deracinated to be credited to a prior torture.

Scarry's torture victim has the luxury of a narrative progression from equilibrium to disequilibrium. And the first of two stages in the narrative progression holds forth the promise of a third stage: equilibrium restored; a closure stage—healing, or what we might call metaphysical renewal: the reinstantiation of objects and their properties, space and time, cause and effect.

But where the black is concerned, we cannot think in terms of stages, much less in terms of narrative. The metaphysics of being (objects and their properties, space and time, cause and effect) cannot be *recalled* by the black psyche without simultaneously recalling what is, for the victim of torture, *merely the second stage of a three-stage progression.*

If, at each version or reemergence of "Dirty Nigger!" in encounters with Human or subaltern subjects, or anti-Human objects (Blacks, pace Wilderson) with media, with and within the state, its institutions and its agents, and in memory, the psychic space breaks again and again, does not the rupture of black psychic space approach infinity?[19]

The world-unmaking catalyst that Scarry posits as a force that moves in a coherent progression from external violence imposition to psychic internalization is not the same for Fanon, Marriott, and Murillo. Torture cannot be blamed for instantiating disequilibrium when disequilibrium constitutes being. In other words, the black arrives at the torture chamber as a victim of metaphysical violence, a state too deracinated to be credited even to prior and coherent violent events. Blackness is constituted by violence with no event horizons.

We need to imagine metaphysical violence rather than a metaphysics that violence destroys. We need to think metaphysically through social death and the figure of the slave. There is no a priori connection between sentience and relation; no natural link between *feeling* and *world*.

Notes

1. See Lewis Gordon's *Bad Faith and Anti-Black Racism* (New York: Humanity Books, 1995).

2. See Hortense Spillers, *White, Black & In Color: Essays on American Literature and Culture* (Chicago: University of Chicago Press, 2003); David Marriott, "'I'm Gonna Borrer me a Kodak': Photography & Lynching," in *On Black Men* (New York: Columbia University Press, 2000); Jared Sexton, *Amalgamation Schemes: Antiblackness and Critique of Multiracialism* (Minneapolis: University of Minnesota Press, 2008); Saidiya Hartman, *Scenes of Subjection: Terror, Slavery, and Self-Making in Nineteenth-Century* (New York: Oxford University Press, 1997); and Frank B. Wilderson III, *Red, White & Black: Cinema and the Structure of U.S. Antagonisms* (Durham, NC: Duke University Press, 2010).

3. Elaine Scarry, *The Body in Pain: The Making and Unmaking of the World* (New York: Oxford University Press,1985).

4. See Jasbir Puar, *Terrorist Assemblages: Homonationalism in Queer Times* (Durham, NC: Duke University Press, 2007).

5. In the interview "*ProudFlesh* Inter/views: Sylvia Wynter," Wynter argues that "genre" represents multiple modes of being human, which is the designation of "kind." Race and gender are spoken to directly in the invocation of genre as a mode of analysis by Wynter and through the contours of the article it is apparent that sexuality and class among other subject distinctions are also fitting to this analysis. Wynter has elaborated upon and engaged the concept of genre in many of her other works as well. See Greg Thomas, "*ProudFlesh* Inter/views: Sylvia Wynter," *ProudFlesh: New Afrikan Journal of Culture, Politics, and Consciousness,* ISSN: 1543–0855 (online).

6. Puar, *Terrorist Assemblages,* p. 36.

7. The phrase "metaphysical violence" was coined by Patrice Douglass in her master's paper "The Claim of Right to Property: Social Violence

and Political Right," submitted to the program in Culture and Theory at the University of California, Irvine, on June 20, 2013.

8. Hartman, *Scenes of Subjection,* pp. 81–82.

9. Puar, *Terrorist Assemblages,* p. 221.

10. This, in part, is why her work has had such an effect on debates within critical theory as well as on philosophical reflection on metaphysics and ethics. In 1999 Edward Said declared, "There is no one even remotely like Elaine Scarry for the depth and originality of her thinking in the humanities today." See Geoffrey Galt Harpham, "Elaine Scarry and the Dream of Pain," *Salmagundi* 130/131 (Spring–Summer 2001): 202–234, quote on p. 202.

11. Ibid., pp. 203–206.

12. Scarry, *The Body in Pain,* p. 49.

13. "Metaphysics," Wikipedia, en.wikipedia.org/wiki/Metaphysics, accessed April 23, 2013. The Merriam-Webster Dictionary definition and Peter van Inwagen's entry in *The Stanford Encyclopedia of Philosophy* enhance and complicate the Wikipedia entry; plato.stanford.edu/archives/win2012/entries/metaphysics. Webster defines metaphysics as "a (1): a division of philosophy that is concerned with the fundamental nature of reality and being and that includes ontology, cosmology, and often epistemology." While van Inwagen attends to the contrariness of any definition at all, "It is not easy to say what metaphysics is. Ancient and Medieval philosophers might have said that metaphysics was, like chemistry or astrology, to be defined by its subject matter: metaphysics was the 'science' that studied 'being as such' or 'the first causes of things' or 'things that do not change.' It is no longer possible to define metaphysics that way, and for two reasons. First, a philosopher who denied the existence of those things that had once been seen as constituting the subject-matter of metaphysics—first causes or unchanging things—would now be considered to be making thereby a metaphysical assertion. Secondly, there are many philosophical problems that are now considered to be metaphysical problems (or at least partly metaphysical problems) that are in no way related to first causes or unchanging things; the problem of free will, for example, or the problem of the mental and the physical."

14. John Murrillo is a graduate student in the department of English, Brown University, and is an emerging Afro-pessimist scholar. Murrillo's current work merges the realms of creativity and intellectualism, drawing from poetry, quantum mechanics, and psychoanalysis to meditate on the political ontology of blackness. See John Murillo, "Smiles Undun, *Django Unchained,*" unpublished manuscript.

15. Marriott, "I'm Gonna Borrer Me a Kodak."

16. Lewis Gordon makes a similar point in *Bad Faith and Anti-Black Racism.*

17. See Murillo.

18. Ibid.

19. Ibid.

Afrarealism and the Black Matrix

Maroon Philosophy at Democracy's Border[1]

JOY JAMES

Our mind is more powerful than anything.
                    —**Amante**[2]

Introduction: Resilience

Black philosophy functions as both a corrective and a creative source for political theory in particular and philosophy in general: it approaches the life of the mind, aesthetics, ethics, and transcendence through the human struggle for "freedom"— not as an abstract value but as concretized in resistance to captivity.

Black philosophy's savant is an Afrarealism that explores its contributions and contradictions. Through black radical, feminist-womanist, queer theories, Afrarealism confronts theoretical limitations and political practices in conceptualizing freedom. It has been operative in the "New World" for half a millennium. It is as old as black theory and philosophy's hunger for liberty. Although Afrarealism often seems relegated to the underground of resistance and to the shadows of formal concepts, its resilience allows for continuous agency.

Fed upon and fetishized by Europe since the 1500s, emerging states in the Americas refined the efficacy of terror and genocide while inadvertently incubating the maroons that birthed Afrarealism. Prefigured in the Atlantic slave trade, and challenged by the maroonage of ship rebellions and mutinies, racial capital and racial rape became the conquistadores of the Americas.[3] Five hundred years of flights from captivity, into communal and conceptual wilderness, created the maroon philosophers' natural habitat at the boundary of democracy. Such outsider terrain superficially appears as a reservation or cell; yet it is in part a trajectory into freedom. For centuries democracy was idealized through the rise of white citizenship,[4] and portrayed as the manifestation of freedom. Black radical thought witnessed it as building democracy's boundaries: establishing the definitional norms for democratic citizenship through racially fashioned captivity.[5]

Afrarealism recognizes two coterminous phenomena: democracy as a boundary defining freedom through captivity, and maroon philosophy at the borders reimagining freedom through flight. Afrarealism does not equate democracy with freedom as some black philosophy does. Rather, Afrarealism's journey moves adjacent to a democracy originating and reproducing amid racial captivity and racial rape. Afrarealism also sojourns with black philosophy's challenges to racial supremacy. Afrarealism sees through the lens of a black matrix. As both spectacle and spec-

Joy James is the F. C. Oakley Third Century Chair, Professor in Humanities and of political science at Williams College. Her most recent book is *Seeking the Beloved Community: A Feminist Race Reader* (Albany: SUNY Press, 2013).

trum, the black matrix allows a broader grasp of anti-black state and citizenship terror, and wounded agency pursuing freedom.[6]

A form of maroon philosophy (all black philosophy is not radicalized as maroon philosophy), Afrarealist political theory treks beyond conventional militarized borders to survey democracy's violence toward the black matrix and black reproductivity. The violent exploitation of black productivity in agricultural, industrial, penal, and cultural markets is a historical and structural feature of democracy. These aggressions and violations I have earlier described as "state violence."[7] Democracy's aggressions against the black matrix, its terror against black reproductive labor, its sanction of racial rape I describe here as state "intimate violence." State violence and intimate state violence are two related but distinct phenomena. Violations of black productivity coexist with terror against black reproductivity. Afrarealism witnesses both and calls for greater scrutiny to assaults against black reproductivity, an under-theorized feature of black captivity.

Reproductivity

Equally violently exploited in labor, black captive males and females enriched racial capital. Yet the inequities of the terror in their reproductive labors were diminished in both enslavement and abolition narratives, initially shaped and controlled by propertied white males. (In fantasies of democracy, the enslaver rescues the savage from barbarity, and the abolitionist saves the savage from the enslaver. Afrarealism sees both forms of "salvation" as captivity.)[8]

Colonial, imperial, and corporate state violence fomented and structured anti-black practices and policies. Productivity in work and labor, based on economic exploitation, and civil and human rights violations became the primary analytical framework for critiquing democracy's rapaciousness toward black captivity—a capacity first legalized in the US Constitution's "3/5 clause" and later in its thirteenth amendment codifying enslavement through imprisonment.

Reproductivity, marginalized as a theoretical space for analyzing (and undoing) democracy's terrors, points to the black matrix as the site for the symbolic and material subjugations that birthed the maroon philosopher. When and wherever the concept of racial capital overshadows the phenomenon of racial rape, the outline of democracy's boundary and the contour of its terrors are obscured. Terror against the black matrix shapes those borders. Afrarealism redirects maroon philosophy to criminal violence and political terror directed toward the exteriority of black productivity *and* the interiority of black reproductivity. Anti-black violence and terror also exist within maroonage complicating the enterprise of freedom; particularly if the terror registers most through forms of sexual predation.

Racial Rape

Historically, captive females were violently forced to labor alongside captive males. This seeming erasure of gendered differences masculinized black suffering. Under patriarchy, violence against the female form is often denied or deflected through language that renders female trauma invisible, inconsequential, or self-inflicted. The "uncut bond" of black exploitation and trauma under white supremacy meant a folding of black female trauma into the black male frame, from which it receded from common view, typically emerging as spectacle only and not as spectrum. Thus common perceptions of black suffering became embodied in and represented by male trauma—emanating from the lash, shackle, the brand, convict lease, lynch mob, death row, mass imprisonment, and "stop-n-frisk." With the norm and apex of black suffering centered on violence in the public realm and the public spaces of the private realm (cloistered plantations and prisons), racial rape became subsumed under racial capital.

The official chronology of and narratives about violence and terror that constitute US democracy's borders—chattel slavery, the convict prison lease system,[9] Jim Crow segregation, mass incarceration, "stop-n-frisk"—crowd out the black matrix, displacing it from philosophical inquiries into subjugation. The interiority of this trauma zone has paltry public record and memory. Racial rape, the dominant threat, appears in black women's writings, memoirs, fiction, and art, but in these forms may be categorized as emotive performance, mere illustrations for rather than inherently forms of critical philosophy.

Racial rape is complicated and mercurial although all blood trails are traceable to the black matrix. Part of the trauma of captive males entails their sexual violations. Boys and men could be forced into being proxy rapists, coerced to rape for the entertainment, edification, or enrichment of their captors or "masters." And black boys and men themselves are rape victims. (Legal discourse has changed to acknowledge male victimization as rape; recently the US Justice Department under Eric Holder redefined "rape" to include males.)

Outside the narratives of compulsory heterosexuality, black males were raped by their white captors or were forced to rape others, or both. Outside of the narratives of compulsory black solidarity, captive males raped for pornographic, sadistic pleasure or material gain (more food and benefits, fewer beatings, etc. from violent authoritarians). Any philosophical aversion, emotional dissonance, political "shame" toward critiques of racial rape leaves black masculinity theory adrift or disengaged. Either it dangles as strange fruit or following the broken branch collapses heavily upon the black matrix. If black philosophy undervalues male entanglement and investment in racial rape and violence against reproductivity, it loses sight of the violence manifested through sexual trauma and denigration, forced breeding or sterilization, or abuse of or contempt for children. Thus the currency of black philosophical engagements with freedom is undermined.

Male captives "feminized" through blackness, and terrorized by mutating manifestations of white supremacy, have structural male supremacy over *black* females. Male captives did and do not, could and cannot suffer rape as routine entertainment or the terrors of forced reproductivity. Hopefully, we agree that this discussion is not about which (trans)gendered being suffers most under racial subjugation; rather the focus rests on the "nature" of the subjugator's extensive reach into interior spaces, its colonization and scarification of black wombs and matrices that have no public record.

American democracy's generative violence uniquely and strategically targets the black matrix because it offers the foundational frame for building the border between democracy and captivity, and deniability of state inmate violence. The black matrix is where patriarchal, racial-sexual violence, economics, and privatized terrors meet. The *maroonage* is where they are dissipated into the dust of Afrarealist departures.

Historically, captives and fugitives painted political ethics and theory so that maroon philosophy could map freedom along the contours and fault lines of colonial and imperial democracies.[10] When early rebellions and multiracial *maroonage* receded to leave only blackness at democracy's outermost borders, that blackness solidified into the silhouette of the black matrix, as the basic boundary between *domination* and *power*,[11] between the violence of productive labor for the marketplace and the terror that reproduces "plantation babies."[12] Encompassing democracy's anti-black animus and maroonage's anti-black feminist sentiments, the black matrix both points to and constitutes uncharted territory on the other side of democracy. Its objective is to destabilize democracy's mythology and *maroonage*'s demystifications as a form of pleasure, as well as justice.

Pragmatic Dance

In perpetual flight from genocide and toward healthy intimacy, maroons crossed the borders of colonies and democracies. Their flights from captivity or toward familial community are viewed as defining moments for

democracy as oppositional to black freedom. Maroon resistance failed to convince the tyrannical majority of the soundness of its reasoning, and the legitimacy of its definitions. Still the diaspora's fugitives fought, fled, and bargained with enslaving armies, and their authorized reformers who followed in their wake. Their ancestral resistance is embodied in contemporary rebels, revolutionaries, and political prisoners and exiles that self-identify as realists rather than idealists.[13]

Realpolitik's lack of sentimentality about domination may still veil violence and terror—justified in the name of deity, family, democracy—against the black matrix.[14] Western democracies manufactured the black matrix as disposable through libidinal, linguistic, and material economies. Yet the tyrannical citizenry, discussed in Alexis de Tocqueville's *Democracy in America*, and dissected in Lani Guiner's *The Tyranny of the Majority*, is reticent about democracy's sexual predations.[15] A founding father and former president illustrates the centrality of the black matrix for predatory nation-state formation.

Thomas Jefferson was an astute consumer of black female reproductivity. In *The Notes on the State of Virginia*, Jefferson differentiates between the Indigenous *social* savage and the African biological or *ontological* savage.[16] He illustrates with bestiary: orangutans, he asserts, prefer black women. Jefferson exempts all other racially subjugated human forms from animalized sexuality (e.g., he does not opine that female orangutans prefer black males or buffalos desire Native women).

Jefferson's political progeny, obsessed with the reproductivity of "Sallys," appear in Daniel Patrick Moynihan's 1965 report on "black matriarchy" as a family pathogen;[17] Reagan Secretary of Education William Bennett's 2005 *Morning America* talk show suggestion that the final solution to crime is anti-black abortion; and the 2011 "Most Dangerous Place" anti-abortion advertisements depicting black women (their absence represented by dark-skinned cherubic toddlers) as mass murderers terrorizing black children (hence the black matrix as a "freak of nature" that harbors both predator and prey in one body).

Afrarealism and realpolitik appear strange, and estranged, bedfellows; yet if one comprehends racial rape, Afrarealism is an advanced level of realism distanced from violent nihilism and denials. "Conventional" wars exemplify male casualties. Yet normative warfare is unconventional: civilians are the primary targets for destabilizing terror. Racial rape is an act of war. Terror against black female matrices and children emanates from varied sectors.[18] The DNA of police, guards and (para)military, of master/mistress races, "civilized" Indians, hardworking immigrants and black captives and maroons, and of intimates—all can be found on the bodies of the black matrix.[19] Afrarealism counters the foundational patriarchs fostering proxies: whatever the "orangutans" prefer, these are not the preferences of black women and girls.

Conclusion: Grieving Beauty

In Euripides's play *Medea*, the Greek chorus of slave women plead against and beautifully grieve Medea's sovereign vengeance expressed in the murder of her and Jason's children and his child-bride. Lacking grieving beauty as an impetus to act, the chorus does not flee or impede their slave mistress's homicidal terror. Euripides, as author, refuses the slaves the agency of defiance, the dance in resistance. They lack the wisdom that rebellion inevitably follows violent tyranny. Hence these women lack the beauty of survival, they have no concept of *maroonage*. Afrarealism respects the complexity of "slave women" who traumatized in the black matrix still view the hangman's noose as a frame intensifying the colors of sky and flowers; still glimpse the decayed child corpse as emerging compost for a riot of red, thorny roses.

This black matrix maroon is terrifyingly beautiful because it is violently transcendent. It ruptures conventional political protest: Mamie Till's open-casket funeral for her mutilated, decomposed teenage son; Soweto mothers' burials of schoolchildren refusing Afrikaans as mandatory instruction; black Brazilian mothers' nonnegotiable demands to democracy's paramilitary police ("Highlanders") who decapitate youth in favelas: "Resurrect the child you have killed."

Politicized black mothers, although prematurely silenced or disappeared through grief or death,[20] transform tragedies into a breech in democracy's concertina wire.[21] In the era of open rebellion against repression, *The Black Scholar* published such women as political prisoners or fugitives, including in one 1970s issue Assata Shakur's article, "Women in Prison: How It Is With Us."[22] Captured and showcased in sensationalized trials, trophies of democracy's police powers, located at the extreme borders of democracy, the Afrarealism of such women illuminated freedom flights and shaped a legacy for black philosophy.

Notes

1. This article, in conversation with "AfroPessimism," is a reflection on the lives of black revolutionary maternals such as Assata Shakur and Afeni Shakur. See Assata Shakur, *Assata: An Autobiography* (Westport, CT: Lawrence Hill Books, 1987); and Jasmine Guy, *Afeni Shakur: Evolution of a Revolutionary* (New York: Atria Books, 2004). Guy's biography of Afeni Shakur offers a poignant description of the betrayal of Shakur's ethics not to reproduce a child as a political prisoner.

2. Amante, Nashville high school student presentation at "School to Prison Pipeline" panel, Rethinking Prisons Conference, Vanderbilt University, May 3, 2013. At the Nashville conference, black activist-educators referred to formerly incarcerated kin as "returning citizens," not "returning maroons."

3. The concept of "racial capital" is developed in Cedric Robinson, *Black Marxism: The Making of the Black Radical Tradition* (Chapel Hill: University of North Carolina Press, 2000); and libidinal economy of sexual terror against enslaved black women is explored in Sadiya Hartman, *Scenes of Subjection* (New York: Oxford University Press, 1997). Here, "racial rape" refers to the implicit and explicit racial value attributed to each sexually violated subject under cultural and judicial racial hierarchies. With such attribution, all accusations of rape and sexual assault are perceived and prosecuted through a racially driven framework. For a discussion of anti-black rape by black males, and police complicity, see Toni Irving, "Decoding Black Women: Policing Practices and Rape Prosecution on the Streets of Philadelphia," *NWSA Journal* 20, no. 2 (2008).

4. See Sharon Block, *Rape and Sexual Power in Early America* (Chapel Hill: University of North Carolina Press, 2006); and Khalil Muhammad, *The Condemnation of Blackness* (Cambridge, MA: Harvard University Press, 2010).

5. Early maroon camps responded to anti-indigenous genocide, anti-black enslavement, and European servitude (racialization of the Irish). Xenophobic nativism, and the heteropatriarchy of racial capital, has been reproduced from the early encounters of "red, white, and black." For a differentiation between political "conflicts" between people of color and white supremacy based in sovereignty, and structural "antagonisms" based in master-slavery legacies of anti-black terror, see Frank Wilderson, *Red, White and Black: Cinema and the Structure of US Antagonism* (Durham, NC: Duke University Press, 2010).

6. *Matrix,* from the Latin "breeding female animal" and "mater" or mother, signifies origins. To encounter black female suffering without mimetic performance is an intimacy and vulnerability to such suffering. The black matrix outlines the limits of the democracy that created it, and the beauty of resistance to denigration.

7. Joy James, *Resisting State Violence* (Minneapolis: University of Minnesota Press, 1996).

8. The US Civil War was followed by three "Reconstruction amendments" that reproduced anti-black violence: the thirteenth amendment, which legalized slavery or involuntary servitude to prisons; the fourteenth amendment, which granted political personhood to (white male–dominated) corporations, not to disenfranchised black masses; the fifteenth amendment, which permitted the evisceration of the right to vote through felon disenfranchisement, poll taxes, and voter ID laws, and intimidation at the polls.

9. For a discussion of the convict prison lease system, mass terror, and transference of black labor as wealth, see Douglas Blackmon, *Slavery by Another Name* (New York: Anchor Books, 2009).

10. All democracies in the Americas are "imperial" if they have colonized or held captive their racially fashioned "inferiors," that is, invaded the "mother country" for conquest. Of course, this is the line of argument here for retrieving the black matrix as a conceptual incubator for maroon philosophy.

11. My use of Hannah Arendt's concept of power as communication, an interpretation of the work of Jurgen Habermas, in relation to antiblack subjugation and black resistance, as well as her uncritical embrace of the Athenian polis whose public realm was predicated on the "private realm" of disenfranchised slaves, women, and children, appears in "'All Power to the People!' Arendt's Communicative Power in a Racial Democracy," in Joy James, *Seeking the Beloved Community* (Albany: SUNY Press, 2013).

12. The term is taken from Afeni Shakur's reflections in her life story; see Guy, *Afeni Shakur.*

13. The most influential and controversial of maroon philosophers are senior noncitizens in captivity or exile, including: Russell "Maroon" Shoatz, Assata Shakur, Mumia Abu-Jamal, Sundiata Acoli, Mutulu Shakur, Leonard Peltier, and Veronza Bowers. Organizing for release of political prisoner Shoatz, artist and writer Fred Ho observed: "It is time to stop writing about history and to start making it" (March 2013 e-mail to author).

See Russell "Maroon" Shoatz, *Maroon the Implacable,* ed. Fred Ho and Quincy Saul (Oakland, CA: PM Press, 2013); Assata Shakur, *Assata;* Joy James, ed., *Imprisoned Intellectuals* (Lanham, MD: Rowman & Littlefield, 2003).

14. For a historical review of the lethal FBI counterintelligence program, see Kenneth O'Reilly, *Racial Matters: The FBI's Secret File on Black America, 1960–1972* (New York: Free Press, 1989).

15. See Alexis de Tocqueville, *Democracy in America* (1864; Chicago: University of Chicago Press, 2000); and Lani Guinier, *Tyranny of the Majority* (New York: Free Press, 1994).

The centrality of the black matrix to the viability of white life can be read into recent media reports of the starvation 1609–1610 winter of Jamestown colony in which "Jane," the fourteen-year-old "pretty" British girl, allegedly was sacrificed in cannibalism. Perhaps only a black female slave could have saved her.

16. See Thomas Jefferson, *Notes on the State of Virginia,* 1785 (electronic text, University of Virginia Library), p. 265. In Query XIV titled "Law: The Administration of Justice and Description of the Laws," Jefferson codifies white supremacy as essentially anti-black, stating: The superior beauty of whites (and Indians); black male preference for white females; "Orantoon" preference for black females as sexual partners over their species female.

17. The Hemings story is a case study of familial pathology determined and denied by white patriarchy while forced into the black matrix. Jefferson met the teenage Sally Hemings when she accompanied his daughters—her nieces by her late, white half-sister, Martha—to France where Sally Hemings's biological brother-in-law and legal owner was US ambassador.

Although not a runaway in the likes of Harriet Jacobs/Linda Brent, Hemings might have engaged maroon philosophy. Interpreting her relationship with the former president as a "love story" ignores that possibility and the fact that property is legally incapable of granting consent; hence nonconsensual (legalized) sex under captivity is racial rape. Productivity from bondage and pornographic pleasure overrides erotic intimacies.

18. Judith Herman notes that during world wars clinicians observed adult male trauma as part of warfare, whereas the trauma of women and girls was experienced in civilian life, through household violence. According to Herman, Sigmund Freud could not conceptually link sexual predation to family and so shifted from talk therapy to theories of female envy and seduction. Herman's notion of recovery occurs only after

traumatization has ceased. See Judith Herman, *Trauma and Recovery* (New York: Basic Books, 1997).

19. Afeni Shakur, former Black Panther Party and Black Liberation Army member, best known as the mother of Tupac Shakur, recounts the myriad violence against children and women, and the sexual duplicity of black men. She also notes black maternal violence against children and "plantation babies." Still her rage and disarray present grief, dignity, and beauty. See Guy, *Afeni Shakur.*

20. Reportedly murdered in Mexico, Malcolm Shabazz, grandson and namesake of Malcolm X, is captured on YouTube offering an analysis of how he killed his grandmother Bettye Shabazz. The young Shabazz acknowledges that he set fire to her apartment in an attempt not to injure his grandmother but to force reunification with his mother Qubilah Shabazz, who was remanded to a drug and mental health rehabilitation center after planning the assassination of Louis Farakkhan, whom she blamed for her father's death. Shabazz recounts that he did not realize that his grandmother, conditioned by political attacks against her, would see the arson on a continuum and as a "strong" black woman would run into the flames to rescue her twelve-year-old grandson (an act of courage and sacrifice not restricted to black resistance). Bettye Shabazz died several weeks later with severe burns on over 80 percent of her body. See "Malcolm Shabazz, Grandson of Malcolm X Killed," *Amsterdam News,* May 9, 2013.

21. Afrarealism and maroon philosophy are expressed in Scientific Soul Sessions; opposition to FBI opportunism; political prisoners literary and film productions; and the repurposing of hospital beds as courtroom or death row for intravenously fed prisoners of war striking against torture and offshore prisons.

22. On the fortieth anniversary of the shooting and killing of New Jersey trooper Werner Forester, the Federal Bureau of Investigation held a May 2 press conference raising the bounty on Assata Shakur to $2 million and placing her as the first woman on the FBI "Terrorist List" with Al-Qaeda. Her attorney Lenox Hinds maintains that it was physically impossible for Shakur to have shot Forester, given that she had already been shot and her right arm paralyzed.

In a May 2013 *Democracy Now!* interview concerning Assata Shakur and the FBI terrorist list, Angela Y. Davis offers insight and context into the black matrix as a female revolutionary positioned at democracy's border:

> The FBI decided to focus quite specifically on black women, because somehow they feared, it seems to me, that the movement would continue to grow and develop, particularly with the leadership and the involvement of black women. I was rendered a target, an ideological target, in the same way that Assata Shakur was called the "mother hen" of the Black Liberation Army. The way in which she was represented became an invitation for racists and . . . the U.S. government to focus very specifically on her, to focus their hate, to focus vendettas on her . . . there is this effort to again terrorize young people by representing such an important figure as Assata Shakur as a terrorist.

Davis references five Cuban political prisoners currently held in Florida, who opposed CIA-backed terrorism that downed a Cuban airliner in 1973, killing all passengers and crew. See "Angela Davis and Assata Shakur's Lawyer Denounce FBI's Adding of Exiled Activist to Terrorist List," *Democracy Now!* Amy Goodman and Juan Gonzales, producers, May 3, 2013. The US State Department has placed Cuba—the only nation in the hemisphere to successfully and militarily defeat a US-backed dictatorship—on its list of terrorist nations, alongside Iran, Sudan, and Syria.

Diversity in Philosophy

D. A. MASOLO

In his keynote address to the Democratic National Convention in 2004, then-senator Barack Obama referred to his relatively fast rise in American politics as an "unlikely story," yet one that could happen only in America. The remark was understood to refer, among other things, to America's final embrace and recognition that a black man could play a key role in helping define and highlight a political course for a white presidential candidate. In his memorable speech, Obama spoke to America's long-standing self-denial in refusing to recognize the social and historical reality about its social, cultural, and racial complexity, or that this mosaic of its social reality can no longer ignore the different narratives that tell its story.

The transformation of the sociopolitical space by the African diaspora is not limited to President Obama's unlikely story, but it remains the highest level of that influence. Besides it, there are or have been others in quite unlikely places: Benin-born Jean Gregoire Sagbo, a council member of Novozavidovo, a town in southern Russia; Guinea-Bissau-born Joaquin Crima, a well-known Afro-Russian dubbed "Russia's Obama" by his admirers and detractors alike; Kenya-born James Atebe, who was elected to two terms (in 2005 and 2008) as mayor of Mission, a town in British Columbia, Canada; and a Nigeria-born member of a town council in Ireland. This list does not include African-American-Russians in nationally visible positions in both the private and public sectors. Their stories, unlikely until recently, definitely have brought permanent changes to the histories of the countries whose narratives will no longer afford to leave them out. Yet, despite them, we by no means can claim finally to have made a breakthrough, or even come close to living the promises of an inclusive world. In some places the changes come fast, and in others they may take four centuries. Sagbo's story is particularly captivating. It goes something like this: when he arrived in this small and impoverished Russian town in 1982, people would stop to stare at him because they had never seen a black man. They may have heard stories about the distant continent and its people, but most likely it was the type that usually gets filtered through Africa-unfriendly media. Seventeen years later, only seventeen, they realized that Sagbo may be black in terms of phenotype, but inside he was a

D. A. Masolo is a native of Kenya and teaches philosophy at the University of Louisville in Kentucky. Previously he taught philosophy at the University of Nairobi, Kenya, and at other several American universities and colleges. He has published widely on African philosophy and philosophy and cultures. His latest work includes *African Philosophy in Search of Identity* (Indiana University Press, 1994), *African Philosophy as Cultural Inquiry* (Indiana University Press, 2000), a collection of essays coedited with the late Ivan Karp of Emory University in Atlanta, Georgia, *Self and Community in a Changing World* (Indiana University Press, 2010), and numerous essays in journals and book chapters.

decent person, one just like them, one they could call their own. In other words, skin color did not define him in his totality.

As a result of colonial settlements—by which I mean also the old Ottoman, Persian, and Omani rulerships abroad as well as the older and more recent European swarms into the so-called new world—people of different world regions have moved and made successful settlements far from home: Indians in east, central, and southern Africa, and Lebanese and other Middle Easterners in West Africa. Their ascendance in the economic and political ranks of the local systems was generally regarded as part of the "normal." There is no doubt that these global transitions and resettlements, especially since the end of World War II, have changed the demographic tapestry of Western nations. Multicolored and multicultured cities, neighborhoods, institutions, and all the way down to the classroom are no longer a surprise. Institutions of learning have been forced to take notice, because they are part of the neighborhoods, cities, and communities in transformation.

For philosophy and education generally, the kind of change we are talking about cannot be limited to having bodies of different appearances. My well-known countryman Ngũgĩ wa Thiong'o has claimed famously that real cultural change occurs in how and what people think about, which was his reason to switch to using his own vernacular as the primary medium of communicating his ideas to his audiences.[1] In so claiming, Ngugi resuscitated, or brought to African literature, a debate begun earlier in African philosophy by Paulin Hountondji's critique of African ethnophilosophy.[2] In a visit to South Africa

last year, I dared to raise an issue along similar lines: the content of the philosophical curriculum since the shelving of the apartheid policy as it applied to education. The answer I got was the familiar refrain: teaching Western philosophy was the easier thing to do because otherwise one only opens an unmanageable can of worms also known as "the plurality of African perspectives." The question, then, is: Is cultural diversity of our classrooms a hindrance to philosophy? It was inconvenient, and there would be no time for it all, I was told. This reality is familiar to many of us who hear it from students of color that the reason they don't flock to philosophy is that it is one discipline of the human sciences that does not speak to their experiences, or that it is a discipline whose language, meaning conceptual language, as addressed by Ngugi, remains foreign to them. Indeed, echoing Ngugi and others who have written on the topic of colonizing by controlling what one should know, or what counts as knowledge, Bernard Cohn, a well-known social anthropologist and historian of British colonization in India, argues that driven primarily by the need to produce usable knowledge for the colonizer, the (British) scholar usually reverted to analytical and historical modalities that explained and historicized local systems and practices as "texts" that could be deconstructed in relation to specific colonial projects. In British India, he writes, "This [historical] modality is the most complex, pervasive, and powerful, underlying a number of the other more specific modalities. History, for the British, has an ontological power in providing the assumptions about how the real social and natural worlds are constituted."[3] To this end, for example, the British system engaged philologists whose task of producing texts for teaching the vernacular languages of Bengali and Hindustani focused mainly on teaching the imperative forms and lexicons relevant to daily intercourse with servants and juniors generally, because they were prejudiced against the Brahmans and the local elites whose interests stood in the path of British social and political order.

Given the above examples of the connection between knowledge and power, there can be no compelling reason to want to teach philosophy to culturally and racially diverse class audiences. In the seminar at the University of Johannesburg, I asked colleagues there whether the obvious needs presented by the post-apartheid era to adjust college curricular content to reflect not just the dismantling of the political and cultural vestiges of the former white minority rule but also to recognize the intellectual content and value of the majority cultures was something they had considered. The answer was disappointing on both ends. Members of the old system argued that giving attention to the intellectual content of African traditions would bog down the system by the sheer number of points of reference as there are "far too many African tribal traditions" with relatively very little time to complete syllabi. Hence the disdain for African values would continue, as teaching political theory is confined to the familiar Western writers and texts. African students entering these once-whites-only institutions claim there are no solid texts or references from African traditions of thought to go by. Unperturbed by the continued dominance of Western knowledge in the new era, curricu-lar, and hence mental apartheid continues unabated. African philosophy is confined to the classrooms of the institutions located in the one-time tribal lands like Kwa Zulu Natal, or the University of the North while it remains shunned by the once-Afrikaans-only elite institutions. Due to the lack of funding and trained faculty, the institutions in the one-time tribal lands lack the capacity to absorb graduate students from other African countries who see South Africa as a closer and more affordable alternative to Europe or the United States. Hence they flock to South African elite universities to obtain degrees in Western philosophy.

Back in the United States, in response to the new demographic patterns of the classroom in the academy, general education committees across the nation, whether they are in the arts and sciences or in the professional schools, are mandating the diversification in the design of the curriculum content to address the social and cultural diversity ubiquitously represented by the visibly diverse student populations in the classrooms here. Humanistic disciplines in the colleges of arts and sciences, and some in the social sciences—such as anthropology, sociology, political science, and in art—are obvious targets of "cultural diversity" statements as their knowledge content is relatively obviously regarded as subject to cultural systems in specific periods. The problem, however, is far greater than the simple mandates of the general education or curriculum committees. It is to be hoped that the mandates of these college committees are driven by an underlying pragmatic goodwill not just of their members, but of the colleges and the education system generally. They all desire that colleges provide an educational experience that gives the students the opportunity to know, understand, and appreciate the fact and history of different cultural systems around the world. Furthermore, the pragmatic expectation for students who go through the educational experience that integrates cultural diversity is that they be able to communicate an understanding of the values of cultural diversity. They can do this partly by showing an ability to perform critical and comparative analyses of the problems of their times, thus making them better people who appreciate the pluralism of cultures and the knowledge systems on which they are erected.

Demanding awareness of cultural diversity in how we design and teach our disciplines alerts us to the ills of our time, and to the need to rectify them. It can be hoped that students everywhere, not just in the United States or in the struggling post-apartheid South Africa, can identify the ways in which perceptions of race, ethnicity, and gender have unjustifiably been used to serve biased interests of dominant groups by controlling the content of the curriculum, and take a stand that this should no longer be the case.

The challenge for the student is to identify and to discern two major yet opposed characteristics of our time, namely that while the development of the natural sciences and technology has revolutionized communication, our time is also marked by the eruption of the ideological storms of our time: the socialist revolutions, totalitarian ideologies of both right and left, nationalisms of all shades, racism, genderism, ethnicism and tribalism, and religious intolerance. Just like the revolutions in communication, the latter, too, begin with ideas in people's heads: ideas about what relations between humans have been, are, might be, or should be. Also, while communication has closed the once-ominous distance between people by virtually placing most people within a click of each other, the ideological movements of our time have the characteristic of pushing people apart and literally and ideologically putting them at war with each other.

Not everyone will be convinced that knowing what writers and thinkers from other cultures say is important, much less that he/she should take them into account. Philosophers are particularly stubborn when it comes to responding to or embracing work from sources they do not consider "mainstream," meaning work produced within the parameters of his/her own set modalities in both content and method. The turn of philosophy in the United States since the 1970s toward social philosophy opened the door to a renewal of the discussion of race as it relates to the idea of justice. Although it is as old as what we know as America today, a systematic discussion of the idea and practices related to race had, until then, been confined to the work of a few African-American philosophers whose impact was likewise limited. Iconic African-American intellectuals like W. E. B. Du Bois and Alain Locke wrote on race and how its perceptions were responsible for the different hierarchical and segregated experiences that privileged some (whites) while victimizing others (blacks). Recent discussions of race and racism among African-American scholars build on the dual legacy of Du Bois[4] that combine scholarship with activist approaches to combating social injustice, but also take advantage of the growth in the United States of social philosophy in the shadow of the influence of John Rawls since the publication of his widely debated book, *A Theory of Justice*,[5] but their work became part of regular academic reading and discussion on the matter only in the past four decades or so, despite the fact that, for example, Du Bois's *The Souls of Black Folk* had originally been published in 1903.

Like the white philosophers in South Africa, American philosophers who are white and male may view the demand for curriculum diversification as a call to diversion from "the norm," or "the canon" in more popular parlance, and may see it as putting too much pressure on the already little time, even if they might agree with the general spirit of the demand. On the other hand, matters of cultural inclusion, especially when they are arrived at as corrective measures, cannot be left to serve mere decorative ends by making a cultural diversity statement at the top of the syllabus. To achieve the ends of sociocultural change that they are deemed to serve, there ought to be principles that are enforceable by requiring that syllabi integrate culturally diverse texts and be examinable at the end of a course with a cultural diversity component. And how does one police this in a liberal society, or in a superliberal community like the university?

Because institutions of learning are, or at least are expected to be, liberal, no discussion of any problem can be considered exhaustive without including in the dialogue people who represent different stances on the issue. Discussions on race and racism should include in the dialogue people from both polar points of the debate, as well as those in the middle of the extremes. If they are genuinely sincere and open with each other in their arguments, there should be an interesting debate, which is always a positive condition and an achievement in itself. Even if there are no substantial changes in the discussants' original positions, they all carry back with them new arguments they had not heard before, examples they probably had not given much thought to before or had understood very differently. Achievement occurs when we have an individual, or more of them, whose conduct, both theoretical and practical, demonstrates with consistency that he/she is aware of, and takes into account, the existence of multiple beliefs and customs that are worthy of serious consideration as he/she lives and values his/her own. Such a person, as a product of a diversified curriculum, will be able to communicate an understanding that different cultures, once ignored in curricular content, may hold different but equally important views on the same issues over which he had hitherto only trusted what his culture taught him. In such an ideal world, no theory is good or true a priori. A truly diverse curriculum calls for and should be the instrument for comparative learning.

For concrete examples, one could mention Charles Mills's now-popular texts for teaching a deconstructive approach to teaching European philosophy that extends from the seventeenth century to our own time as a model for discussing non-reflexive philosophical practice.[6] Also, one could use Kwasi Wiredu's magisterial texts to teach non-Cartesian metaphysics and epistemology or anti-Kantian moral theory.[7] Both Mills and Wiredu give us a glimpse of the possibilities of comparative philosophy. They represent, in a significant way, suggestions that much of what takes place in philosophical texts is built upon the implicitly given, or the cultural axioms that writers share with their defined readership who do not need to be led through the basics they already share with the writer. I call these axioms the ideological roots of philosophy. Many sociopolitical problems are driven by this kind of ideology, which I believe stems, consciously or not, from some ideas of personhood. In this sense, one could also cite John Rawls as yet another example, especially in light of the fact that *A Theory of Justice* is a liberal manifesto that builds on the position that it clearly is all about the individual whose primacy is beyond question, and so should be read as the antonym to *The Communist Manifesto*. In philosophy, this phenomenon has been addressed by some contemporary critical social theorists like Charles Mills, but also by a host of other thinkers who have paid attention to some of these issues. Beneath such issues, of course, is the subtle interrogation of the idea of universality in both normative and descriptive domains of thought. Here is the question: How does one teach the chunk of philosophical thought that develops between the seventeenth and nineteenth centuries? Who has the critical preparation that makes it a worthwhile question? It is just a question, but one which, despite bearing the ingredients for multicultural and comparative critiques, may well lie beyond the disciplinary peripheral vision of the Western philosopher. Yet, I think, it is the kind of question that can make us approach teaching diverse audiences in our philosophy classes with useful traveling ideas for

analysis. And is the student prepared to deal with self-critique using categories supplied by sources other than her own? Let me put it thus, which is the same question I posed to a young black South African graduate student after she told me how she starts her Introduction to Philosophy class to freshmen at the University of Johannesburg: How many different ways are there to teach *The Euthyphro* as an introductory reading for the first two classes of freshman philosophy?

I am assuming that the circumstances under consideration here would be similar to those of a classroom anywhere in the world regardless of the demographic or cultural composition. In other words, we live in a world where much of the rest of it is brought to our awareness daily through different media types. Most people in the world watched the so-called Arab Spring unfold right before their eyes, just as they watched Russian police assault protesting women singers in Moscow's Red Square. Currently, as we write these pages, we have just been watching as Brazilian police assault demonstrators expressing dissatisfaction with their government's mismanagement of the country's economy. The lesson of standing up for what is right, even if it implies going against authority of any kind, resonates with many people around the world today. Sometimes the price may be high, as we all observed in the exemplary life story of the now-ailing South African Nelson Mandela, or even terminal, as has been the case with so many people, individuals and groups in movements, who have given their lives for good causes. The good is a just society in which no one individual or group deserves any more or any less than another, which should apply to our cultures and the importance for educational diversification.

Notes

1. wa Thiong'o, Ngũgĩ, *Decolonizing the Mind: The Politics of Language in African Literature* (London: James Currey, and Nairobi: Heinemann Kenya, 1981).

2. See Paulin J. Hountondji, "Remarques sur la philosophie africaine contemporaine," in *Diogène* 71 (1970): 120–140.

3. Bernard S. Cohn, *Colonialism and Its Forms of Knowledge: The British in India* (Princeton, NJ: Princeton University Press, 1996), p. 5.

4. W. E. B. Du Bois, *The Souls of Black Folk*, with introductions by Dr. Nathan Hare and Alvin F. Poussaint, MD (New York: New American Library, 1969).

5. John Rawls, *A Theory of Justice* (Oxford: Oxford University Press, 1971).

6. Charles W. Mills, *The Racial Contract* (Ithaca, NY: Cornell University Press, 1997); and *Blackness Visible* (Ithaca, NY: Cornell University Press, 1998).

7. Kwasi Wiredu, *Philosophy and an African Culture* (Cambridge: Cambridge University Press, 1980); *Cultural Universals and Particulars: An African Perspective* (Bloomington: Indiana University Press, 1996).

Particularity and Situated Universality

Problems for a Black Feminist Philosophy

DONNA-DALE MARCANO

In 1977, the *Philosophical Forum* published a volume of essays whose topic was "Philosophy and the Black Experience." No doubt, this represented an important collection of essays that served to become part of the slow movement to address the appalling absence of discussion on race and racism at philosophy's roots and at the same time argue for the acknowledgment that blacks and/or Africans did indeed possess philosophical thoughts and systems. And while there were at least two female contributors, there were no papers that could become an example of any nascent consideration of black feminist philosophy despite the analogous development of feminist analytic/Anglo-American philosophy at the time. This volume, and others that followed, constituted the foundation for the slow inclusion of blacks in philosophy, and more recently, black women in philosophy. And yet, the paltry numbers of black women in philosophy is certainly a sign of how much further along the queen of the sciences and humanities has to go.

In 1977, however, the concern was to defend and justify the existence of black intellectual thought as philosophical and deserving a rightful place in what and who is considered philosophy and the philosopher. William R. Jones in his essay "The Legitimacy and Necessity of Black Philosophy: Some Preliminary Considerations" begins the task of justifying the existence of black philosophy in addition to critiquing the philosophical marketplace in which black philosophy, *unlike other new entries* to the philosophical arena, must not merely justify its adequacy and significance but "respond to the prior question of its legitimacy; It must establish its right to exist as an appropriate philosophical position."[1] Thus, Jones's essay is a response to the fundamental question of whether the history of black/African-American intellectual thought and writing done by blacks and concerning the experiences of blacks could be legitimately considered philosophy.

Many of us do not necessarily have a sense of the arguments both for and against a black philosophy that contextualized the professional philosophical landscape then

Donna-Dale Marcano is currently a professor at Trinity College, where she teaches courses on race and philosophy, feminism, existentialism, and the philosophy of human rights. Marcano is a coeditor of the volume *Convergences: Black Feminism and Continental Philosophy* (SUNY Press, 2010) and has published articles on the social construction of race, black feminism and philosophy, and race and philosophy. Professor Marcano's most treasured achievement, however, was coteaching a community-based course titled "Politics, Power and Rights: Engaging Women of Color in Hartford" (spring 2012) with a former student and including Trinity students and the Hartford-based Voices of Women of Color, LLC.

and now. This can only lead to an unfortunate lapse in the discursive sphere and lineage that philosophy inherently tends toward. It remains significant that we have access to and continuously engage those philosophers who were first on the scene in order to obtain greater clarity regarding the philosophical challenges that advocates of subdisciplines such as black philosophy confronted. This essay, then, is, in the spirit of Jones's essay, a preliminary consideration for the legitimacy of black feminist philosophy. The criticisms from within the discipline of philosophy, which held for the foundation of a black philosophy, still holds sway in the consideration of a black feminist philosophy. Ultimately I suggest that recognizing "situated universality" of philosophy and its methods will help ease the way for the future inclusion of black feminist philosophy.

I.

Jones identifies four primary criticisms, all of which attempt to delineate the boundaries of philosophy. The first criticism of the legitimacy of a black philosophy contends that ethnic qualifiers of philosophy are inconsistent with the universality inherent to the nature of philosophy. This criticism asserts that what constitutes philosophy *as* philosophy is its grounding in norms, for example, reason that transcends the particular individual or a community.[2] Qualifiers like "black" presume or at least indicate that there exists something like black logic when there is only LOGIC: "Philosophy is one and has no color."[3] Thus, the project of black philoso-

phy threatens the very nature and existence of philosophy itself by applying particular perspectives and experiences as legitimate departure points for "universal thought." This criticism may also underlie the assertion that philosophy is a tool for perfecting and identifying arguments. Thus, good arguments are grounded in logical form and identifying an argument's form is a universal skill that is not determined or shaped by the context and content of the particular individual or community.

The second criticism envisions a slippery slope of qualifiers to philosophy. It suggests that once modifiers like "black" are added to philosophy, the door would be open to an absurd and dizzying array of increasingly detailed philosophical monikers. This path surely would lead us to an absurd variety of specific and detailed modifiers "until it is reduced to the philosophy of precise spatio-temporal coordinates, i.e. philosophy of X at point Y and Z."[4] Black philosophy, then, is "ultimately self-refuting because it collapses into an ad absurdum position" that would not only threaten the nature of philosophy itself but make attempts at black philosophy ultimately obsolete.[5] We would be left with such a specificity and proliferation of philosophical viewpoints that neither philosophy nor the particularities themselves will survive.

The third criticism challenges the use of a racialized identity as "determinative for one's world view or philosophical orientation."[6] Since "race" is a sociological rather than an ontological category, in order to utilize a racialized qualifier one must justify "race" as having ontological primacy such that a correlation between race and one's philosophical orientation stands. Thus, "we are bound, logically to argue for a black logic, a black epistemology, etc."[7] This criticism ultimately challenges the significance of situated perspectives in philosophy. Indeed, once one does insist on such significance, the advocate is doomed to an ongoing essentialism that maintains an ontological primacy of that situated perspective.

Lastly, the fourth criticism argues that while some qualified philosophies, like Jewish philosophy, do exist, this is not the case for black philosophy. One cannot point to a concrete philosophical tradition of black philosophy that exists in order to evaluate its legitimacy: "There is no concrete Black philosophy because a black philosophy is akin to a married bachelor; it constitutes a null class."[8] This criticism seems to link the *recognition* of the existence of any particular philosophy to the possibility of its existence in any and all historical time. The argument implies that if a specific instance of black philosophy cannot be located by the established purveyors of philosophy, namely white men, then it cannot be possible. Indeed, it suggests that blacks have never engaged in philosophizing and should they do so this would not itself constitute grounds for a black philosophy. This challenge provided the impetus to prove, for instance, that African worldviews were more than primitive and ritualistic, but were instead self-sufficient philosophical systems. It is no wonder then that black women's intellectual works are often assigned only as political "writings" rather than philosophy or even political philosophy. What seems to confuse people is that the history of black women's speeches and writings were responses to the pressures of living as an underclass in a racist, sexist, exploitative society (e.g., lynching, starvation, rape, forced domestic exploitation, etc.). Their intellectual works have the clear goal of surviving, analyzing, and challenging the overwhelming social, psychical, and material conditions resulting from comprehensive economic, political, and social suppression. It is quite disconcerting that real people responding to and creating arguments in order to live and to do so well in a world with its own "rational" arguments dismissing the uniqueness of their lives, their flourishing, their thoughts, are barely rated as rigorous philosophical thinkers. This can only lead to the conclusion that oppressed people, especially those whose indigenous metaphysics, epistemology, languages, and social and political systems have historically been deemed inferior and even constructed as illegal, are incapable of philosophical thinking as they confront the conditions of their existence.

William Jones admits that these four criticisms do not exhaust the various sentiments and arguments of *both black and white philosophers* who understood the emergence of black philosophy as something of a monstrosity, a bastard of philosophy, "a concern of the unphilosophical mind."[9] Nonetheless, these criticisms center first on the debate of the nature of philosophy and second on the meaning of black philosophy.[10] In response to the first general concern, Jones argues that any debates or discussions around the existence or possibility for a black philosophy "inaugurate a crucial and unavoidable *philosophical* debate about the nature of philosophy itself. Individuals on either side cannot appeal to unexamined, unsupported, self-serving stipulations about the essential character of philosophy."[11]

The nature of philosophy—what distinguishes it from other ways of knowing or questioning, the limits of philosophical thinking as well as its breakthroughs and expansions, the duties and obligations of philosophers and philosophy to society and to itself—includes all of these questions as the hallmarks of great philosophical thinking throughout the philosophical tradition. Thus, the question and debate regarding the nature of philosophy is itself the *task* of philosophy. Philosophers who take philosophy's "universality" for granted and those non-philosophers who criticize and focus on philosophy's abstractions fail to see that this thing we call philosophy isn't at all times absolutely certain of itself and thus requires continuous self-reflection and self-justification.

Since Jones admits his project is apologetic, I understand that he also apprehends his task as a defense of the value of philosophy to the exploration and articulation of African-American lives, experience, and culture and additionally a defense of what philosophy understands itself to be and to do. In doing so, Jones defends not the universality of philosophy but its nature as particular. Jones defends and argues four claims:

(1) all philosophies are particular. This will establish the foundation for the remaining propositions, (2) a statement expressing the black perspective is an indispensable ingredient in an authentic philosophical and cultural pluralism, (3) blacks dehumanize themselves if they fail to philosophize from their cultural perspective, and (4) the self-critical task of philosophy demands the formulation of a statement that expresses the black experience.[12]

It is the notion of particularity, in fact, that must be defended. It is the fact of particularities that critics of philosophy claim are ignored and subsumed in philosophy's tendency toward universalizations, generalizations, and abstractions. It is in the service of particularities that many black female students (and other women of color), despite their interest and pleasure in philosophy, continue to feel as if philosophy has nothing in common with their desire to contribute in some concrete and "real" way to their communities.

Despite the established existence and acceptance of monikers such as Greek, medieval, Anglo-American, French, and British philosophies, the particularity of black philosophy appears to some as overly determined and unusually so. Let us be clear what is at stake in this over-determined particularity. No one thinks that Greek philosophy is only applicable to ancient Greeks or that French philosophy is confined to the French, and yet the particularities of situated qualifiers such as black or African-American are interpreted as so particular as to only account for, be applied to, or provide knowledge of a specific associated group. Jones argues that philosophy is always particular and thus "you will discover only particular philosophies."[13] Therefore, to assert particularity is to affirm that materially each concrete expression of a cultural reality posits specific questions and answers, and, thereby, effectively excludes the opposite answers. It is to acknowledge that the limits of each cultural tradition or perspective are increasingly becoming obvious. Finally, it is to demand from those who challenge the hegemony of particularity that they represent to us the alleged universal perspective that does not require supplementation or modification in light of opposing viewpoints.[14]

II.

I propose that we consider understanding that philosophy is always engaged from the position of "situated universality." The term "situated universality" expresses the historicity and thus situated perspective of any philosophical position or movement but nonetheless engages in questions, ideas, and answers that are universal because it addresses varieties of human knowing, experiencing, and willful transformations of the many possible human conditions. The relationship between the universal and the particular constitutes a major philosophical problem that is often confined to technical discourse around abstract entities. However, it is the fundamental problem around which the question of a black philosophy or black feminist philosophy depends. Situated universality offers us another perspective on the paradox of the philosopher and philosophy—the paradox of the necessity of using her particular location in time, history, and culture to transcend her particular interior-

ity and offer responses to the reasons for the current shape of her world. I take my cue from Simone de Beauvoir, who understood the relationship between particularity and universality thus:

> But man is man only through situations whose particularity is precisely a universal fact. There are men who expect help from certain men and not from others, and these expectations define privileged lines of actions. It is fitting that the negro fight for the negro, the Jew for the Jew, the proletarian for the proletarian, and the Spaniard in Spain. But the assertion of these particular solidarities must not contradict the will for the universal solidarity and each finite undertaking must also be open on the totality of men.[15]

Beauvoir apprehends particularity in the situatedness of individuals who also make up collectives. The conditions that constitute a situation for a particular "solidarity" also express a universal fact of the human condition.

To the first criticism that argues that philosophy is grounded in norms that transcend the particular individual or community, we respond that *should* we agree that reason is the norm that grounds philosophy, it certainly will be expressed in the service of the conditions that face a community and the individuals who make that community. There may not be a black logic if logic is an intellectual abstraction, but why can we not suggest a black logic if logic represents an attempt at a system of coherent reasons, beliefs, or arguments? In the face of the logic of colonialism or racism or sexism, there must be its counter. In so doing, we understand logic as systems in which we analyze points and possible counterpoints within the conditions that shape a world.

The second criticism, which argues that the admittance of qualifiers to philosophy can lead down the slippery slope of increasingly detailed philosophical monikers, need not appear so absurd. As some situated conditions become less important, others will come onto the philosophical scene.

In regard to the third criticism that race is not ontological but sociological, I suggest that situated universality would force us to rethink all of philosophy as partially sociological. As a conceptual lens, it enables philosophers to seriously consider social ontology as an important factor in the kinds of questions and answers we put forth in the philosophical discursive space. No longer can we ignore collectives or groups in favor of a neutral, abstract individual. To be situated is to be situated in contexts that are shared with other individuals.

Finally, to the last criticism that denies the existence of a qualified philosophy because we cannot point to it, we would ask, "But, sir, who's doing the pointing? Who's looking for it?" Situated universality offers the opportunity to understand philosophy as a continuous process of discovery gained in order to address inconsistencies in experience of self and world. Discovery is an important task for black women in the United States. Denied access to educational institutions, black women thought and wrote about their condition even as their role was limited to the drudgery of domestic caretaking of white society and subservience to men. Nonetheless, in 1832 Maria Stewart, a free black woman born in Hartford, Connecticut, calls: "O ye daughters of Africa, awake! Awake! Arise! No longer sleep nor slumber, but distinguish yourselves. Show forth to the world that ye are endowed with noble and exalted faculties."[16] And again,

> I have heard much respecting the horrors of slavery; but may Heaven forbid that the generality of my color throughout these United States should experience any more of its horrors than to be a servant of servants, or hewers of wood and water! Tell us no more of southern slavery; for with few exceptions, although I may be very erroneous in my opinion, yet I consider our condition but little better than that. Yet, after all, methinks there are no chains so galling as those that bind the soul, and exclude it from the vast field of useful and scientific knowledge. O, had I received the advantages of an early education, my ideas would ere now, have the expanded far and wide; but alas! I possess nothing but moral capability—no teachings but the teachings of the Holy Spirit![17]

Stewart, uneducated and self-taught, was the first American woman to give a public lecture in front of a mixed audience of blacks and whites and men and women.[18] She asks the ultimate question for those "servants of servants"—those who lived beneath the servitude of blackness and maleness—"what is a self that can only be constituted as a servant of servants and who and what are the horizons of this self?" Who will look for Maria Stewart but the daughters of her legacy?

Like Jones, I believe that philosophy and philosophizing reflects a greater project of humanity's attempts to understand itself, to view all of its transformations and incarnations. Like Jones, I also think it is important that blacks, particularly black women, participate in this project because to not have that opportunity is to miss the chance to express humanity in this way called philosophy. Just as important, by acknowledging that philosophy is always thought and/or written from the vantage of a situated universality, we can then acknowledge that black women have a history of engaging in the greater project of humanity's contemplation upon itself.

Notes

1. William R. Jones, "The Legitimacy and Necessity of Black Philosophy: Some Preliminary Considerations," *Philosophical Forum* 9, no. 2–3 (1977): 149.

2. Ibid., pp. 150.

3. Ibid.

4. Ibid.

5. Ibid.

6. Ibid.

7. Ibid.

8. Ibid., p. 151.

9. Ibid.

10. Ibid.

11. Ibid., p. 152.

12. Ibid., p. 155.

13. Ibid.

14. Ibid., p. 156.

15. Simone DeBeauvoir, *Ethics of Ambiguity* (New York: Citadel Press, 2000), p. 144.

16. Beverly Guy-Sheftall, ed., *Words of Fire* (New York: New Press, 1995), p. 27.

17. Ibid., p. 30.

18. Ibid.

The Reality of Black Philosophy

BLANCHE RADFORD-CURRY

My stance for the ontology and the importance of black philosophy begins with my graduate studies journey as well as the foundation I used to develop a course on African-American philosophy. First, then, I would like to focus on aspects of my graduate studies journey about black philosophy and its impact on my stance for the ontology and the importance of black philosophy. Second, I would like to present the essence of the African-American philosophy course I developed in support of my thesis.

My personal graduate studies journey resulted in my earning a PhD and being among the trailblazers of approximately twenty-five black philosophers across the United States, and I was also among the two or three black women philosophers at the time. I was the second African-American graduate student at my institution. There was an African-American male who preceded me. He was a great study partner. During his graduate studies there, we shared many discussions about the academics of philosophy, as well as philosophy for our culture and other cultures. My graduate studies were devoid of any discussions, historically or otherwise, about black philosophy or black philosophers. Moreover, among the philosopher-giants who were presented to me, there was no hint or discussion of the racism that I later learned was woven throughout their great works.

What was invisible in my graduate studies and what I learned elsewhere provided me with a formative introduction that prepared me to advocate for the ontology, as well as the importance of black philosophy. I received that informal learning elsewhere at a series of conferences founded by Everet Green known as "Philosophy Born of Struggle," which celebrated its twentieth annual conference in October 2013 at Purdue University in West Lafayette, Indiana. My informal education in black philosophy surged as I later read an edited book of the same title by Leonard Harris, *Philosophy Born of Struggle: An Anthology of Afro-American Philosophy from 1917.*[1] I was motivated by knowledge about many philosopher-giants from my graduate studies who regarded the black experience or black philosophy as negative or invisible. With my introduction to "Philosophy Born of Struggle" conferences, my knowledge of black philosophy and its value was enhanced, providing me with a critical perspective on the philosophy giants presented to me during my graduate studies as objective and open-minded intellectuals. Learning of black philosophers and black philosophy shined much light on those other giant philosophers and philosophy in general. From black philosophy, real light was being birthed for philosophy.

Blanche Radford-Curry is a professor of philosophy and assistant dean of the College of Arts & Sciences at Fayetteville State University in North Carolina. Her areas of research include African-American philosophy, multicultural theory, and feminist theory.

Not only was this greater knowledge of philosophy valuable for me and those who looked like me, it was or should also be for all other philosophers. It is valuable for philosophers who look like me from the perspective of acknowledging the contribution of black philosophy and black philosophers. It is valuable for all philosophers because it can significantly impact the ideas espoused by them. For the contribution of those philosophers had been limited to the extent that philosophy demands further analysis of their ideas and rethinking their ideas and soundness of those ideas against the context of black philosophy.

According to William Jones in "The Legitimacy and Necessity of Black Philosophy: Some Preliminary Considerations," analysis of the acceptance of black philosophy as an "appropriate philosophical position" requires "the prior question of its legitimacy."[2] I take the same position, and accordingly, I use the format of questioning the legitimacy of the course as the foundation for my African-American philosophy course. In addition to Jones's essay, I also address essays by Bruce Kuklick, Lucius T. Outlaw, Alain Locke, Johnny Washington, and others as evidence for the ontology and the importance of black philosophy. Their essays represent units one and two of my course: "Concerning the Character of Philosophy" and "Debate Concerning Black Philosophy." The essays for each unit reflect evidence of the ontology and value of African-American philosophy.

Among the essays in unit one are Bruce Kuklick's "The Changing Character of Philosophizing in America," Lucius T. Outlaw's "Philosophy, African-American, and the Unfinished American Revolution" and "The Future of Philosophy in America," Alain Locke's "Good Reading," and Cornel West's "Philosophy, Politics, and Power: An Afro-American Perspective." Among the essays in unit two, "Debate Concerning Black Philosophy," are Paul Jefferson's "The Question of Black Philosophy," William Jones's "The Legitimacy and Necessity of Black Philosophy: Some Preliminary Conditions,"[3] Johnny Washington's "What Is Black Philosophy?", and Lucius Outlaw's "Black Folk and the Struggle in Philosophy."

For further analysis, I address renowned black thinkers and black philosophers such as Frederick Douglass, W. E. B. Du Bois, Malcolm X, Martin Luther King Jr., and Angela Davis. All of their works are critical to black philosophy found in units three through eight of the course. This approach is more systematic to an analysis of the ontology and importance of black philosophy. Prior to these works, there was no traditional academic text as such titled "Black Philosophy." Later to be published was *Reflections: An Anthology of African American Philosophy*[4] and *African American Philosophy: Selected Readings*.[5] Earlier, there was also *African-American Philosophers: 17 Conversations*.[6] This work provides us with a notable preview of African-American philosophers, but is *not* an introductory text. The other texts offer, as suggested by their titles, a composite of well-written individual essays on an array of topics critical to the discussion of black philosophy. For me, this preview of African-American philosophers and collection of essays needed to be preceded by a sound foundation grounded in argument for the ontology of black philosophy and then linkage to the analysis of the varied philosophical concepts addressed by this array of essay topics. While I use the former approach, it is also important that my students are knowledgeable about benefits from anthologies like those mentioned above. Accordingly, students engage in close readings from the anthology/collection of the essays on African-American philosophy.

Let me begin my advocacy for the ontology of black philosophy by examining Bruce Kuklick's essay.[7] He addresses the meaning of philosophy, the purpose of philosophy, and who the philosophers were through a historical synopsis of philosophy from the mid-seventeenth century through the post–World War II era. We learn that the meaning of philosophy, the purpose of philosophy, and who the philosophers were are not static, but fluid and rooted in the "power" of the "gatekeepers" of philosophy. Moreover, Kuklick concludes with concern about the estrangement of philosophy from our everyday world. His discussion provides a beginning justification for the ontology of black philosophy and African-American philosophers. It reflects that there is no one standard sense of the meaning of philosophy, its purpose, and who constitutes philosophers. In particular, it rejects the Eurocentric standard, which necessarily questions the ontology of black philosophy.

Jones argues against four frequent criticisms that question the possibility of black philosophy as presented by Paul Jefferson in "The Question of Black Philosophy." [8] Jones notes that the development of black philosophy is the result of the emergent contemporary trend toward the concept of an ethnic approach to philosophy addressing the "characteristics of a given cultural, racial, religious, or national grouping and to establish its history, perspective, culture, agenda, etc. as indispensable for the content and method of the various disciplines. Black philosophy is a representative of this development."[9] The four criticisms by Jefferson are as follows: (1) the appropriateness of ethnic categories as legitimate qualifiers of philosophy, namely there is no black logic, philosophy has no color; (2) the argument that justifies the legitimacy of "black" as an appropriate modifier for philosophy leads to the legitimacy of absurd categories, for example, "bald-headed or flat feet philosophy" to reducing philosophy X at point Y and Z; (3) the support for the legitimacy of black philosophy is the result of confusing ontological and sociological categories, and to propose a black philosophy suggests that race is "determinative for one's world view or philosophical orientation," leading us to accept, for example, black logic or epistemology; and (4) the claim of a black philosophy is not concretely identifiable in the sense that we understand, for example, Jewish philosophy or a black theology.[10]

For Jones, Jefferson's four criticisms are based on hidden presuppositions beginning with the nature of philosophy. Jones points out that beginning with certain presuppositions about the nature of philosophy and the appropriate standards and methods for philosophizing leads to a particular view of philosophy, and its standards and methods. Accordingly, it is necessary to be clear about the implicit definition of philosophy that informs these four criticisms. The merit and legitimacy of a black philosophy involves a decisive and inevitable philosophical debate regarding the nature of philosophy. Clearly the essential character of philosophy cannot rest on a normative stance that includes "unexamined, unsupported, and self-serving stipulations," which would beg the question. Jones's response to the criticism regarding the nature of philosophy involves reference to historical models of philosophy that support the "peculiarities" of black philosophy, resulting in the development of the importance of contextualism in philosophy. Jones notes further that the meaning of "black" in black philosophy connotes an ethnic or cultural grouping, not racial, and also it is not intended to make "race its organizing principle." It is a reference to the cultural experience and history of African Americans.[11]

Johnny Washington considers a comparative approach to explain the legitimacy and necessity of black philosophy.[12] He begins by reminding us of the meanings of philosophy from culture to culture and philosopher to philosopher. Next he points out the common threads between accepted historical philosophers and issues, and black thinkers and issues. In his elaboration of these common threads, Washington distinguishes the role of philosophy as a scholarly enterprise and its cultural and social relevance. Of particular interest, Washington discusses Socrates. It is the philosophical work of Socrates that examines values within the social context, making philosophy practical, and enabling a flourishing life for all that is mirrored by black thinkers and philosophers, such as Booker T. Washington, Frederick Douglass, W. E. B. Du Bois, Martin Luther King Jr., Angela Davis, and many more. Indeed, for Washington, Socrates's revolutionary view on the importance of reason in criticizing society is a political philosophy model for examining black philosophy.[13] Washington notes:

> Socrates saw philosophy as beginning in perplexities and social crises. And so, for Black Philosophers, philosophy is neither luxury nor leisure for the isolated individual. It involves a struggle against the unjust society from which it arises and against which it is primarily directed.[14]

In "The Future of Philosophy in America," Lucius Outlaw traces the lineage of philosophy to its Western European roots with elaboration on its racist foundation, the failure to question its Euro-racism, and to sanction it. Like Kuklick, Outlaw also underscores concerns regarding the stagnant perception of American philosophy today and suggests that this void can be filled by African-American philosophers with the aim of redefining American philosophy, resulting in revolutionizing the American society and culture.[15]

In "Good Reading,"[16] Alain Locke defines philosophy as the map of the culture's historicity for discovering a pattern of meaning and truth in the universe. Although the history of American philosophy does not echo this position, he stresses that philosophy can provide us with a panoramic view of life along with insights into transforming our lives for the better, that is, in terms of quality of life. To this end, Locke challenges us to engage in reading philosophy, which he admits can be difficult at times. Locke notes, "All philosophies, it seems to me, are in ultimate derivation philosophies of life and not of abstract, disembodied 'objective' reality; products of time, place and situation, and thus systems of timed history rather than timeless eternity."[17] Philosophy for Locke is truth "founded on collective vision" for the black community and American society.[18] Contextuality is as much a part of philosophy as is black philosophy characterized as pertaining to the social and cultural settings of blacks.[19]

Outlaw advocates further for the legitimacy and necessity of African-American philosophy in "Black Folk and Struggle in Philosophy" by examining the importance of having a global view of reality in order to pursue a quality of life for all people, including African Americans.[20] This global view of reality for Outlaw involves such issues as the value that black philosophy brings to this global view of reality; acknowledging the problematic professionalization of contemporary philosophy and the increasing irrelevance of philosophy in today's world; and the need for social critics, advocates of justice, and moral philosophers committed to changing the status quo of race, gender, class, and other biases. Angela Davis, in *Lectures on Liberation,* states, "I think that Socrates made a very profound statement when he asserted the raison d'etre of philosophy is to teach us proper living. In this day and age, 'proper living' means liberation from the urgent problems of poverty, economic necessity and indoctrination, mental oppression."[21]

Despite his preoccupation with analytic and linguistic philosophy, Wittgenstein affirms the value of philosophy for addressing social issues when he asks rhetorically,

What is the use of studying philosophy if all that it does for you is to enable you to talk with some plausibility about some abstruse questions of logic, etc. and if it does not improve your thinking about the important questions of everyday life?[22]

The point here is that philosophers should not acquire analytic or linguistic skills for their own sake, but as a means for solving existential problems to make life more worth living.

This approach to philosophy was demonstrated in the life of King as an educator, philosopher, leader of the civil rights movement, and minister. He was less interested in academic discussion or abstract debate of philosophic issues and more about philosophic justification for civil disobedience and demonstrations with the goal of liberating both blacks and whites with the aim of creating the Beloved Community in which there would be peace, freedom, and justice for all.[23]

In conclusion, it must be stressed that the best way to understand and to appreciate the ontology and importance of contemporary black philosophy is not to think of professional philosophy as a melting pot within a European furnace, but as a salad bowl consisting of various historical and cultural orientations with their distinct colors and flavors. Black philosophy would then be appreciated as one of these significant elements within the salad bowl, proudly showing off its distinct color and flavor based on its unique historical experience as "philosophy born of struggle."

Notes

1. Leonard Harris, *Philosophy Born of Struggle: An Anthology of Afro-American Philosophy from 1917* (Dubuque, IA: Kendall Hunt, 1993).

2. Lucius T. Outlaw, *On Race and Philosophy* (New York: Routledge, 1996), p. 149.

3. Ibid.

4. James A. Montmarquet and William H. Hardy, *Reflections: An Anthology of African American Philosophy* (Belmont, CA: Wadsworth/Thomson Learning, 2000).

5. Tommy Lott, *African American Philosophy: Selected Readings* (Upper Saddle River, NJ: Pearson, 2002).

6. George Yancy, *African-American Philosophers: 17 Conversations* (New York: Routledge, 1998).

7. Bruce Kuklick, "The Changing Character of Philosophizing in America," *Philosophical Forum* 10, no. 1 (Fall 1978): 4–13.

8. Paul Jefferson, "The Question of Black Philosophy," *Journal of Social Philosophy* 20, no. 3 (June 28, 2008): 99–109.

9. Outlaw, *On Race and Philosophy,* p. 149.

10. Ibid., p. 150.

11. Ibid., pp. 151–152.

12. Johnny Washington, *Alain Locke and Philosophy: A Quest for Cultural Pluralism* (New York: Greenwood Press, 1986).

13. Ibid., p. 4.

14. Ibid., p. 5.

15. Outlaw, *On Race and Philosophy*.

16. Leonard Harris, *The Philosophy of Alain Locke: Harlem Renaissance and Beyond* (Philadelphia: Temple University Press, 1983).

17. Horace M. Kallen and Sidney Hook, *American Philosophy Today and Tomorrow* (Freeport, NY, 1968), p. 313.

18. Alain Locke, *Four Negro Poets* (New York: Simon & Schuster, 1927), p. 5.

19. Washington, *Alain Locke and Philosophy,* p. 21.

20. Outlaw, *On Race and Philosophy*.

21. Angela Davis, *Lectures on Liberation* (New York: NY Committee to Free Angela Davis 1st Edition, 1971), p. 14.

22. Howard Kahane, *Thinking About Basic Beliefs: Introduction to Philosophy* (Belmont, CA Wadsworth, 1983), p. xv.

23. Washington, *Alain Locke and Philosophy,* pp. 17–19.

Book Review

STEPHANIE LEIGH BATISTE

Prove It On Me: New Negroes, Sex, and Popular Culture in the 1920s, by Erin D. Chapman. Oxford: Oxford University Press, 2012. $21.95 paperback; $66.79 hardback. 189 pages.

Erin Chapman's *Prove It On Me* follows a recent flush of creative scholarship on early twentieth-century black history and performance published since the millennium including work by Jacqueline Stewart, Jayna Brown, Davarian Baldwin, and Shane Vogel. These studies and work by canonical black feminist scholars like Hazel Carby, Tera Hunter, Ann Ducille, Angela Davis, bell hooks, Claudia Tate, Darlene Clark Hine, and Deborah Gray White provide a duly acknowledged scaffold upon which Chapman advances her discourse analysis of black women's double bind of sexism and racism during the New Negro era.

Prove It On Me is most effective in its demonstration of the texture and operation of racism and sexism in confining conceptions of black womanhood within "iron cages" of stereotype and social restriction. Chapman explores texts by and about women to show (1) how sexism worked to restrict women's liberation and freedom of choice during a time period commonly romanticized; (2) the ways black womanhood was manipulated culturally to serve black masculinity and black patriarchy to the stultifying detriment of black women's spiritual and political fulfillment; and (3) the texture of a notion of race progress that gained traction only when women subordinated their own needs to those of men, children, the community, and more abstractly, the "race."

There is much in this book to recommend it to undergraduates. Chapman's comprehensive and concise introduction details the major forces culminating in and accomplished by the Harlem Renaissance and New Negro era. This summary will prove useful for those seeking a clear synthesis of the era. Four compact chapters source conventional American studies materials: a film, journal articles, advertisements, editorials, photographs, and literature. The author includes a brief study of professional sociological scholarship and social work as well to advance an argument that women were relegated to a role of "race motherhood." Chapman's first chapter, on Oscar Micheaux's *Within Our Gates,* competently analyzes the positioning of its heroine to advance patriarchy and modern black man-

Stephanie Leigh Batiste is an associate professor in English and Black Studies at the University of California at Santa Barbara. She received her PhD in American Studies from The George Washington University in Washington, DC, and her AB in sociology from Princeton University. Her book *Darkening Mirrors: Imperial Representation in Depression Era African American Performance* (Duke University Press, 2011) received the Modern Language Association William Sanders Scarborough Prize and Honorable Mention for the Association for Theater in Higher Education Outstanding Book Award.

hood. Her most lively chapter, on celebrity photographs and advertisements of beauty products and women's blues records, examines the contradictions of stereotype, modernist "feminism," and sexual representation in black women's self-fashioning and a bell hooks–esque "sex/race marketplace." The chapter touches on race motherhood only to criticize Mme. C. J. Walker's deft use of respectability and health promotion to market her product line. The book's analyses are somewhat cursory and derivative for the interests of the scholar, however.

Chapman defines race motherhood, her central conceptual model, as subordination, invisibility, self-sacrifice, and support of others. Throughout, the concept is more asserted than proven. Various modes of race uplift or gendered service are concluded to represent race motherhood because women appear to prioritize others above themselves. Although described repeatedly, particularly after historical women do or encourage "race work," Chapman's concept lacks coherence, precision, and punch. Chapman herself ignores motherhood, mothering, and mothers in her blanket denigration of the category as an iconic, secondary, undesired, meaningless, and oppressed role. She offers little material or theoretical evidence of experience or sentiment from early twentieth-century discourse or current theory for deploying "motherhood" in this way and positions what she does relate in less than helpful ways. Motherhood included not just the grueling domestic work many black women also did for pay, but the complicated rigors and pleasures of childbirth, childrearing, and parenting as well. One need not necessarily identify a direct historical analog to

proffer a conceptual model. Without some basis upon which to thicken the notion and add meaning to its self-alienated womanhood, however, the model remains a vague catchall for the consequences of sexism— one lacking an affective, physical, labor, or even feminist component. Each chapter's primary resources seem thin, particularly with regard to illustrating the cultural ethos of something as sweeping as an era. Chapman offers a condensed, cursory, and curious analysis of Charles S. Johnson's fact-based editorials regarding women in *Opportunity Magazine* (pp. 71–73). In Chapter 4, Nella Larsen's character Helga Crane stands as one of few examples of Chapman's much-maligned motherhood (pp. 139–40). The fictional Crane expires from pregnancy and childbirth in the surrealist folk nightmare of *Quicksand*'s final pages. Stephanie Shaw and Anne Stavney, both of whom Chapman cites, accomplish arguments akin to race motherhood more effectively.

In Chapter 1 character Sylvia Landry in Micheaux's *Within Our Gates* becomes relegated to something like "race *wifehood*" in her marriage to the New Negro race man as hero (p. 52). In Chapter 2, women social workers writing about social intervention advocate something that looks like "race *teacherhood*," a manifestation of one of few professions actually open to women (pp. 71–76). Chapman's presentation and use of evidence does not always serve the author in the most efficient ways. It could be argued, from the evidence presented, that black women *justified* newfound professional freedoms by applying them to a discourse of race progress. The possibility of women's discursive manipulation is neither offered nor foreclosed in Chapter 2's discussion of women's professionalization, self-conception, gender liberation, and race progressivism. Chapman gives Reconstruction-era Club Women credit for eking a measure of freedom out of domestic discourses and social activism that was firmly rooted in manipulations of domestic ideologies including marriage and motherhood. In contrast, she finds "New Negro" women oppressed for apparently doing the same without fully examining the terms of the shift. These and other partially fleshed out, or footnoted, theoretical and historical slides undermine the strength of Chapman's otherwise useful analysis of the nature and consequences of the sexism black women faced during an era misunderstood as overwhelmingly "progressive."

While Chapman's arguments are heartily plausible, there is precious little analytical display of the exhaustive research her archival acknowledgments indicate she accomplished. The three sections in Chapter 3 analyze a handful of images each. Chapman's assertion that *all* black women were blues-women, including "regular" women caught up in the representational matrix of a familiar sex/race marketplace, rests on analysis of a single photograph from a single pageant. Analysis that displays much insightful sartorial comment offers no theorizing of style. A broader use of resources like visual materials from additional pageants, gatherings, protests, or documentary and promotional film material from the era might more fully support this claim while remaining consistent with Chapman's methodology. The blend of critical strategies and disciplinary methodologies in this text never quite reaches fruition, unfortunately, leaving even its lovely hypotheses, intimations, and provocative examples under-theorized, under-analyzed, and, seemingly, under-researched. A more strategic positioning of her arguments combined with greater attention to detail might put this discussion of New Negroes, sex, and popular culture over a bit more effectively. One can only hope this lively scholar follows the archival potential and expertise in the field this work demonstrates with further writing on the period.

Book Review

TOIVO ASHEEKE

Black Power Beyond Borders: The Global Dimensions of the Black Power Movement, edited by Nico Slate. New York: Palgrave MacMillan, 2012. $28.50 paperback. 212 pages.

Over the past decade and a half there has been an explosion of academic interest on the Black Power movement, producing recuperative and rehabilitative works that have formed what Peniel Joseph in 2001 described as "a new phase of civil rights history that might best be described as Black Power Studies" (p. 2). Black Power studies' reconceptualization of the civil rights–Black Power era deconstructs the polarities created by popular literature of the two movements in which the former is stereotyped as integrationist, nonviolent, nationally focused, Southern-rural, and moderate/liberal while the latter is described as separatist, violent, internationalist, Northern-urban based, and radical/revolutionary (Harris 1998; Umoja 1999; Joseph 2001, 2006, 2009; van Horne 2007; Slate 2012).

Additionally, the world-historical/cultural nature of Black Power that electrified the Black Atlantic is being connected to the constant resistance of enslaved Africans of which the greatest expression is the Haitian revolution (Harris 1998; Singh 2004; West 2005; Martin, West, Wilkins 2009; Bogues 2009; Barlow 2010). Returning from its banishment to the periphery of mainstream academic interest, Black Power studies has made it unequivocally clear that it is here to stay.

Nico Slate's edited volume *Black Power Beyond Borders: The Global Dimensions of the Black Power Movement* is one of the newest works in this field that "examines how concepts of Black Power were translated not just across national boundaries but also across time, political movements, and race itself" (p. 5). What makes this contribution unique are the geographical spaces selected to analyze Black Power as well as little-known stories brought to light that help us reimagine Black Power's origins and influences. Despite utilizing a shorter and less provocative stance on the world-historical nature of Black Power in comparison to William Martin, Michael West, and Fanon Che Wilkins's 2009 *From Toussaint to Tupac: The Black International Since the Age of Revolution,* Slate's edited text does capture the powerful influence this movement had on dispossessed peoples outside the Black Atlantic.

Tracing Black Power's roots to the 1930s, Part I of this volume traces narratives of black strivings for freedom beginning with the NAACP decolonization efforts at the UN

Toivo Asheeke is a sociology PhD student at Binghamton University studying pan-Africanism, Black Power, the Haitian revolution, black revolutions, black radicalism, and black internationalism. He is working on linking the Haitian revolution and Black Power explicitly as global black revolutions against capitalism.

after WWII, the unceasing search for self-emancipation that took the pan-Africanist labor organizer George McCray across the world, and the Southern groundings of newly immigrated blacks in the urban North, particularly in California, that gave birth to the Black Panther Party. The authors who cover these respective themes—Carol Anderson, Yevette Richards, and Donna Murch—do much to reconceptualize how we think of black radicalism by highlighting the NAACP's international radicalism post-WWII, exposing McCray's labor-race struggles in Africa and the United States, and calling into question Northern versus Southern antagonism as regarding the origins of black radicalism in the 1960s.

These essays form the roots of Black Power while Part II, the meat of the text, focuses on how the rhetoric of Black Power, if in some cases not its substance, influenced dispossessed peoples in Israel, New Zealand, and India. Oz Frankel, Robbie Shilliam, and Nico Slate demonstrate how these deprived peoples appropriated certain symbols, styles, and strategies to reinvigorate their own domestic struggles. The Mizrahi Jews (Israel), Maoris (New Zealand), and Dalits (India) all tapped into the global Black Power movement to fuel local struggles and strivings for equality, emancipation, and egalitarianism; these local struggles in turn refueled the global movement.

Returning to the theory of Black Power in Part III, Yohuru Williams's essay cautions that even though Black Power was global, he believes it was powered by the oppression and exploitation of blacks locally in the United States. Scott Kurashige, through an in-depth analysis of the political and intellectual maturation of Grace Lee Boggs and Dr. Martin Luther King, illustrates how Black Power transformed and was in turn transformed by its participants. Using Boggs's rereading of King and his revolution of values, Kurashige believes the Black Power movement ultimately evolved to a revolution of values as the only way to address the structural and social inequalities inherent in the US system. In the final chapter, Kevin Gaines elucidates how the music of the Black Power era in many ways captures the essence of what people were fighting against and what they imagined as the new reality. Gaines frames this essay around a detailed look at how the blind genius of musician Stevie Wonder and others blended their interpretations of the Black Power movement into the rhythms, beats, and lyrics of their music.

The strengths of this edited volume revolve around the unique case studies selected to show the influence of Black Power globally. Generally, in the US-centered/-bounded interpretations of Black Power in the literature, places like Israel, India, and New Zealand unfortunately slip beyond our notice. Furthermore, this well-written and -researched text makes a strong effort to uncover stories of black radicalism that generally are not well known. This makes each chapter an invigorating learning experience as to the contours and influences of black internationalism.

However, although this book describes the influence of Black Power, it does not explain the context within which the movement emerged or its genesis, purpose, and importance. Tracing the origins of Black

Power from radicalism in the '30s is problematic because as it has been argued in *From Toussaint to Tupac,* the movement has its roots in the slave revolts/rebellions/revolutions of the late eighteenth century. The Haitian revolution's challenge to the dominant institution of capital accumulation at the time, slavery, is essential to understanding the world-historical roots of Black Power. It was from this monumental revolution that Black Power was to emerge during its historical conjuncture as a challenge to the contradictions inherent in the reproduction of the welfare state fueled by global imperialism, internal colonialism, colonialism, and neocolonialism. Contextualizing Black Power is not done sufficiently by Slate's volume and so it misses that, like the Haitian revolution, Black Power was, to quote Walter Rodney's 1969 *The Groundings with My Brothers,* "a doctrine about black people, for black people, preached by black people," and so was a move toward studying, understanding, and then fighting for freedom from the perspective of the oppressed (p. 16).

All in all, *Black Power Beyond Borders: The Global Dimensions of the Black Power Movement* gives a fair descriptive treatment of a movement that until recently has served the role as the ugly duckling to the swan that is the civil rights struggle. This book is a commendable contribution to Black Power studies that realizes C. L. R. James's prophetic observation in 1967 that Black Power would be remembered as "the symbol of a tremendous change in life and society as they have known it" (p. 4). Touching on geographical areas, struggles, and individuals that in this type of work are not household names expands the borders of what, where, and who are to be studied when looking at Black Power.

References

Andrew Barlow, "The Contemporary Crisis of Neo-Liberalism and Black Power Today," *The Black Scholar* 40, no. 2 (2010): 24–33.

Anthony Bogues, "Black Power, Decolonization, and Caribbean Politics: Walter Rodney and the Politics of 'The Grounding with My Brothers,'" *Boundary* 2, no. 36, 1 (2009): 127–147.

Daryl Harris, "The Logic of Black Urban Rebellions," *Journal of Black Studies* 28, no. 3 (1998): 368–385.

Cyril L. R. James, "'Black Power' on Black Power," speech, London, 1967.

Peniel Joseph, "Black Liberation Without Apology: Reconceptualizing the Black Power Movement," *The Black Scholar* 31, no. 1 (2001): 2–19.

Peniel Joseph, ed., *The Black Power Movement: Rethinking the Civil Rights–Black Power Era* (New York: Routledge, 2006).

Peniel Joseph, "The Black Power Movement: The State of the Field," *Journal of American History* 96, no. 3 (2009): 751–776.

William Martin, Michael West, and Fanon Che Wilkins, eds., *From Toussaint to Tupac: The Black International Since Age of Revolution* (Chapel Hill: University of North Carolina Press, 2009).

Walter Rodney, *The Groundings with My Brothers* (London and Tanzania: Bogle-l'Ouverture Press, 1969, 1986).

Simboonath Singh, "Resistance, Essentialism, and Empowerment in Black Nationalist Discourse in the African Diaspora: A Comparison of the Back to Africa, Black Power, and Rastafari

Movements," *Journal of African American Studies* 8, no. 3 (2004): 18–36.

Nico Slate, ed., *Black Power Beyond Borders: The Global Dimensions of the Black Power Movement* (New York: Palgrave Macmillan, 2012).

Akinyele Umoja, "The Ballot and the Bullet: A Comparative Analysis of Armed Resistance in the Civil Rights Movement," *Journal of Black Studies* 29, no. 4 (1999): 558–578.

Winston van Horne, "The Concept of Black Power: Its Continued Relevance," *Journal of Black Studies* 37, no. 3 (2007): 365–389.

Michael West, "Global Africa: The Emergence and Evolution of an Idea," *Review* (Fernand Braudel Center) 28, no. 1 (2005): 85–108.

Book Review

JARED RICHARDSON

Looking for Leroy: Illegible Black Masculinities, by Mark Anthony Neal. New York: New York University Press, 2013. $22 paperback, $65 cloth. 224 pages.

"Can a nigga be a cosmopolitan?" (p. 35). In his book *Looking for Leroy: Illegible Black Masculinities,* Mark Anthony Neal poses this question and plumbs popular culture for fresh, close readings of black male entertainers. *Fame* character Leroy, played by Gene Anthony Ray, signifies Neal's search for a radical black masculinity, one that exceeds and queers trite grammars around black male performativity and its attendant epistemologies. Neal, for instance, expresses "the act of looking for Leroy, like the search for Langston before him, might represent a theoretical axis to perform the kind of critical exegesis that contemporary black masculinity demands. . . . Leroy serves as a jumping-off point to examine other illegible black masculinities"(p. 8). Hip-hop mogul Jay-Z, actor-turned-scholar Avery Brooks, the late rhythm-and-blues crooner Luther Vandross—all of these black men become newly animated by Neal's use of black feminist theories and queer frameworks vis-à-vis historically and sociologically based analyses that interrogate the visual, the lyrical, and the biographical.

In Chapter 1, "A Foot Deep in the Culture: The Thug Knowledge(s) of *A Man Called Hawk,*" Neal examines how Avery Brooks's television performances create a cosmopolitan black masculinity that complicates spatial politics and belonging. Neal analyzes several episodes of *A Man Called Hawk*— a 1980s spin-off of the ABC series *Spenser for Hire*—in which Brooks plays a black enforcer named Hawk. Hawk, according to Neal, embodies a combination of intellect and unapologetic itinerancy that rendered him indecipherable to mainstream American audiences. In relation to Hawk's roving identity, Neal explains, "Though audiences never see Hawk's place of residence, he is often shown in public settings that suggest his connection to a community" (p. 19). Neal also argues that Hawk's recurrent visits to spaces such as Mr. Henry's, a Washington, DC, jazz club, constitute black publics as his home. As a vigilante with a gun for justice and a mind for ethics, Hawk functions as the black male outlaw who, ironically, works with the law.

Neal also considers how Brooks's performance as spaceship commander Benjamin Sisko engages issues of time. In the speculative drama *Deep Space Nine,* the sci-fi iteration of Brooks grapples with temporality, race, and suffering. Neal contextualizes Sisko within the rise of black male global icons—such as Michael Jordan and Michael Jackson—and the Rodney King incident; this maneuver highlights the competing

Jared Richardson is a PhD student in art history at Northwestern University. In addition to modern and contemporary art, Richardson's research interests include popular culture, speculative genres, and art of the black diaspora.

ontologies of historical pain and commercial transcendence. Consequently, Neal directs our attention to two rival schemes: first, how black (and brown) bodily trauma writes itself onto corporeality and collective memory; and second, how this same trauma ironically coexists with the prospect of crossing over—becoming a "timeless," and potentially "raceless," icon ready for mass consumption. Additionally, Neal notes how Brooks navigated the structural limitations of the television network, negotiating the development of illegible characters with a predominantly white staff of writers.

In Chapter 2, "'My Passport Says Shawn': Toward a Hip-Hop Cosmopolitanism," Neal situates Jay-Z within the hip-hop's postmillennial milieu of global marketing and local authenticity; subsequently, Neal queers Jay-Z's performance in virtue of his non-normative performances (e.g., transnational mobility and sartorial choices) and lyrical flow. As Neal puts it, his project concerns "the productive value of having the theoretical worlds of black feminist and queer theory—rendered as discursive interventions—travel through the body of a highly visible and influential masculine icon of hip-hop, as alternative diaspora" (p. 39).

Among Neal's many queer readings of Jay-Z, two of his most superb examinations include analyses of the videos "03 Bonnie and Clyde" (2003) and "Excuse Me, Miss" (2002). For "03 Bonnie and Clyde," Neal notes that Beyoncé's hook was appropriated from Prince's 1987 song "If I Was Your Girlfriend," a recording whose chorus concatenates a series of gender reversals and same-sex relationships; such an appropriation, according to Neal, implies a sexual fluidity

between Jay-Z and Beyoncé. Notwithstanding the lyrical connection, Neal does not discuss how queerness unfolds itself visually in the video. As for his reading of the "Excuse Me, Miss" video, Neal identifies the elevator in which Jay-Z fantasizes about a woman as a "proverbial closeted space" (pp. 62–63). According to Neal, the upwardly mobile and concealed space of the elevator functions as a cosmopolitan closet, which opens up an interstice for the non-normative sexuality in a genre whose vehement homosociality—a social order that, according to scholar Eve Kosofsky Sedgwick, favors same-sex interactions and institutions—warrants a queer inquiry. This detail troubles the presumed heterosexual gaze of the scene, a regard thrown into further uncertainty given Jay-Z's reverie of opposite-sex interaction.

In Chapter 3, "The Block Is Hot: Legibility and Loci in *The Wire*," Neal furthers his discussion of black male cosmopolitanism and queerness by way of the HBO drama. In a conceptual move similar to that of theorists Hortense Spillers and Darieck Scott, Neal clarifies how black bodies are inherently constructed both as queer and as incapable of occupying normative gender roles. Neal supports his study with an overview of black female masculinity and then connects it to the butch-queer iterations in *The Wire* (e.g., lesbian detective Shakima "Kima" Greggs and erudite "homo-thug" Omar Little).

Further into the chapter, Neal illuminates the erotic and biographical parallels between Black British actor Idris Elba and his character Stringer Bell, a black American drug dealer who peddles cosmopolitan masculinity and cooperate savvy. Connecting Bell's urbane sensibilities to those of Elba, Neal asserts that the actor and his character are able to navigate disparate spaces and wield an erotic appeal, the latter of which Neal articulates through scholar James S. Williams's notion of homoerotic cinematics within *The Wire*. It remains unclear as to whether these queer cinematics, in their erotic pivot on black male bodies in urban settings, engender a form of violability for heterosexual audiences. Here, scholar Maurice O. Wallace's concept of "enframement" could offer headway in conceptualizing a racializing, cinematic gaze that is simultaneously sexual, violent, stagnantly taxonomic, and mobile.

In Chapter 4, "R. Kelly's Closet: Shame, Desire, and the Confessions of a (Postmodern) Soul Man," Neal parses the R&B's pied piper's *Trapped in the Closet* series (2005 and 2007), a "twenty-two chapter episodic music video" that "examines black interpersonal relationships in the age of DL (downlow) sexuality" (p. 119). Juxtaposing Kelly's sex crimes with the singer's own narration of deviant sexuality, Neal offers a challenging portrait of anxieties around black sexuality vis-à-vis AIDS and narratives of respectability.

For his examination of Kelly, Neal returns to the figurative space and interpretive power of closet to scrutinize the sexual and epistemological stakes of the post–soul man's melodrama. Neal describes Kelly's narrative position in the closet as a "privileged site of knowledge and surveillance" that contains "archival knowledge—music and extramusical—of the soul men who preceded him" (p. 125). Given the arguable immateriality of music, the metaphors of queerness, and the physicality of closet within the video series, the "archival knowledge" of Kelly's closet

could arguably register as both a physical space of sexual record and a lateral epistemological process. In terms of the latter mode, one could understand the antics of Kelly's *Trapped in the Closet* as a complex palimpsest of black sexualities, a queer surface that obfuscates the heteronormative projections of black middle-class respectability. With this said, Neal unfurls a patrilineal genealogy of past soul men—from Sam Cooke to Al Green—in which Kelly is situated. Toward the end of the chapter, Neal makes a plausible yet controversial speculation about Kelly's initial exposures to sex within the domestic sphere. Neal imagines that this (postmodern) soul man could have used the closet either as a furtive space from which he viewed adult sexual interactions or as an escape from sexual abuse. Neither lyrical nor biographical material can be found to validate Neal's diagnosis of Kelly's sexual appetites.

Finally in Chapter 5, "Fear of a Queer Soul Man: The Legacy of Luther Vandross," Neal discusses how Vandross's masculinity as a sensitive balladeer occupied a delicate position between respectability and pathology. Setting Vandross's career against both the height of the Black Power movement in the late 1960s and 1970s, and the desire for black respectability and aspiration in the 1980s, Neal explains that the singer eschewed the hypermasculine vocals and hypersexual bravado favored by a majority of his fellow soul men. Such an avoidance of black macho tropes queers Vandross, positioning him as an entertainer who commiserated with female audiences.

In addition to mapping a series of disconnections between Vandross and his fellow soul men, Neal also examines the disparity between the singer's girth and the cultural labor of his vocals. Neal argues that Vandross's corpulence "became a visual stand-in for the pathological excesses of the Chitlin' Circuit and segregation" (p. 149). However, Vandross used his voice and his music as a form of black respectability that emblematized "the refined sensibilities of the new black middle class" (p. 149). Yet, as Neal notes, rumors connecting Vandross's drastic weight loss to an alleged HIV infection corralled his body into public worries over lethal contagion and queerness. "In a broad cultural sense, with his increased popularity," Neal writes, "Vandross's body became a source of anxiety for some black audiences, initially because of his girth and later with the advent of the AIDS/HIV crisis" (p. 156). Neal juxtaposes the public panic over Vandross's supposedly homosexual corporeality with the heterosexual cooptation of his ballads in an effort to highlight the dichotomy of the queer soul man.

Leroy mines the contradiction between epistemologies of realness and self-making in relation to black men in popular culture. Neal has crafted an accessible text that creatively renders our understanding of black men as alien, offering complex connections between spatiality, cosmopolitanism, sound, and desire.

Book Review

MICHAEL O. WEST

Black Against Empire: The History and Politics of the Black Panther Party, by Joshua Bloom and Waldo E. Martin Jr. Berkeley: University of California Press, 2013. $34.95 cloth. 539 pages.

Coming of age in scholarship—the Black Power movement in the United States, formerly maligned or ignored by scholars, may now be so described. Beginning in the 1990s, and accelerating since the turn of the century, the study of Black Power has become one of the more dynamic subfields in African-American and US history. *Black Against Empire,* by Joshua Bloom and Waldo E. Martin Jr., is among the latest additions to the literature on the Black Power phenomenon. Bloom and Martin focus on the Black Panther Party (BPP), the most conspicuous Black Power formation in and out of the United States.

Presented more or less as the definitive text on the BPP, this is a hefty book, both in size and ambition. (It runs to 401 pages of text, backed up by eighty-odd pages of footnotes, plus some gorgeous images.) No previous account, the authors write, offers "a rigorous overarching analysis of the Party's evolution and impact" (p. 4). They attribute the lacuna to state repression and internal disputes, which have conspired to render the BPP's past "nearly impenetrable" (p. 9). Consequently, "no one has presented an adequate or comprehensive history" of

the party (p. 5). Nor has anyone offered "a complete picture of the Black Panther Party, or an adequate analysis of its politics" (p. 9). *Black Against Empire* is said to be such an account, penetrating and complete—in short, a "forbidden history" (p. 2). This is a hefty claim indeed.

As a movement with national and international resonance, the BPP was short-lived. Founded in Oakland, California, in late 1966, it remained, the authors of *Black Against Empire* assert, "a small local organization" as late as February 1968 (p. 2). By the end of 1968, that fateful year of antinomian insurgencies worldwide, everything had changed. The BPP, Bloom and Martin continue, had become "the center of a revolutionary movement in the United States" (p. 2). But things quickly fell apart, the BPP's precipitous fall rivaling its sphinxlike rise. In less than two years, the BPP "rapidly declined" (p. 3). By 1972 it had come full circle, becoming "a local Oakland community organization once again," before formally closing its doors in 1982 (p. 3).

The main lines of the story, as told in *Black Against Empire,* are familiar enough to students of the Panthers. With the passage of the Civil and Voting Rights Acts of 1964 and 1965, respectively, the principal civil rights organizations either "imploded" or "declined" (p. 11). Meanwhile, many young

Michael O. West teaches at Binghamton University. He has written widely on Africa, the African diaspora, and the interlocutions between them. He is working on Black Power in global perspective.

blacks considered the new anti-discrimination laws "limited, even illusory" victories (pp. 11–12). "Into this vacuum" entered Panther founders Huey P. Newton and Bobby Seale, advancing a "black anti-imperialist politics that powerfully challenged the status quo yet was difficult to repress" (p. 12). Presumably it is this black anti-imperialism, described by Bloom and Martin as the BPP's "unchanging core," that provides the inspiration for the title of their book (p. 312).

Black Against Empire contributes to Panther studies from the standpoints of both documentation and interpretation. Consider the collapse of the BPP, accounts of which generally privilege two factors: state repression and internal dissension. In common with other Panther scholars, Bloom and Martin document the sordid history of vicious and deadly attacks on the Panthers by governmental entities at all levels, including the notorious COINTELPRO program. Bloom and Martin are also attuned to the destructive internecine conflicts within the BPP, some of which were conceived or abetted by state disinformation and dirty-trick campaigns, or else by government informers and *agents provocateurs*. That there was a relationship between the external and internal factors, state repression and internal dissension, Bloom and Martin also acknowledge. Ultimately, though, it is the external argument that concerns them the most. They reject the view that ultimately the BPP was routed by state repression. If anything, Bloom and Martin argue, the Panthers thrived under persecution: "The year of greatest repression, 1969, was also the year of the Party's greatest growth" (p. 4). The BPP, they insist, fell victim not to state repression, but rather to state neu-

tralization of its program. In fine, the Nixon regime, in alliance with the wider political establishment and the ruling class, defeated the Panthers by stealing their thunder.

This argument, which will be called here the state cooptation thesis, is not new. Others have made it in respect to the Black Power movement more generally. Some iterations of the state cooptation thesis include as a key component Nixon's promotion of black capitalism, offered as an antidote to militant Black Power. Bloom and Martin have little to say about Nixon's black capitalism. Their innovation, rather, is to elevate the state cooptation thesis, making it the primary factor, not just a contributory one, in the demise of the BPP. Central to this argument, in turn, is the relationship between the Panthers and the New Left, by which Bloom and Martin mean mainly the white left.

The single most important point of connection between the BPP and the New Left was the Vietnam War, as the Americans call it, or the American War, as the Vietnamese call it. This connection, like the BPP's putative vanguardism, was short-lived. By the beginning of the 1970s, Bloom and Martin note, radical and revolutionary forces no longer monopolized the antiwar opposition, which now included important segments of the US Congress. In response, Nixon reduced the military draft and increasingly turned over the fight to the puppet regime in South Vietnam—in a word, Vietnamization. Meanwhile, Bloom and Martin go on, the number of black elected officials had increased, thanks to the Voting Rights Act. Affirmative action opened up greater access to employment and education for black folk. On campus, black studies had become an accepted fact. As it successfully diminished the BPP's appeal at home, the US government worked to do the same abroad. Cuba, Algeria, and China, all of which had supported the BPP in multiple ways, including offering asylum to Panthers fleeing the wrath of US lawmen, became the focus of new US diplomatic overtures. Such efforts undermined the BPP's international network of support, with negative consequences for Panthers in search of asylum. White liberals also fell in line. With their scions no longer in much danger of dying on some Vietnamese battlefield, and the Negroes finally getting a fair shake, leading white liberals turned on the misbehaving Panthers with a vengeance. It was this combination of forces, Bloom and Martin contend, not state repression, that led to the collapse of the BPP.

Black Against Empire, then, has brought an old idea—the state cooptation thesis—to the center of Panther studies. But while offering future Panther scholars food for thought, the argument advanced by Bloom and Martin is based more on assumptions than evidence. Relationships between symmetrical historical events cannot be assumed; cause and effect must be demonstrated, for example, by showing that a particular action by, say, the Algerian government, was a direct outcome of requests, demands, or threats by the US government. Further, the fact that the BPP initially thrived under repression is no evidence that, cumulatively and over time, the repression did not have the desired effect. In the absence of further research, this book's version of the state cooptation thesis lacks the explanatory power of the much better documented arguments in favor of state repression and internal dissension.

Argumentation, in the form of the state cooptation thesis, is one of two notable features of *Black Against Empire.* The other is documentation. The primary source for their book, the authors proudly note, is the *Black Panther.* This, too, is not new. The *Black Panther,* the BPP's official organ, has long been a staple of Panther scholarship. Still, Bloom and Martin's claim of unprecedented mining of the *Black Panther* must be credited. Theirs is truly commendable work, assembling and digitizing 520 of the reported 537 issues of the paper published between 1967 and 1971. Moreover, this entire collection has been put online. It is no poor reflection on the authors to say that so generous an act—digitizing and making publicly available almost the entire run of the *Black Panther*—will have a greater impact on the field than their book. As if one good deed was not enough, Bloom and Martin have made a second noteworthy contribution to Panther historical documentation. Their research resulted in the discovery of a trove of documents on Bay Area movements, including the BPP. Named the H. K. Yuen collection, after its collector, this discovery is now housed at the University of California, Berkeley.

All the more uncomprehending, therefore, that Bloom and Martin would make a documentary blunder as serious as the one in *Black Against Empire.* Initially, the authors say, they intended to write their book using mainly interviews with former Panthers and others. But they soon noticed a disturbing pattern: "The more interviews we conducted, the clearer the limits of that medium became. Retrospective accounts decades after the fact—with memories shaped by intervening events, interests, and hearsay—are highly contradictory" (pp. 9–10). Consequently the oral evidence, although not totally discarded, was largely put aside in favor of "documentary or recorded evidence that was temporally proximate to the events" (p. 10).

This is a grave matter, with profound methodological and conceptual implications, not least for the study of the black experience. Since when did scholars, least of all historians, begin to reject, virtually *in toto,* an entire stream of evidence because it is "contradictory"? What body of evidence is not contradictory, in some form or fashion? Certainly not the main one on which *Black Against Empire* is based, namely the *Black Panther,* which is chock-full of contradictions, biases, even outright defamation, a good deal of which is directed against dissenting or disfavored Panthers. The *New York Times,* another important stream of evidence for *Black Against Empire,* shares many of those pitfalls. This is all well and good, since historical scholarship thrives on contradiction. The investigator's task is not to seek out documentary consistency, which is neither attainable nor desirable, but rather to critically interrogate all sources, oral and written alike. Besides, oral evidence sometimes has the extra benefit of adding a spicy helping of levity and joy to labored and uninspiring prose of the kind often encountered in *Black Against Empire.*

Significantly, Bloom and Martin do not discredit just the particular interviews they did, but the very "medium" of oral methodology. Of course, informants will always make errors of fact or interpretation. However, they cannot be blamed for the shortcomings of researchers, who have a responsibility to engage informants on any known or perceived contradiction or error; and also to cross-check all sources, oral and literary. The conceit that contemporary written evidence is inherently more accurate or reliable than oral source material gathered after the fact is sheer fallacy. A rejection of oral sources is a rejection of African historiography, which pioneered the use of such sources in modern world historical studies. It is not just African historiography, however, that is at issue. Panther scholarship is also deeply indebted to oral sources. To cast aspersions on that entire medium, therefore, would seem to unjustly invite questions about the documentary integrity of much of the existing, and fine, scholarship on the BPP. With the digitization of the *Black Panther* and the H. K. Yuen collection, Bloom and Martin have already contributed much to the documentation of the Panther story. They could augment that contribution by also making their interviews available to other scholars, who may yet find use for the detritus of *Black Against Empire.*

The a priori rejection of oral evidence on grounds of inconsistency speaks to a wider problem with *Black Against Empire*—namely, a pursuit of consistency and coherency where there is little to be found. Here, the book's greatest strengths also become a weakness. Using the *Black Panther,* their prized source, Bloom and Martin carefully document various twists and turns in the BPP. The resulting study, although not unmindful of BPP chapters and leading Panthers across the United States, largely focuses on the Oakland headquarters and on the thoughts and actions of the Oakland-based leaders, who edited the *Black Panther* and determined its contents. Constantly, the Oakland leadership sought to impose its writ and its ever-changing political line on the branches. As Bloom and Martin write: "The survival of the Party depended on its political coherence and organizational discipline" nationally (p. 344). This, however, remained an aspiration, never to be realized. Oakland had neither the personnel, nor the organization, nor the money to work its will on the far-flung and often headstrong branches.

Accordingly, an Oakland-centric teleology beholden to notions of ideological coherence and organizational discipline emanating from above is necessarily limited and limiting. Bloom and Martin wax enthusiastic about the vanguard role of the BPP, which throughout the book they call the "Party," with an uppercase "P." Intended or not, the impression of a Leninist-style vanguard party is created. If so, nothing could be further from the reality. Bloom and Martin's is an internal history, one that presents the Oakland-based headquarters as the institutional linchpin of a national movement. In truth, the BPP was at least as much inspiration as institution. It was not so much a party, Leninist or not, as a model of organization and agitation that could be readily replicated at the local level, not just in the United States but beyond. In this sense, the BPP has something in common with Marcus Garvey's Universal Negro Improvement Association, which in a previous era also served as a prototype for disparate organizational initiatives throughout the African diaspora and the African continent. Bloom and Martin acknowledge the connection, noting that without Garveyism "it is hard to imagine the emergence" of the BPP, although they do not elaborate (p. 391).

Far more perplexing is the failure to develop a seemingly key Chinese angle to the Panther story. The book calls attention to Panther founder Huey Newton's well-known fascination with the writings of Mao Zedong. Mao also appears to have been an archetype for Newton, the helmsman presiding over the vanguardist BPP, with the attendant Mao-like cult of personality. Yet Bloom and Martin are inexplicably silent on the evident parallels, and possible source of inspiration for Newton's approach to leadership, the destructive consequences of which are documented in *Black Against Empire*. It is perhaps symptomatic of their inattention to things Chinese that the authors should write about "the Red Guard, Mao's army in China" (p. 290). Actually, the Red Guards were largely students without military training whom Mao used to smash his enemies in the state-party apparatus. Their work complete, Mao then used the army to smash the Red Guards. In a work on the Panthers, the misidentification of the Red Guards is a minor point, although there are other similar errors in the book, including in the discussion of other events outside the United States. Small problems are sometimes indicative of larger ones.

Whatever the problems with the book, they do not extend to the authors' knowledge of the secondary literature on the Panthers, which is very firm. The problem, rather, is Bloom and Martin's approach to that literature. The introduction to *Black Against Empire* lists the names of some of the noted Panther scholars, and provides a footnote to some of their productions. Bloom and Martin then offer the following assessment: "These previous treatments are invaluable, and the depth of our analysis is much richer for them" (p. 9). Alas, Bloom and Martin did not see fit to substantively engage this rich body of scholarship in the text of their book, treating it instead as so much documentary backdrop, useful for enhancing the "depth" of *Black Against Empire*. This dismissive attitude, which smacks of an unwarranted haughtiness and a concomitant devaluation of the work of other scholars, is both regrettable and wrongheaded. Amazing indeed that scholars as generous as Bloom and Martin—witness their making publicly available the digitized *Black Panther* and the Yuen collection—could also be so ungenerously and unjustifiably withholding. Some of the secondary literature Bloom and Martin withhold from consideration in the text of their book differs significantly from *Black Against Empire* on various points of interpretation. Many of those works also show a greater appreciation of oral evidence than do Bloom and Martin, who opted to circumvent a potentially productive historiographical and methodological debate. The book would have been the richer for such a debate, enabling readers of *Black Against Empire* to see exactly where and why it differs from other works on the Panthers. Instead, Bloom and Martin offer *ex-cathedra* puffery about having written a forbidden history.

The accomplishments of *Black Against Empire* are more modest—which, however, is not to say inconsiderable. From the em-

pirical standpoint, for one, the book has few if any significant new revelations. Readers familiar with the broad outlines of the Panther story will find little that is really pathbreaking here. Rather, what the book does, and does well, is to widen and deepen the known Panther narrative, making particularly skillful use of the *Black Panther*. *Black Against Empire* also adds usefully to the debate on the decline of the BPP, as noted. Altogether, Bloom and Martin provide a rounded picture of the BPP, if not exactly the "complete" one they claim. Theirs is a tightly focused portrait, one that accords pride of place to the Oakland-based headquarters. Such a focus has merit. Without Oakland, there would have been no BPP. But as a national, even international, sensation, the Panther phenomenon was far beyond the commanding capacity of the Oakland-based leadership. Operationally, most of those assuming the Panther label were quite independent of Oakland, in part or in whole. *Black Against Empire* presents the BPP as a "Party," an institution. Mostly, though, the BPP was experienced as an inspiration, a model of political possibilities. In the nexus of the two, institution and inspiration, may be found an outline of the fuller portrait Bloom and Martin were seeking to sketch. Indeed, that nexus is already evident in some of the existing literature they unhappily declined to engage.

CPSIA information can be obtained at www.ICGtesting.com
Printed in the USA
LVOW01s0523300114
371504LV00001B/1/P